Advances in
Clinical Child Psychology

Volume 12

ADVANCES IN CLINICAL CHILD PSYCHOLOGY

A Continuation Order Plan is available for this series. A continuation order will bring delivery of each new volume immediately upon publication. Volumes are billed only upon actual shipment. For further information please contact the publisher.

Advances in
Clinical Child
Psychology

Volume 12

Edited by

Benjamin B. Lahey
University of Georgia
Athens, Georgia

and

Alan E. Kazdin
Yale University
New Haven, Connecticut

Plenum Press · New York and London

The Library of Congress cataloged the first volume of this title as follows:

Advances in clinical child psychology. v. 1–

  New York, Plenum Press, c1977–

  v. ill. 24 cm.
  Key title: Advances in clinical child psychology. ISSN 0149-4732

  1. Clinical psychology — Collected works. 2. Child psychology — Collected works. 3. Child psychotherapy — Collected works.
RJ503.3.A37 618.9′28′9   77-643411

ISBN 0-306-43271-4

© 1989 Plenum Press, New York
A Division of Plenum Publishing Corporation
233 Spring Street, New York, N.Y. 10013

Printed in the United States of America

*This series is dedicated to
the children of the world, especially
MEGAN, EDWARD, ERIN, NICOLE, and MICHELLE*

Contributors

Joanna Basta

Department of Psychology, Michigan State University, East Lansing, Michigan 48824

Karen Linn Bierman

Department of Psychology, The Pennsylvania State University, University Park, Pennsylvania 16803

Lawson Crowe

Institute for Behavioral Genetics, University of Colorado, Boulder, Colorado 80309

William S. Davidson II

Department of Psychology, Michigan State University, East Lansing, Michigan 48824

Rex Forehand

Department of Psychology, University of Georgia, Athens, Georgia 30602

Brian Forsyth

Department of Pediatrics, Yale University School of Medicine, New Haven, Connecticut 06510

Christoph M. Heinicke

Department of Psychiatry and the Biobehavioral Sciences, University of California at Los Angeles, Los Angeles, California 90024

Alan E. Kazdin

Department of Psychology, Yale University, New Haven, Connecticut 06520

Benjamin B. Lahey — Department of Psychology, University of Georgia, Athens, Georgia 30602

Rolf Loeber — Department of Psychiatry, Western Psychiatric Institute and Clinic, School of Medicine, University of Pittsburgh, Pittsburgh, Pennsylvania 15213

Nicholas Long — Department of Pediatrics, University of Arkansas for Medical Sciences, Little Rock, Arkansas 72202

Steven G. Vandenberg — Institute for Behavioral Genetics, University of Colorado, Boulder, Colorado 80309

Bahr Weiss — Department of Psychology and Human Development, Vanderbilt University, Nashville, Tennessee 37203

John R. Weisz — Department of Psychology, University of North Carolina, Chapel Hill, North Carolina 27599

Joseph L. Woolston — Child Study Center, Yale University School of Medicine, New Haven, Connecticut 06510

Carolyn Zogg — Child Find of America, Inc., 7 Innis Avenue, New Paltz, New York 12561

Preface

The goal of *Advances in Clinical Child Psychology* is to provide clinicians and researchers in clinical child psychology, child psychiatry, and related mental health disciplines with an annual compilation of statements that summarize the new data, concepts, and techniques that *advance* our ability to help troubled children. Looking forward, the series intends to highlight the emerging developments that will guide our field of inquiry and practice. Looking back, the dozen volumes in this series chronicle the changes in our attempts to understand and solve the psychological problems of children and adolescents.

Each year, scholars are chosen whose recent work is on the leading edge of clinical child psychology and related disciplines. They are selected either because their own work offers potentially important new information or theoretical viewpoints or because they are especially well qualified to discuss critical topics in the field that are not identified with one particular research program.

In this context, the editors wish to comment on the inclusion of chapters in Volume 12 that were authored or co-authored by the editors themselves. We agreed at the onset of the series that we would not use these volumes as a soapbox for our own views. Our belief in the wisdom of that agreement has not changed, but circumstances led us to make an exception to it for this volume. Because of understandable but unforeseen events, three authors were unable to write chapters for this volume as they had agreed to do. Given our wish not to delay publication of the other chapters, we found ourselves in search of authors at a very late date. We therefore chose two authors (and an exceptionally talented co-author) who had topics about which they wished to write and whom we felt comfortable incommoding with a very short deadline—ourselves.

The chapters in this volume reflect a welcome return to innovative research on psychological intervention. Heinicke tackles the extremely difficult but enormously important task of specifying the assumptions and methods of psychodynamic psychotherapy in sufficient detail to allow the conduct of meaningful research on its effectiveness and parameters. Weisz and Weiss cogently discuss the role of cognitive mediators of the outcome of psychotherapy with children. Bierman outlines an innovative strategy for intervention with socially rejected children that is solidly based in the data and theory of developmental and clinical psychology. Davidson and Basta similarly describe the development of a promising approach to the prevention of recurrent juvenile delinquency. Forehand, Long, and Zogg describe the psychological effects of abduction of children by their own separated parents and outline an innovative attempt to cope with this rapidly growing problem.

The five chapters on intervention are complemented by four chapters dealing with fundamental issues of psychopathology. Vandenberg and Crowe summarize the now formidable body of evidence that suggests that genetics play an important role in the etiology of at least some forms of childhood psychopathology and sketch out the clinical implications of these findings. Woolston and Forsyth discuss the important medical–psychological problem of obesity in infancy and early childhood and suggest a new conceptualization of this issue. Kazdin summarizes and integrates information on the apparently important changes in depression that occur during childhood and adolescent development. Loeber and Lahey close the volume with a discussion of serious shortcomings in our current database on the disruptive behavior disorders of childhood and make suggestions for research that may help clarify future understandings of these disorders.

We sincerely appreciate the roles played by the advisory editors and by the editorial staff of Plenum Publishing Corporation. As always, our strongest thanks go to the chapter authors for their important contributions.

BENJAMIN B. LAHEY
ALAN E. KAZDIN

Contents

Chapter 3. Improving the Peer Relationships of Rejected
Children   53

Karen Linn Bierman

Chapter 4. Diversion from the Juvenile Justice System:
Research Evidence and a Discussion of Issues   85

William S. Davidson II and Joanna Basta

Chapter 5. Parental Child Abduction: The Problem and
Possible Solution   113

Rex Forehand, Nicholas Long, and Carolyn Zogg

Chapter 9.   Recommendations for Research on
Disruptive Behavior Disorders of Childhood and
Adolescence   221

Rolf Loeber and Benjamin B. Lahey

1 Psychodynamic Psychotherapy with Children

Current Status and Guidelines for Future Research

CHRISTOPH M. HEINICKE

In 1957, Levitt concluded from a review of research that "there is no evidence to indicate that child psychotherapy is effective" (Eysenck, 1965; Levitt, 1957a). In 1988, Tuma, reviewing a set of studies published from 1953 to 1986, concluded that "two-thirds of the studies [reviewed] find treatment effects showing that treated children achieve positive changes over control children" (Tuma, 1988). The first task of this chapter will be to elucidate these different conclusions and to suggest that both are based on the review of incomplete data. As Tuma (1988) indicated, there are too few well-described and executed studies to group them in a manner that allows generalization.

Three responses to this situation are developed in this chapter. We will first consider previous reviews and recent research to clarify what can be said about the effectiveness of nonbehavioral child psychotherapy. A second response to the present state of nonbehavioral child psychotherapy research will be to abstract and critique three research programs that report findings relevant to certain more specific theoretically articulated questions. Finally, we outline and illustrate from an existing study several guidelines for planning and executing further productive research in this area.

1. Nonbehavioral Child Psychotherapy

Even though this may be seen as an inadequate question, a series of reviewers (Casey & Berman, 1985; Tuma, 1988) continue to ask whether

CHRISTOPH M. HEINICKE • Department of Psychiatry and the Biobehavioral Sciences, University of California at Los Angeles, Los Angeles, California 90024.

nonbehavioral child psychotherapy has any differential positive effect when subjects are compared with a control group. The nature of this question has been repeatedly challenged (Heinicke & Goldman, 1960; Heinicke & Strassmann, 1975; Kiesler, 1966), but one could still argue that if there is not even an overall outcome effect, why bother to study the conditions under which carefully described treatments do or do not work? Nor can one ignore the fact that both the public and mental health professionals do at some level want an answer to the emotionally charged question. Does it do any good? Whatever way one views the question or the answers, it is helpful to review what the answers have been.

From the very beginning of the development of child psychotherapy approaches, the question has been asked as to whether in comparison with children not receiving treatment children in therapy improve completely, partially, or not at all. Thus, following a model suggested by Eysenck (1952), Levitt (1957a) derived mean figures of improvement as based on 18 studies of child psychotherapy. At closing, 67% were found to be improved and 33% unimproved. At follow-up, the figures were 78% and 22%.

To provide a baseline of child patients who were "similar to treated groups in every respect except for the factor of treatment itself," those who were accepted for treatment but "voluntarily (broke) off the clinic relationship" were used (Levitt, 1957a, p. 190). Studies by Witmer and Keller (1942) and Lehrman, Sirluck, Black, and Glick (1949) indicated a closing baseline figure of 72.5%. This rate of improvement was not significantly different from that for the treated group, and thus the conclusion that whereas many child patients improve as a function of both their own resources and certain environmental facilitators, the child psychotherapeutic situation is not one of those facilitators.

Levitt (1957a) himself demonstrated that the results of the individual studies differed significantly, the rate of improvement at follow-up ranging from 43% to 86%. In a further examination of these issues, Heinicke and Goldman (1960) reasoned that it was most appropriate to examine only those treatment studies that also generated control groups as part of the total research design. As did Levitt (1957a), these authors used the Lehrman et al. (1949) and Witmer and Keller (1942) "control" groups, but confined comparison of those groups with the treatment groups reported by these same researchers. This again follows Levitt's (1971) own reminder that the treatment and control group should be selected from the same population. Heinicke and Goldman (1960) further reasoned that if one is trying to test whether the psychotherapeutic situation is an important facilitator of development, the distinction between successful adjustment and partial improvement becomes very important.

Even though these two studies gave clear evidence that the control groups were favored in terms of the resources of the child and the adequacy of the parents, and even though they received some help, the development of the members of the treatment group as opposed to that of the control groups was a more adequate one. That is, despite this "favoring" of the control group, the evaluation of the treatment groups at follow-up showed a significantly higher percentage of successful adjustments as opposed to partial improvements and a significant increase in successful as opposed to partial improvements in the period from the end of treatment to the follow-up point. The more precise application of the model proposed by Levitt (1957a) seemed, therefore, to lend some support to the hypothesis that child psychotherapy is one of the facilitators of more successful development in a child. Heinicke and Goldman (1960) made it clear, however, that the model proposed by Levitt was at that point in the development of psychotherapy research no longer a useful one.

The first serious question was and still is in regard to the nature of the "control" used and whether indeed the treatment and defector group were equivalent at the initial assessment point. In 1960, and even following the further review by Levitt (1963), the evidence tended to be contradictory. Studies by Levitt (1957b, 1958) indicated no difference, whereas those by Lehrman et al. (1949), Witmer and Keller (1942), and Ross and Lacey (1961) found a great number of differences. One could continue to investigate this question, but other difficulties with the model make such research of doubtful value. As in 1960, we would still conclude that a "family and child who wait and then pursue treatment are likely to be a different family than one who does not" (Heinicke & Goldman, 1960, p. 491).

Another serious reservation about the nature of Levitt's (1971) review is raised by the reviewer himself. If the rate of improvement ranges from 43% to 86%, there must be a number of important variables that account for such striking variation in effectiveness. Hood-Williams (1960) pointed out that the date of the studies reviewed by Levitt (1957a) correlated with effectiveness and suggested that the more recent studies dealt with more severe pathology and were therefore less successful.

Following Eisenberg and Gruenberg (1961), Levitt (1963) suggested an initial refinement of the research approach: that it would be important to define carefully the different diagnostic groupings involved in the psychotherapy research. He demonstrated that children with "special symptoms" show a significantly better rate of improvement than those placed in the "acting-out" category and consequently should not be automatically combined into one group.

In 1985, a quantitative study of 75 psychotherapy outcome studies with children (Casey & Berman, 1985) demonstrated that the effectiveness of child therapy is similar to that with adults (Smith, Glass, & Miller, 1980). Treated children achieved outcomes about two thirds of a standard deviation better than untreated children. In this analysis, the superiority of behavior treatments appeared to be largely due to the types of outcome and target problems included in these behavioral studies. When the data were examined for generalizability of outcome (that is, eliminating outcomes that were essentially identical to therapy activities), there appeared to be no difference between the type of therapy. In addition, Casey and Berman (1985) found no differences in outcome due to treatment characteristics such as the use of play in therapy or the administration of treatment individually or in groups or to whether parents were also treated. Further, experience, education, and sex of therapist were not related to treatment success, nor was length of treatment related; in fact, length of treatment was negatively related to mean effect size for studies ($r(59) = .28, p = .02$).

The review by Casey and Berman (1985) included the various modalities of child therapy: individual, play, psychoanalytically oriented, client-centered, nonspecific–nonbehavioral, behavioral, and group. Tuma (1988) reviewed only the nonbehavioral individual psychotherapy studies as well as the two studies of this type (Heinicke & Ramsey-Klee, 1986; Zelman, Samuels, & Abrams, 1985) that had appeared since the Casey and Berman review. Her final sample included 31 studies published between 1953 and 1986.

Although expressing a major reservation regarding the poor description of subjects, diagnosis, and treatment procedures, Tuma (1988) reported that 62% of the studies showed a significantly better outcome for children receiving therapy than those in control groups. Within this total sample of studies, only 25% of the counseling studies showed a positive effect whereas 80% of play therapy and 82% of the child therapy studies showed such an effect.

In view of the above findings from systematic reviews of the literature from 1960 to 1988, one can conclude that nonbehavioral child therapy is a process that facilitates child development. The description of the therapy and under what conditions it is indeed an effective facilitator of development is not well documented. Because individual parent and child psychotherapy continues to be practiced widely, and even though both the practitioners and consumers attest to its validity, it is imperative that systematic knowledge regarding the factors that influence the course and efficacy of this treatment be studied. In the hope of encouraging such research, the remainder of this chapter first gives examples of research that has begun to provide some specific and reliable knowledge regarding such factors. Both the strengths and limitations of each project will be highlighted and summarized. These conclusions will in turn be incorporated in the presentation of guidelines and an example of how to design a project that is likely to provide reliable and more specific knowledge as to factors affecting child psychotherapeutic outcome.

2. Brief Abstracts of Research Providing Findings on the Factors Affecting the Process and Outcome of Parent and Child Psychotherapy

2.1. Psychotherapeutic Treatment of the Maladjusted Child in the Ordinary School

One of the best designed, described, and executed psychotherapy projects is reported by Kolvin *et al.* (1981) in a book entitled *Help Starts Here*. The primary aim of the project was to identify maladjusted children in ordinary schools and to evaluate the effectiveness of different treatment approaches. Approximately 4,300 school children were screened with multiple assessments to select almost 600 children who showed clear-cut disturbance on a variety of social–emotional and cognitive criteria. Seven schools were involved and each type of treatment and control was executed in each school to avoid the effect of school differences. Once a maladjusted population in a given school was selected, children were assigned at random to either a control or treatment group. Not only would this tend to ensure equivalent status at baseline but in analyzing the differential improvement of the various groups, initial differences were allowed for and that difference removed by analysis of covariance. The design thus chooses a no-treatment control from the same setting, ensures that initial group differences do not compromise the outcome results, and at the same time includes the concept of contrast groups by comparing the impact of different forms of treatment.

There were two different age groups: 7 to 8 (juniors) and 11 to 12 (seniors). Each group experienced three different forms of treatment. Both groups experienced parent-counseling–teacher consultation and group therapy that was psychodynamically oriented and involved play for the younger children. For the younger children, the third form of treatment involved a nurturing relationship with a teacher aide and for the older children consisted of behavior modification carried out by their teacher.

For each form of treatment, the authors reviewed the relevant literature, articulated the rationale for the choice of treatment, and then
carefully described what was done. Although extensive training, supervision, and support of the therapist was provided, the authors acknowledged that the evidence as to whether the treatment was actually being
executed was limited.

Before turning to the description of each treatment and the results
obtained, the general hypotheses guiding this study and the results
supporting or not supporting them will be summarized. The first hypothesis stated that some forms of treatment are less effective in reducing maladjustment; parent counseling as used in this project was in fact
less effective. The second hypothesis stated that one or more of the three
treatments would be more effective than the no-treatment regime; a
central finding was that all treatment groups differed significantly from
their controls. As hypothesized, children in all treatments improved
differentially as a function of the diagnosis (conduct disorder versus
neurotic) and the sex of the child. It was also hypothesized that some
treatment regimes would be better for certain diagnostic groupings or
for girls as opposed to boys; there was no support for these hypotheses.
We turn next to the description of and findings in relation to each treatment mode.

In using a 20-week program of behavior modification with the senior children, the authors stressed the teacher's use of positive reinforcement in relation to the child's task behavior. A review of the literature on the importance of on-task behavior in promoting academic
achievement and the greater effectiveness of positive reinforcement as
opposed to other behavioral techniques provides the rationale for the
method used by the classroom teachers. Improvement in these children
including assessments at an 18- and 36-month follow-up was greatest in
the social–emotional and academic motivation areas. The treated children were less antisocial, less neurotic, less anxious, more creative, had
a more positive attitude to school, and were closer to their teacher. In
contrast, at the final follow-up, there were no significant changes in the
cognitive or achievement scores. This was in fact true of all the treatment
regimes. The above-mentioned changes that did occur varied as a function of the number of consultations that a teacher received from the
psychologist as well as the motivation that the teacher had in carrying
out the program. For this treatment module, the research also planned
direct classroom observation of both teacher and target child. Most interesting, whereas the children's on-task behavior improved, the teacher's specific responses, such as the rate of approval, did not change.

The treatment involving a nurturing relationship between a teacher
aide and the young child over a five-term period was based on the

assumption that a warm, empathic guiding relationship with an adult would develop the intrinsic motivation for learning. The teacher aides felt that for 87% of the pupils, an excellent or good relationship developed and that 87% of the children also improved in their relationship to adults and peers. Independent evaluations were consistent with this improvement. At follow-up, there were no differences in peer or cognitive development but when compared with their control group, the children were less antisocial, less neurotic, and showed particularly striking changes in task-oriented behaviors. For example, they were less impatient and less likely to blame external circumstances for school difficulties.

Under parent counseling–teacher consultation, trained social workers both visited the family and consulted with the teacher regarding the child and his or her family. The description of the contacts makes it clear they were diluted. In 91% of the cases there were nine or fewer contacts with the family over a period of a year. Similarly, the contacts with the many teachers was most frequently catch-as-catch-can. Systematic data on how the participants viewed this intervention are available. The teachers felt supported and appreciated having access to information on the family but did not really feel helped with the management of the child. The parents felt they understood the child better but did not experience help for themselves or their family. The social workers felt there was increased understanding within the family and a more individualized approach to the child in the school but also that only one fourth of the families received considerable help. The teachers and parents did note improved comprehension on the part of the junior children and less isolation in the senior group, but though showing overall improvement when compared with the controls, the findings indicated minimal differences.

Ten group therapy sessions were conducted in the second year of the project by the same social workers who had done the parent counseling in the first year. For both junior and senior children, the emphasis was on promoting communication and setting limits. For the junior children, the promotion of play greatly assisted the communication. The training and support provided this treatment was again excellent. Striking for both age groups was the increase in expressed negative affect and the resentment that the sessions were ending. Both of these indicators suggest that the children were intensely involved in the therapy. The therapist's expectation for this treatment tended to match the outcome. Overall, there were improvements in global adjustment and in neurotic and antisocial behavior. The junior children showed improvement in task behavior and the senior children were less isolated.

From the above descriptions, as well as further comparative analysis by the authors, it is clear that the parent-counseling–teacher-consultation approach made the least impact on the maladjusted children. The authors suggest several possible explanations for this difference. They point out that because this was the first treatment approach to be used in the schools it may have encountered the maximum resistance from school personnel. Similarly, because the parents did not ask for help the social workers may have been seen as uninvited guests. The authors also suggest that the intervention may simply have been insufficient in relation to the multiple and severe nature of the family problems. A median number of four home visits in a year's time is indeed very likely insufficient. In a recent review of controlled early family intervention studies, a significant impact on family functioning involved at least eleven contacts (Heinicke, Beckwith, & Thompson, 1988).

Apart from frequency or duration of contact, the parent-counseling–teacher-consultation approach can be differentiated from the other more successful treatments by the lack of evidence of the development of an emotional relationship between social worker and either parent or teacher. By contrast, in the behavior modification regime, a greater closeness between pupil and teacher emerged, the highly motivated teachers had particularly good results, and this commitment was not evidenced in a change in the frequency of such specific behaviors as rate of approval. The development of a positive relationship between teacher and pupil is suggested. The teacher aides in the nurturing program clearly developed a meaningful relationship with their pupils. Similarly, the children in the group therapy approach made their involvement with the group and its social work leader known by protesting the termination of the treatment. Such evidence of the development of an emotionally meaningful relationship in the parent-counseling–teacher-consultation group was not reported by the authors. A review (Heinicke et al., 1988) of subsequent early family intervention studies supports the authors' interpretation that the intensity of this type of intervention interacting with the multiple-problem nature of the family was not sufficient to lead to a positive therapeutic relationship and outcome.

Another finding invites comment. The lack of academic achievement or cognitive changes in this well-executed study is striking. One possible explanation is that the determinants of these behaviors are more likely to be either genetic factors like parental IQ or early infancy characteristics like attention decrement (Heinicke, Diskin, Ramsey-Klee, & Oates, 1988). Early intervention research has indeed tended to show that the social–emotional as opposed to such factors as IQ and sustained attention are more subject to change as a function of environmental intervention (Heinicke et al., 1986).

The authors discuss two further features of their study highly relevant to this review. They conclude first "that improvement continues and may, indeed, become demonstrable for the first time long after active therapy has finished" (p. 316). To support this conclusion they cite a review of six reasonably well-controlled studies by Wright, Moelis, and Pollack (1976) in which only one showed a significant improvement by the end of treatment and for four that improvement was not seen until follow-up.

Finally, the study provides important evidence on the issue of rate of improvement in nontreated control groups. Returning to the questions raised in the first part of this review, of junior children (7 to 8) showing a good to moderate outcome the findings were 44% for the control, 53% for parent counseling, 67% for the nurture work, and 78% for the playgroup. Similarly, for senior children (11 to 12) showing a good to moderate outcome the findings were 39% for the control group, 52% for the parent counseling group, 73% for the behavior modification group, and 75% for those in group therapy. Clearly, the children receiving treatment had a more favorable development during and after treatment than their matched controls.

We turn to two other studies investigating the efficacy of certain treatments in relation to certain diagnostic groupings.

2.2. The Outcome of Psychotherapeutic Intervention with Delinquent Boys

Shore and Massimo (1966, 1969, 1973); Shore, Massimo, Kisielewski, and Moran (1966); Shore, Massimo, Mack, and Malasky (1968a, 1968b); Shore, Massimo, and Ricks (1965); Massimo and Shore (1963); and Massimo and Shore (1967) developed a comprehensive, vocationally oriented, psychotherapeutic program for delinquent boys and carried out an extensive evaluative follow-up of their efforts. The basic study included 10 delinquents who received treatment and 10 who did not. Subjects were included in the sample on the basis of having dropped out of school or been expelled from it and other criteria, such as IQ and a history of antisocial behavior. After assigning subjects randomly to experimental and control groups and finding no significant difference between the two in terms of age, IQ, or socioeconomic status, the treated group was seen for a period of 10 months. A variety of elements characterized the program, the most crucial of which was the focus on reality-oriented factors relating to getting and keeping a job, as well as the intense involvement of the therapist (i.e., available just about any time or any place). Other help was provided when the patient requested it.

To evaluate the program, the authors had data from pretesting, posttesting, after 10 months, follow-up testing for half the sample at 2 years, and the other half at 3 years, a 5-year follow-up, and a 10-year follow-up. Assessment measures administered at these various testing points included thematic stories to measure personality changes, Metropolitan Achievement Tests for academic progress, and descriptive statements of overt behavior (e.g., job performance, antisocial behavior).

On each of these indices, and most of their various subcategories, the treated group functioned in a demonstrably superior manner, and this improved level of functioning tended to be sustained even 10 years after treatment. Most dramatically impressive were the descriptive contrasts of overt behavior. Thus, most of the treated group had good jobs and little if any antisocial behavior, in comparison with many more arrests and typically poorer employment records for the untreated group. Thus, of the treated group, at the 10-year follow-up, one subject had had four arrests since January 1969 and was serving 3 to 5 years for armed robbery and another subject had had one arrest and a suspended sentence for disorderly conduct. In contrast, seven of the control subjects had known arrest records, not counting the one control subject whose whereabouts were unknown.

In addition to significant and maintained improvement in academic areas, the various analyses performed on the thematic stories supported the overt behavioral gains. Ratings pertaining to self-image, control of aggression, attitude toward authority, object relations, and guilt were made at various points. Illustrative of the kind of findings revealed was the increase in positive interaction with people (object relations) for the treated group and the close association between changes in self-image and academic achievement. Shore et al. (1966) concluded, "The changes noted in object relations are clearly not isolated changes but most certainly reflect a generally higher level of over-all ego functioning and integration" (p. 103).

Analyzing both the strength and limitations of this study helps to formulate the guidelines for future research. There is first of all a carefully thought out fit between the form of treatment and the child's difficulty. A reality-oriented program relating to getting a job as well as the ready availability of the therapist would be needed to make an impact on children involved in severe antisocial behavior (Kazdin, 1987). The multiple assessments effectively reflect these major areas, namely the record of overt behavior (jobs, antisocial behavior, academic achievement) as well as demonstrated changes in the capacity for relationships and overall ego functioning. Thus, the choice of a homogenous treatment population, the method of treatment, and the mode of assessment are carefully integrated. A more detailed description of the treatment procedures would have made replication of this work more accurate.

A further strength of the study lies in the repeated and lengthy follow-up. The combination of a well-articulated approach and highly relevant long-term outcome results is impressive. The size of the sample does introduce some caution in generalizing these results. Even though the subjects were assigned randomly to the experimental and control groups and did not differ in age, IQ, or socioeconomic status, matching them on the initial assessments with respect to, for example, the severity of antisocial behavior would increase the power of the findings.

2.3. Outcome of Child Psychotherapy as a Function of Frequency of Session

Kazdin (1987) has suggested that an important direction in identifying effective treatments is to increase the strength or intensity of existing treatments. The author and his colleagues (Heinicke, 1969; Heinicke & Ramsey-Klee, 1986) have focused on the impact on outcome of the intensity or frequency of treatment. Three groups of boys carefully matched on a number of baseline measures including their main symptom, namely, a deficit in academic achievement, were seen by psychoanalytic child therapists at differing frequencies. One group was seen once a week, another four times a week, and the third was initially seen once a week and after a year four times a week. A psychotherapeutic contact with the mother and father was also established.

As in the Shore et al. (1966) research, the treatment approach was linked to a conception of the cause and resolution of the difficulty. It was assumed that the learning disturbance was associated with the child's inadequate resolution of external and internal conflicts. Also as in the Shore et al. (1966) research, the multiple outcome measures focussed on key overt behaviors (tests of academic achievement) and a profile of personality functioning particularly relevant to children with learning difficulties: effective adaptation and self-esteem, capacity for relationships, frustration tolerance and the ability to work, and flexible adaptation (Heinicke & Ramsey-Klee, 1986).

As in the Kolvin research (Kolvin et al., 1981), the most striking outcome findings did not appear until the follow-up point. It is assumed that structural changes in the child's personality had taken place during treatment that in interaction with a favorable environment continued to exert a positive impact on development in the period after treatment. Comparison of the three groups showed that children seen more frequently as opposed to once a week had a greater rate of improvement in reading in the year after the end of treatment and were in particular characterized by being more flexible in their adaptation and having a greater capacity for relationships at both the end and a year after the end of treatment (Heinicke & Ramsey-Klee, 1986).

The strength and limitations of this research are similar to the Shore *et al.* (1966) project. A homogenous sample, children with a learning deficit, are treated with a theoretically relevant mode of therapy and assessed with multiple methods reflecting both their overt behavior and their personality functioning. Even though careful baseline matching on all relevant indices was done and showed no initial significant difference between the three frequency groups, the samples are small and further replication of the findings on frequency are needed. As outlined in the next section, the further research comparing once- and twice-a-week therapy addresses this issue and also attempts to provide a more articulate description of the nature of the therapy used in this research.

2.4. Concluding Remarks

The three projects described were abstracted to indicate what type of research has gone beyond the initial question, Is child psychotherapy research effective? Other studies could have been cited. Those included do highlight certain design features that are likely to promote meaningful research in the future.

In each case a rationale for the likely effectiveness of a given form of treatment in relation to a diagnostically defined disturbance is specified. The baseline and subsequent status is measured using overt and personality variables relevant to the diagnostic grouping. Control and/or contrast groups are integrated into the design. The importance of both end-of-treatment and subsequent follow-up assessment is stressed. In terms of current research experience, more could have been done to describe via manuals the treatment approach being used.

3. Guidelines in Formulating Nonbehavioral Child Psychotherapy Research

The guidelines developed below are not unique to nonbehavioral research but do need to be applied to this area. After stating the guidelines in general terms, we will illustrate each from an ongoing psychotherapy research project with children who in relation to their potential are one or more years behind in reading, arithmetic, and/or spelling. We have used an index developed by Bond and Tinker (1973) to define academic underachievement.

3.1. Defining the Conceptual Link between the Characteristics of the Children and Families Being Treated and the Nature of the Therapeutic Process

It is crucial to delimit the children being treated (broad diagnostic considerations), to describe their specific characteristics, and to link these conceptually to what the therapy is designed to accomplish. We will follow these steps in the sections below.

3.1.1. Defining the Characteristics That Promote Amenability to the Treatment Chosen: Broad Diagnostic Considerations

To match the children being treated with the treatment chosen, namely, nonbehavioral individual psychotherapy and parallel contacts with the parent, certain diagnostic groupings need to be included and excluded. Certain broad DSM-III diagnoses are first of all excluded: children suffering from mental retardation, schizoid disorders of childhood, pervasive developmental disorders and syndromes where the organic impairment or physical disease process is clearly related to the difficulties the child has in reaching his or her learning potential. Furthermore, children with learning potential that is intact but for whom educational stimulation has been insufficient are excluded. In these cases, new or additional educational input as opposed to psychotherapy is most appropriate.

More positively stated, we are including children where learning has failed to reach its potential as a function of the child's and family's inadequate adaptation to certain developmental psychological issues. Broadly speaking, this includes the DSM-III categories of attention deficit disorders, conduct disorders, anxiety disorders, reactive attachment disorders, oppositional disorders, and the specific developmental disorders. It is recognized that in the case of attention deficit disorder with or without hyperactivity the etiology and determinants may be such that the disturbances respond best to pharmacological and alternate treatment approaches. Similarly, specific learning disabilities may best respond to certain educational training methods. Moreover, the determinants and thus treatment of severe conduct disorders represent a different prognosis to children showing milder forms of antisocial behavior combined with underachievement. To ensure the amenability of the child and family to a nonbehavioral psychotherapeutic approach the primary determinant of the underachievement in the above diagnoses should be inadequate psychological adaptation to past and present psychological developmental issues.

A further critical criterion is the child's and family's motivation to seek help. Is there an experienced sense of discomfort and is there (particularly in the family) a determination to pursue and continue treatment?

3.1.2. Defining the Child Characteristics That Promote Amenability to a Treatment: Specific Considerations

Having established the diagnostic categories to be included and excluded, the specific characteristics of the children and families need to be defined and their potential to change as a function of the treatment chosen needs to be at least conceptually feasible.

To illustrate, the set of determinants impeding the learning process in a particular child and family is highly idiosyncratic and requires thorough initial and continuing formulation. Certain characteristics do appear frequently, can be conceptually linked to the therapeutic process (see section below), and have been shown to be subject to change by that process (Heinicke, 1977; Heinicke & Ramsey-Klee, 1986). Thus, the different areas of child functioning relevant to underachievement have been grouped by cluster analysis of multiple assessments as follows: effective adaptation and self-esteem, capacity for relationships, frustration tolerance and the ability to work, and indices of flexible adaptation (see Table 4, Heinicke & Ramsey-Klee, 1986). These are elaborated below. Most important, experience has shown that adequate but especially inadequate functioning in these areas is in part dynamically linked to the nature of the child's adaptation to the external and internal conflicts that are presented (repeated) in the real and transference relationship to the therapist.

3.1.2.1. Indices of Effective Adaptation and Self-Esteem. Central to effective adaptation and self-esteem is the child's effective defense organization in dealing with the anxiety that is experienced in relation to learning and performance. Adequate self-observation further ensures that learning experiences are defined and followed through as opposed to, for example, expressing the anxiety through hyperactivity, distractibility, or dreamlike inattention.

The quality of the self-esteem and the related issue of depressed mood is also likely to be related to underachievement. The fear of failure is seen in the child being unable to achieve at all or worrying that his or her performance will not meet either internal or external standards. Some may be so depressed that they simply cannot muster the energy to confront a task.

3.1.2.2. Capacity for Relationships. A prevalent relationship characteristic of underachievers is the tendency to externalize the control of their initiating, staying with, and completing a task unto others. For example, a child twiddles pencils or goes to the bathroom to force the teacher to stand over him. Or a child consistently waits to complete things until the last minute knowing the parent will come to the rescue. These characteristics are frequently repeated in relation to the therapist and are thus subject to change.

Insofar as learning represents a challenge that needs to be met on one's own, a sense of security in relation to adults and peers may be crucial in promoting comfort with that autonomy.

3.1.2.3. Frustration Tolerance and the Ability to Work. Central to behaviors with regard to frustration is the child's task orientation: the capacity to become involved in, persist in, and accomplish and take pride in a task. Together with IQ, it is a powerful predictor of school achievement (Heinicke, 1980). Task orientation as a whole and its components can be linked to past and current adaptations and recreated in individual treatment. Thus the child may be unable to persist in any task (including those defined in therapy) because he or she feels that before the first one is finished, other involvements are already being demanded.

All learning and performance tasks require some level of frustration tolerance. Relevant to this characteristic in turn are the child's experience of having been satisfied and/or having learned to expect satisfaction. Although infants vary at birth in their soothability, the quality and continuity of parents' responsiveness and such events as being replaced by a sibling affect the development of frustration tolerance. The state of that development can be recreated and addressed in psychotherapy.

3.1.2.4. *Flexible Adaptation.* Central to the definition of flexible adaptation is the balanced use of various defenses and/or modes of coping. For example, as a function of repeated failure and humiliation, the underachiever relies heavily on one defense: avoiding any learning task.

Also frequently associated with low academic achievement is the extensive repression of aggression. This may lead to severe inhibition or provocative acting out in order to be punished. The individual psychotherapeutic process focuses on the excessive use of such types of defenses and has been shown to bring about a greater balance in their use (Heinicke & Ramsey-Klee, 1986).

3.1.3. Defining the Parent Characteristics That Promote Amenability to Treatment

Parallel to linking the characteristics of the underachiever to the potential of the child's psychotherapeutic process are the characteristic themes that emerge and can be potentially dealt with in the treatment of the parents. It is crucial that these parallel themes be integrated both conceptually and in terms of collaborative communication between the therapists.

The characteristics of family transactions and the personality functioning of the parents again have to be understood in their idiosyncratic form. Certain themes do frequently emerge and will be discussed in relation to the typical characteristics of the academic underachiever.

Thus, with regard to adaptation and self-esteem, the child's sense of being able to succeed may be highly affected by parental expectations. A parent's need to realize himself or herself through a genius son or identifying this child as the "stupid one" to maintain a family equilibrium are powerful influences and are subject to change in a non-behavioral psychotherapeutic process. Just as underachievers typically invite control by others so their parents frequently "take over" by not, for example, allowing the child the psychological space to initiate a learning task or take responsibility for it.

As indicated above, encouraging the child's autonomous exploration while at the same time providing sufficient guidance is crucial to an inner sense of "I can cope." This must, however, be seen in the context of a psychologically secure and safe place as provided by the primary caretaking environment. Children may be unable to learn to their full potential because their sense of inner and outer support from adult figures is inadequate. An inconsistent father who has separated from the family is reflected in an inner fluctuation in commitment to learning. In turn, marital discord undermines a sense of security necessary to face challenging learning tasks. Children may be preoccupied with the psychological safety of a depressed parent, the uncontrolled outbursts of a severely disturbed parent, or the fate of a dying parent. The psychotherapeutic work with the parents focuses on their struggle with these issues and in the process hopefully enhances the security felt by the child.

Insofar as the resolution of repressed anger toward effective assertiveness is a major goal of the therapeutic process with the underachiever, extensive parallel work with the parents is necessary for both tolerating and limiting the transitional expression of aggression. A 10-year-old boy who refused to finish the last piece of his homework and was hit by a helpless single mother needed to test whether defiance and calling her a stupid helpless person would again lead to abusive outbursts or effective control. The mother needed help in understanding this repetition, how important it was to ignore her son's jibes, and if necessary to stop his explosions in a firm manner even if it meant calling on another adult to help her.

In tracing the link between the characteristics of the families being treated and the nature of the nonbehavioral therapeutic process, we have so far conceptualized those characteristics of the underachiever that are likely to appear and are amenable to change in that process. A next issue in developing a particular psychotherapeutic study is to outline and describe the particular method chosen to treat the children and families.

3.1.4. Conceptualizing and Describing the Child and Parent Psychotherapeutic Process: The Development of Manuals

Whatever form of nonbehavioral child psychotherapy is chosen for a particular study, its characteristics and its relevance to the children being treated need to be described. Thus for the study under discussion a manual entitled *Framework for Psychodynamic Psychotherapy with School Aged Children and their Parents* has been developed to state the working assumptions and procedures of this treatment approach (Heinicke, 1988). The beginning phase, the emergence of the first major focus, and the emergence of a dynamically linked set of foci are outlined. Further sections describe the historic reconstruction of the subjective foci, the simultaneous confrontation and working through of the issue of internal and external control in relation to adult figures, and how a key event serves as the focus of the repetition of a past trauma and working toward a new adaptation. Finally, the termination of treatment is discussed as an opportunity for further resolution and the assessment of the ending level of adaptation.

Detailed case vignettes from two treatments further define the meaning of the above therapeutic process description and are easily linked to the characteristics of the underachieving child and his or her family described earlier. To illustrate, the beginning of the third section of the manual is given below.

3.1.5. An Illustration from the Parent and Child Psychotherapy Manual

A section of the manual entitled "Beyond the Beginning: A Major Focus Emerges," starts as follows:

> Typically, as issues of trust, confidentiality, and the extremes of subjective stress are no longer as salient, so the work focuses on *certain* intrapsychic and external conflicts. These are seen in the transference and resistance to the transference and especially so if the frequency of the treatment is twice-a-week or more.

3.1.5.1. The Focus in the Child's Treatment. Although in any treatment session, several subjective foci are potentially present either at the same time or in time sequence, one issue typically soon dominates both during the session and over a number of sessions. Most therapists can specify either to themselves or the patient: We are working on so and so.

For example, the major focus of John's treatment became the anger he felt when his mother did not protect him by ensuring that he was on time for this treatment. She had overslept. Yet he could not express his anger directly and instead tried to manipulate the therapist into making up for his felt deprivation.

For Judy, the major focus that soon emerged was the anxiety that if she initiated full communication and told her secrets, her mother and therapist would find out how angry and jealous she was of her younger brother. It was safer to let the mother and therapist ask *and* answer all the questions.

3.1.5.2. The Therapist's Subjective Recognition of the Patient's Central Issue. An essential first step in the process of the therapist's subjective recognition of the patient's central issue is the sufficient and specific communication of that issue by the patient. The therapist in turn communicates his or her understanding. Just as the patient communicates feelings and ideas in a variety of ways (words, gestures, affects, play, and sequences of meanings) so the therapist can react by affects, gestures, play, and certain sequences of communication without saying a word. We assume, and have experienced, that just on the basis of this recognition the patient feels understood, relieved, and is likely to adapt better.

For example, when the therapist simply reflected John's disappointment at being made late by his mother, he communicated his distress by whining in a pained way, by having a little car go off the cliff, and by responding with an intense "Hurry up, let's get going and play."

Similarly, through her silence, her insistence on showing her mother the pictures she had made during the session, and her constant bodily stance inviting question, Judy communicated her feelings of being afraid to share her secrets.

3.1.5.3. The Focus in the Transference and Transference Resistance. Typically, especially in the more frequent dosage of treatment, the central subjective issue is also focused in the transference and the resistance to the transference. The transference provides the emotional and ideational display that both therapist and patient can experience and observe. Patients have commented on the paradox of both repeating a certain intense relationship and feeling from the past and present toward the therapist and then being asked through rational means to gain perspective on and/or change that repetition.

Although the therapist's failure to recognize the transference reaction can lead to nonadaptive developments like negative acting out and even termination of the treatment, it is often the case that the very emergence of the transference with the accompanying experience that the feared associated consequences do not occur that is likely to lead to relief and even better adaptation. If a patient, out of his feeling of not being helped by this adult either, suddenly screams at his therapist "I could kill you" and, though clearly affected, the therapist does not retaliate in kind as the patient's father was inclined to do, then relief and a greater sense of safety is likely to follow.

John's anger toward his mother, who was late and did not protect him, was soon repeated as well in relationship to the therapist. When the therapist was a few minutes late, John at first said it didn't matter. Further resistance to discussing the underlying feeling took the form of the provocative throwing of balls at the therapist and his plant. In subsequent play, two ferocious catlike animals threatened to destroy each other. The therapist interpreted both the resistance and the underlying anger: "It is very difficult for you to let me know how angry you were at being kept waiting because your anger might really destroy me and I would in turn destroy you." "No, no, no," he replied. "Let's get on with the game."

Judy's reluctance to express any feelings and her insistence that the adult control everything by both asking and answering questions also developed in relation to the therapist. Because she was still electively mute she could not respond verbally to the interpretation articulating this repetition. However, both her subsequent painting and Playdoh expressions expanded and included expressions of anger and jealously directed toward her younger brother.

Further subsections of this part of the manual deal with how the central focus is also worked with in the real relationship to the therapist, how this focus is evidenced in the therapist's feelings and countertransference reactions, and the parallel working through of the major focus in different parts of the family system.

3.2. The Research Design and Hypotheses

Having defined the characteristics of the children and families to be treated, how these are amenable to the psychotherapy being used, and having described the therapeutic process, certain influences on that process are defined and systematically varied through a particular research design. For example, on the basis of past research (Heinicke & Ramsey-Klee, 1986), it is hypothesized that twice-a-week as opposed to once-a-week psychotherapy will make a more significant impact on the developmental outcome of families being studied. It is further hypothesized that the differential improvement will be particularly noticeable in the children's flexible adaptation and their capacity for relationships. Moreover, and again particularly in the above two areas of functioning, the differential improvement of children seen twice a week will be particularly noticeable in the period *after* treatment. The research design of course needs further elaboration. It is important to stress in developing the guidelines being presented here is the systematic variation of influences felt to be significant in affecting the process and outcome of therapy. Simply determining whether a given therapy makes a difference is no longer of sufficient value.

3.2.1. Control and Contrast Groups

To answer certain questions a randomized trial that assigns families to a treatment group as opposed to a no-treatment control group may be necessary. To use as a control families who seek treatment but do not follow through seems inappropriate. As in 1960 and 1975, we would conclude that a "family and child who wait for and then pursue treatment are likely to be a different family than one who does not" (Heinicke & Goldman, 1960).

The most promising approach is to find a control sample in the same setting as the treatment group but that has not sought or been offered treatment. Studies by Shore and Massimo (1966) and Shepherd, Oppenheim, and Mitchell (1966) use examples of this approach. Applying this to underachievement, for each child undergoing treatment another child preferably in the same classroom is found that matches him or her in terms of the initial assessments being used. The limitation of the approach may still lie in the fact that families experiencing difficulty that do not seek help even if matched on known variables may nevertheless have less visible associated variables that compromise the findings. Moreover, if such a control group is used, then one has to determine if those families did or did not eventually receive some sort of help.

An alternate approach to the use of a no-treatment control group is the use of contrast groups that systematically vary the influence being studied. In the study being proposed here, the contrast is between a once- and twice-a-week frequency of session. Adding a no-treatment control group clearly enhances the power of such a comparison. That is, children and families from the same classroom matched on the initial assessment would be randomly assigned to one of three groups: twice-a-week sessions, a once-a-week session, and a no-treatment control.

3.2.2. The Initial Assessments

Psychotherapy researchers generally agree that given our present state of knowledge, both multidimensional, multiple rater, and multiple data source assessments are necessary to obtain a reliable and valid measurement of the initial status and outcome. In the study of psychotherapy for school-aged underachievers, "multiple dimensions" refers to the profile nature of such an assessment, ranging from child's fantasies as to why he or she can't learn to parental reports of the child's involvement in sports. "Multiple rater" refers to therapist, parents, the child, the child's teacher, and the psychological examiner. "Multiple data source" refers to the fact that the assessments are based on observations of the child and family in a variety of settings: interviews, test situations, the classroom, the home setting, and the playground. These assessment instruments will be described below in the sequence they are administered in the project being used as an illustration.

Following the referral of the child to the outpatient intake team, the suitability of the case for the project is reviewed. Initial primary criteria are that the family is in a psychological and resource position to bring the child once or twice a week and is willing to sign the human subjects protocol. A further major criterion is that the symptom picture is part of an emergent but internalized and external set of conflict and adaptation issues that is potentially subject to repetition and resolution in a psychodynamic treatment process.

Following the intake, four further steps are taken:

1. *Initial unstructured interview between therapist, parent, and child*

The initial interview is with both parents or other primary caretakers. This interview is unstructured except for the general focus of realizing certain major goals:

a. Determining the nature of the difficulty for which the parents and the child are seeking help.

b. Determining the nature of the quality of family functioning affecting the child as well as other significant environmental events influencing that child.

c. Gathering sufficient developmental history on the child and family.

At the end of the interview, the parents are given the Family Assessment Measure (Skinner, Steinhauer, & Santa-Barbara, 1983), the Yale Neuropsychoeducational Assessment Scales, (Shaywitz, 1979), and the Achenbach Child Behavior Checklist (Achenbach & Edelbrock, 1983). They are asked to fill these out and return them at the subsequent visit with the therapist. They are also given the Achenbach Teacher Report Form (Achenbach & Edelbrock, 1986) to hand to the child's teacher that is most knowledgeable about his or her functioning. This battery provides parallel interview and inventory data for the following areas: family functioning, the nature of the child's problems, details of functioning in various setting, and developmental level.

Further appointments are then set up for the child. He or she first sees the therapist in an unstructured set of two or three interviews and this is followed by the educational testing. The purpose of the unstructured interviews with the child is to assess the nature of the difficulty as experienced by the child and to provide initial formulation of the child's external and internal conflicts. Such information as is necessary for the mental status exam is also gathered during these interviews. The Youth Self Report is also administered by the therapist toward the end of the sessions with the child (Achenbach & Edelbrock, 1987). All initial interviews with the parents and child are dictated after the session in process detail.

2. *Educational testing*

As part of the standardized assessment battery, our education consultants administer the WISC-R, the reading section of the California Test of Basic Skills, and the arithmetic part of the Wide Range Achievement Test, Form R. If the child is younger than 6 years of age, a specialized version of this assessment battery is given. This testing should be done after the initial unstructured interviews between therapist and child.

3. *Physical examination and other additional evaluation procedures*

If there has not been a recent physical examination of the child and the clinic has no access to pediatric records, this type of examination may need to be arranged. Other types of considerations, such as speech and language development, may arise during the evaluation procedure. All assessments should be completed before the formulation of the case and feedback to the parents. Subject to the availability of the educational testing results and the teacher report form, a conversation over the phone between therapist and teacher may well be in order to further gain a qualitative picture of the child's situation in school.

4. *Diagnostic formulation and ratings pertaining to the initial status of child and family*

The integrating formulation both for the purposes of diagnosis and treatment recommendation takes several forms. The first is a qualitative statement in the form of the central intake psychiatric evaluation, which then also leads to the DSM-III diagnosis. The second type of formulation is reflected in the ratings done by the therapist. The first of these is a series of ratings based on the Anna Freud Diagnostic Profile (Heinicke & Ramsey-Klee, 1986). The second set of ratings is entitled The Psychodynamic Child Ratings. Each of these sets of ratings is defined by accompanying manuals (Szapolznick, Rio, Richardson, Alonso, & Murray, 1987). The third form of rating is the Children's Global Assessment Scale by Shaffer (Shaffer *et al.*, 1985). Here the form itself defines the rating. These three sets of ratings are also done by an outside clinician who reads the reported material. Finally, these various formulations include a treatment recommendation. In the context of feedback, the therapist will communicate these recommendations to the parents at the end of the diagnostic interview.

3.3.3. *The Outcome Assessments*

After a year of treatment and at the end of one and two years after treatment, all of the above instruments are repeated except the Yale Inventory, which is not given again, and the WISC IQ test, which is given again only at the end and 2 years after treatment. Both the absolute and change measures (including rates of change) constitute the outcome measures. (See Heinicke & Ramsey-Klee, 1986, for further description of the methodology.)

It is the combination of initial and subsequent repeat assessments (outcome measures) that are used to test the hypotheses in regard to the impact of frequency of treatment on the development of children with a deficit in academic achievement. Is the rate of reading achievement, the ease of flexible adaptation, and the capacity for positive relationships greater for the children seen twice as opposed to once a week? Such information would be of immense value to the practitioner trying to advise parents as to which of these two forms of treatment is likely to be the most efficient in helping their child.

4. Concluding Remarks

In an effort to encourage theoretically based and well-articulated research on the outcome and process of nonbehavioral individual child and parent psychotherapy, we have presented three arguments: (1) that much of the past research was a response to an inadequate question but that nevertheless repeated reviews of this literature support the conclusion that nonbehavioral child therapy does facilitate child development; (2) that some research projects have been executed that provide reliable and valid data in relation to specific hypotheses; and (3) that the accumulation of specific knowledge as to the factors influencing the efficacy of nonbehavioral parent and child psychotherapy research is more likely to occur under the following conditions:

1. There is a general and specific conceptual link between the characteristics of the children being treated and the nature of the therapy being used.
2. There is a multidimensional, multiple-rater, multiple-datasource, and multiple-assessment-point approach to constructing the profile of child and family functioning.
3. The assessment profile includes measures of overt and personality functioning specifically relevant to the symptomatology of the children.
4. There is a manual describing the conceptual framework and specific steps of the treatment process.
5. Follow-up assessments are an integral part of the design.
6. Control and/or contrast groups are compared with treatment groups.
7. The total design is guided by specific hypotheses that have been generated in relation to theory-based questions.

5. References

Achenbach, T., & Edelbrock, C. (1983). *Manual for the Child Behavior Checklist.* Burlington: University of Vermont, Department of Psychiatry.

Achenbach, T., & Edelbrock, C. (1986). Manual for the teacher's report form. Burlington: University of Vermont, Department of Psychiatry.

Achenbach, T., & Edelbrock, C. (1987). Manual for youth self-report. Burlington: University of Vermont, Department of Psychiatry.

Bond, G. L., & Tinker, M. A. (1973). *Reading difficulties: The diagnosis and correction.* New York: Appleton-Century-Crofts.

Casey, R. J., & Berman, J. S. (1985). The outcome of psychotherapy with children. *Psychological Bulletin, 98,* 388–400.

Eisenberg, L., & Gruenberg, E. M. (1961). The current status or secondary prevention in child psychiatry. *American Journal of Orthopsychiatry, 31,* 355–367.

Eysenck, H. J. (1952). The effects of psychotherapy. *Journal of Consulting Psychology, 16,* 319–324.

Eysenck, H. J. (1965). The effects of psychotherapy. *International Journal of Psychiatry, 1,* 99–142.

Heinicke, C. M. (1969). Frequency of psychotherapeutic session as a factor affecting outcome. *Journal of Abnormal Psychology, 74,* 553–560.

Heinicke, C. M. (1977). Changes in the preschool child as a function of change in the parent–child relationship. (ERIC Document Reproduction Service No. ED 138 377)

Heinicke, C. M. (1980). Continuity and discontinuity of task orientation. *Journal of the American Academy of Child Psychiatry, 19,* 637–653.

Heinicke, C. M. (1988). Framework for psychodynamic psychotherapy with school aged children and their parents. Unpublished manuscript, University of California at Los Angeles. Department of Psychiatry.

Heinicke, C. M., Beckwith, L., & Thompson, A. (1988). Early intervention in the family system: A framework and review. *Journal of Infant Mental Health, 9,* 111–141.

Heinicke, C. M., Diskin, S. D., Ramsey-Klee, D. M., & Oates, D. S. (1986). Pre- and postbirth antecedents of 2-year-old attention, capacity for relationships, and verbal expressiveness. *Developmental Psychology, 22,* 777–787.

Heinicke, C. M., & Goldman, A. (1960). Research on psychotherapy with children. *American Journal of Orthopsychiatry , 30,* 483–494.

Heinicke, C. M., & Ramsey-Klee, D. M. (1986). Outcome of child psychotherapy as a function of frequency of session. *Journal of the American Academy of Child Psychiatry, 25,* 247–253.

Heinicke, C. M., & Strassman, L. H. (1975). Towards more effective research in psychotherapy. *Journal of the American Academy of Child Psychiatry, 14,* 561–588.

Hood-Williams, J. (1960). The results of psychotherapy with children. *Journal of Consulting Psychology, 24,* 84–88.

Kazdin, A. (1987). *Conduct disorders in childhood and adolescence.* Newbury Park, CA: Sage.

Kiesler, D. J. (1966). Some myths of psychotherapy research and the search for a paradigm. *Psychological Bulletin, 65,* 110–136.

Kolvin, L., Garside, R. F., Nicol, A. R., Macmillan, A., Wolstenholme, E., & Leitch, I. M. (1981). *Help starts here.* London: Tavistock.

Lehrman, L. J., Sirluck, H., Black, B., & Glick, S. (1949). Success and failure of treatment of children in the child guidance clinics of the Jewish Board of Guardians, New York City. *Jewish Board of Guardians Research Monograph, 1:*1–87.

Levitt, E. E. (1957a). The results of psychotherapy with children. *Journal of Consulting Psychology, 21,* 189–196.

Levitt, E. E. (1957b). A comparison of "remainers" and "defectors" among child clinic patients. *Journal of Consulting Psychology, 21,* 316.

Levitt, E. E. (1958). A comparative judgmental study of "defection" from treatment at a child guidance clinic. *Journal of Clinical Psychology, 14,* 429–432.

Levitt, E. E. (1963). Psychotherapy with children. *Behaviour Research and Therapy, 1,* 45–51.

Levitt, E. E. (1971). Research on psychotherapy with children. In A. E. Bergin & S. L. Garfield, (Eds.), *Handbook of psychotherapy and behavior change,* New York: Wiley.

Massimo, J. L., & Shore, M. F. (1963). The effectiveness of a comprehensive, vocationally oriented psychotherapeutic program for adolescent delinquent boys. *American Journal of Orthopsychiatry, 33,* 634–642.

Massimo, J. L., & Shore, M. F. (1967). Comprehensive vocationally oriented psychotherapy. *Psychiatry, 30,* 229–236.

Ross, A. O., & Lacey, H. M. (1961). Characteristics of terminators and remainers in child guidance treatment. *Journal of Consulting Psychology, 25,* 420–424.

Shaffer, D., Gould, M., Brasic, J., Ambrosini, P., Fisher, P., Bird, H., & Aluwahlia, S. (1985). A children's global assessment scale (CGAS) (for children 4 to 16 years of age) *Psychopharmocological Bulletin, 21,* 747–748.

Shepherd, M., Oppenheim, A. N., & Mitchell, S. (1966). Childhood behaviour disorders and the child-guidance clinic. *Journal of Child Psychology and Psychiatry, 7,* 39–52.

Shaywitz, S. (1979). Yale Neuropsychoeducational Assessment Scales—Children's Personal Data Inventory. New Haven, CT: Yale University.

Shore, M. F., & Massimo, J. L. (1966). Comprehensive vocationally oriented psychotherapy for adolescent delinquent boys. *American Journal of Orthopsychiatry, 36,* 609–615.

Shore, M. F., & Massimo, J. L. (1969). Five years later. *American Journal of Orthopsychiatry, 39,* 769–773.

Shore, M. F., & Massimo, J. L. (1973). After 10 years. *American Journal Orthopsychiatry, 43,* 128–132.

Shore, M. F., Massimo, J. L., Kisielewski, J., & Moran, J. K. (1966). Object relations changes resulting from successful psychotherapy with adolescent delinquents and their relationship to academic performance. *Journal of American Academy of Child Psychiatry, 5,* 93–104.

Shore, M. F., Massimo, J. L., Mack, R., & Malasky, C. (1968a). Studies of psychotherapeutic change in adolescent delinquent boys. *Psychotherapy, 5,* 85–88.

Shore, M. F., Massimo, J. L., Moran, J. K., & Malasky, C. (1968b). Object relations changes and psychotherapeutic intervention. *Journal of American Academy of Child Psychiatry, 7,* 59–67.

Shore, M. F., Massimo, J. L., & Ricks, D. F. (1965). A factor analytic study of psychotherapeutic change in delinquent boys. *Journal of Clinical Psychology, 21,* 208–212.

Skinner, H. A., Steinhauer, P. D., & Santa-Barbara, J. (1983). The family assessment measure. *Canadian Journal of Community Mental Health, 2,* 91–105.

Smith, M. L., Glass, G. V., & Miller, T. I. (1980). *Psychotherapy.* Baltimore, MD: Johns Hopkins University Press.

Szapolznick, J., Rio, A., Richardson, R., Alonso, M., & Murray, E. (1986). *Manual for the Psychodynamic Child Ratings.* Unpublished manuscript, University of Miami.

Tuma, J. M. (1988). Current status of insight oriented therapy with children. Unpublished manuscript. Louisiana State University, Department of Psychology.

Witmer, H., & Keller, J. (1942). Outgrowing childhood problems. *Smith Coll. Studies in Social Work, 13,* 74–90.

Wright, D. M., Moelis, I., & Pollack, L. J. (1976). The outcome of individual psychotherapy: Increments at follow-up. *Journal of Child Psychology and Psychiatry, 17,* 275–285.

Zelman, A. B., Samuels, S., & Abrams, D. (1985). I.Q. changes in young children following intensive long-term psychotherapy. *American Journal of Psychoanalytic Psychotherapy, 39,* 215–227.

2

Cognitive Mediators of the Outcome of Psychotherapy with Children

John R. Weisz and Bahr Weiss

Those of us who conduct child psychotherapy would like to believe that the outcome of the process is influenced by our efforts. On the other hand, few of us would argue that the outcome is determined solely by what we the therapists do. Instead, we recognize that children and adolescents (herein referred to collectively as "children") begin psychotherapy with a form and substance of their own and that what each youngster brings to the process will help determine its outcome. In this chapter, we focus on how *cognitive* aspects of the child's makeup may mediate the outcome of psychotherapy.

1. Rationale for This Review

Psychologists interested in children and development have studied cognitive development for years, stimulated in part by such theorists of conceptual development as Piaget (e.g., 1970), and in part by process-oriented research within the information-processing tradition. In the past two decades, there has been a burgeoning emphasis on cognitive processes in the clinical area too. Several recent theories of psychopathology (e.g., Peterson & Seligman, 1984) and of behavior change (e.g., Bandura, 1982) feature cognition as a centerpiece. And one of the most prominent psychotherapeutic methods presently employed with children and adults is the cognitive–behavioral approach.

Thus, there is reason to believe that human behavior, and changes

John R. Weisz • Department of Psychology, University of North Carolina, Chapel Hill, North Carolina 27599.   Bahr Weiss • Department of Psychology and Human Development, Vanderbilt University, Nashville, Tennessee 37203.

in behavior, are mediated by cognitions. This, in turn, suggests that the kinds of change associated with psychotherapy may be mediated by cognitive processes. Because we now have a number of relatively reliable means of measuring cognition, it would seem that we are in a strong position to study the impact of cognitive factors on the outcome of psychotherapy.

Despite this positive state of affairs, there has been (as we shall see) surprisingly little effort to explore the possible mediational role of cognition, particularly in the area of *child* psychotherapy. In this chapter, we review the rather limited evidence that we have been able to identify. We then discuss gaps in the evidence and questions that may be usefully addressed in the future, and we suggest research strategies for addressing these questions.

2. Method Used to Identify Studies

To identify literature relevant to the topic of this chapter, we carried out a three-step search. The search revealed surprisingly little research evidence, raising the question of whether our procedure may have missed important studies. Given this possibility, we provide a rather detailed description of the search procedure, partly for the benefit of readers who may wish to take additional steps.

One step involved a computer search. We surveyed all journals in the PSYCLIT system, extending back to 1967. We searched for articles involving the conjunction of the following terms: *psychotherapy* or *training* or *treatment; child* or *adolescent; cognitions* or *beliefs* or *attributions* or *cognitive (adj.) ability* or *intelligence* or *IQ* or *internal-external-locus-of-control* or *self-efficacy; outcome* or *efficacy* or *effectiveness* or *effects* or *success.* We ruled out studies focused on mentally retarded children, subjects over 18 years of age, and (except in the theoretically interesting case of studies by Schleser, Meyers, and their colleagues—see below) youngsters who had no identified psychopathology. We also excluded studies designed to increase children's ability in school subjects (e.g., math or spelling). And we ruled out unpublished dissertations, because these studies would not consistently have had the quality control associated with journal review.

As a second step, we reviewed all issues from January 1980 to March 1988 of the following journals: *Behavior Therapy, Journal of Abnormal Child Psychology, Journal of the American Academy of Child and Adolescent Psychiatry, Journal of Clinical Child Psychology,* and *Journal of Consulting and Clinical Psychology.* As a third step, we reviewed the 108 articles included in a recent meta-analysis of child psychotherapy outcome research (Weisz, Weiss, Alicke, & Klotz, 1987).

The two-part search process generated 166 candidate articles. More careful scrutiny of the computer-generated list, however, revealed that many of the 166 were speculative articles or nonempirical reports based on clinical experience rather than research. The winnowing process generated a very modest number of truly relevant studies. These form the core of what we discuss in the remainder of this chapter.

3. Theoretical Perspectives on a Linkage between Cognitive Factors and Therapy Outcomes

Before examining these studies, we should first consider theoretical arguments bearing on the relation between cognitive factors and therapy outcomes. As several writers (e.g., Bower, 1975; Meichenbaum, 1977; Meyers & Cohen, 1984; Neisser, 1976) have suggested, the term "cognition" has been used to refer both to the *processing* of thought and the *content* of thought. Accordingly, in this chapter, we focus on both of these aspects of cognition.

One part of this chapter addresses the possibility that children's processing capacity, or cognitive ability, influences the outcome of child therapy. Kendall, Lerner, and Craighead (1984), in their discussion of self-instructional training programs for children with self-control problems, offer a relevant perspective. These authors note that effects of such programs may depend on the cognitive capacity of the youngsters being treated. Below certain levels of capacity, the cognitive demands of the self-instructional programs may be beyond the reach of the children. Thus, one might expect certain treatment approaches to be more effective with increases in cognitive capacity.

One can also imagine circumstances, however, in which advanced cognitive capacity might *attenuate* the impact of certain interventions; for example, interventions that rely heavily on compliance with the therapist's instructions and trust in the authority of the therapist might be less effective with youngsters who are so cognitively advanced as to resist blind compliance and question authority.

Cognitive capacity may be conceptualized in terms of such variables as psychometric mental age and cognitive developmental level construed in Piagetian terms. One might even consider such a gross indicator of cognitive level as age. Finally, it may also be useful to consider whether rate of cognitive development, as indexed by IQ, might be related to training effects. In this chapter, we review the few studies we found that bear on the predictive power of cognitive level as detailed above and cognitive rate operationalized as IQ.

In a second part of the chapter, we focus on cognitive *content* as a possible mediator of therapy outcomes. One body of thought that has broad, general relevance to this topic, though it has developed outside the clinical literature, has come to be called action theory (see Chapman, 1984; Frese & Sabini, 1985). According to action theory, a person's behavior with respect to a goal will be influenced by that person's cognitions about that goal—for example, its attainability. Applying action theory to the process of psychotherapy suggests that the client's pursuit of therapeutic goals will be influenced by his or her cognitions about those goals. Are the goals involving behavior change construed by the client as appropriate, desirable, or even attainable? If the answer to such questions is *no*, then action theory suggests that the client may invest less than maximum energy in pursuit of the therapeutic goals.

Applied in this manner, action theory suggests that cognitions with respect to therapeutic goals can be used to predict the client's attainment of those goals. A number of theorists in the clinical area have suggested specific kinds of cognitions that may influence therapy effects with children. We address these specific cognitions in the material that follows.

4. Research on Cognitive Capacity as a Mediator of Therapy Effects

We focus first on research in which various measures of cognitive capacity have been used to predict outcomes of psychotherapy. Before considering direct measures of cognitive capacity, such as mental age (a measure of *level* of cognitive development) and IQ (a measure of *rate* of cognitive development), we first consider an indirect measure, age.

4.1. The Problem of Age as a Mediator

There has been some discussion, in fact, of age as a predictor of therapy effects with children. For example, Kendall *et al.* (1984), in discussing such cognitively weighted programs as self-instructional training, note that age may be a determinant of effects. They point out that researchers such as Kendler and Kendler (e.g., 1962) have identified ages 5–7 as the period in which mediational thinking is likely to emerge. Because self-instructional training appears to require an ability to use cognitive/verbal mediation, such training may not be effective prior to this period. In support of this view, Kendall *et al.* (1984) note that literature reviews that have reached relatively pessimistic conclusions about the efficacy of self-instructional training (e.g., Hobbs, Moquin, Tyroler, & Lahey, 1980), unlike those that have reached relatively optimistic conclusions (e.g., Urbain & Kendall, 1980), have included several studies in which subjects were younger than 6.

Reviews focused on a broader range of treatments and ages, however, have left the picture rather mixed. In a meta-analysis of psychotherapy outcome studies with youngsters aged 4–18 (with many different therapy methods included), Weisz *et al.* (1987) found that therapy effects were more pronounced the *younger* the treated subjects were. This relationship also held when the sample was confined to studies involving subjects younger than 13. By contrast, in Casey and Berman's (1985) meta-analysis of psychotherapy outcome studies among children younger than 13, effect sizes did not differ substantially with age of the treated youngsters.

Thus, the two most comprehensive meta-analyses of child psychotherapy outcome studies present different pictures of the relation between outcome and age. Having noted this, we should indicate a conceptual problem: chronological age is a very gross index of cognitive level. Besides being correlated with cognitive level, age is also correlated with such diverse characteristics as biological maturity and social competence, which in turn might be related to therapy outcomes. Age is simply a less precise index of cognitive level than are either psychometric mental age or Piagetian conceptual level. For this reason, we give primary attention to those two, more precise, indices, and we do not attempt a comprehensive review of age effects.

4.2. Mental Age

We found only one study in which mental age was studied as a possible mediator of treatment effects. Barkley, Copeland, and Sivage (1980) studied the efficacy of a combination of self-control procedures in a classroom with six hyperactive boys aged 7–10. A within-subjects reversal design was used in assessing effects of the procedures. Dependent variables included measures of on-task behavior, class misbehavior, and activity level. The first two measures, but not the third, showed evidence of improvement overall. However, for on-task behavior, improvement also appeared to be related to mental age of the youngsters, as assessed on the Peabody Picture Vocabulary Test. Mental ages ranged from 6 years, 6 months to 10 years, 2 months. There was a trend for boys of higher mental age to show (1) higher levels of on-task behavior during all phases of the program but particularly during treatment phases, (2) less variability over time in each treatment phase, and (3) less deterioration in performance with changes in schedules of self-monitoring.

4.3. Piagetian Cognitive Level

Taking a different approach to assessment of cognitive level, Cohen, Meyers, Schleser, and their colleagues have conducted a series of studies exploring the effects of self-instructional training with children at different Piagetian cognitive levels. These investigators have been particularly interested in the contrast between children at the preoperational and concrete operational stages of development (see Flavell, 1977, for descriptions). To summarize, preoperational children are said to be (1) more influenced by their perceptions than by conceptual understanding or general principles, (2) relatively unable to shift from their own perspective to the perspective of another person, and (3) relatively unable to shift their attention from one dimension of a problem to another. Concrete operational children, as compared with preoperational children, are said to be (1) more systematic in their reasoning, more oriented toward general principles, and able to overrule perceptual appearances by conceptual knowledge; (2) more adept at taking the perspective of others; and (3) more skilled at reasoning about multiple dimensions of a problem concurrently. In short, concrete operational children show reasoning that is more logical, flexible, and powerful than preoperational children. Thus, one might expect that preoperational and concrete operational children would differ in their response to cognitively oriented interventions.

In one study exploring this possibility, Schleser, Meyers, and Cohen (1981) used self-instructional methods designed to enhance children's reflectivity and accuracy on tasks requiring focused attention. The groups contained children of similar age (mean age = 7.8 years), half of whom were classified as preoperational and half of whom were concrete operational, based on their performance on two Piagetian conservation tasks. The design included a no-instruction control group plus four treatment groups, each involving a somewhat different self-instructional procedure to enhance self-control. Across the various groups, concrete operational children did outperform preoperational children on various assessments. However, *changes* from pretest to posttest were similar for children at the two different cognitive levels. In other words, there was no evidence that Piagetian cognitive level was a mediator of treatment effects.

In another study in the series, Cohen, Meyers, Schleser, and Rodick (1980) again used self-instructional procedures with same-age group of preoperational and concrete operational children. Here, too, the purpose was to enhance children's reflectivity and accuracy. In this study, however, in addition to traditional self-instructional procedures, a *discovery* condition was included. Youngsters in the discovery group eventually received the same set of self-guiding statements used by children in the other groups; however, the discovery youngsters were induced to discover these statements through a programmed dialogue with the experimenter. For example, rather than simply instruct the child to begin a task by asking "What is it I need to do?", the experimenter would ask the child "What's the first thing you should ask yourself when given this task?" In the ensuing dialogue, the experimenter would lead the child to "discover" the key initial question: "What is it I need to do?"

In this study, as in Schleser, Meyers, and Cohen (1981), Cohen *et al.* (1980) did not find Piagetian cognitive level to be a mediator of outcome with the traditional self-instructional procedures. However, with the discovery procedure, only the concrete operational children showed significant generalization of performance to a new (perspective-taking) task. From this finding, Cohen *et al.* conclude that concrete operational children, in contrast to their preoperational counterparts, are able to distinguish form from content. That is, unlike preoperational children, whose cognitive limitations confined their learning to a set of specific self-guiding statements, the concrete operational youngsters learned not only a set of specific statements but also *a procedure* for generating such statements. Thus, when faced with a new task requiring new statements, the concrete operational children were well-equipped to proceed on their own, whereas the preoperational children were not.

In a follow-up study, Nichol, Cohen, Meyers, and Schleser (1982) tested the robustness of these findings. Instead of offering specific self-guiding statements tailored to a specific training task, they taught children to use more general self-guiding statements that might be applicable to multiple tasks (e.g., "I'm going to answer a question: I have to stop and think about what the question is asking."). Even with the procedure changed in this way, the investigators found that the discovery procedure led to significant generalization only among concrete operational children, not among preoperational youngsters. These findings, too, suggest that concrete operational children are more likely than preoperational children to use training procedures to internalize general principles that can be flexibly applied to new situations.

In a related study, Goodnight, Cohen, and Meyers (1983) took preoperational and concrete operational children through a three-step sequence. The first step involved conventional self-instructional procedures applied to the Matching Familiar Figures Test. The second step involved training in learning to transfer self-instructional procedures to a new task. The third step involved a test of generalization to a third task. Here, again, only concrete operational children showed significant generalization to the third task.

The findings of these studies by Cohen, Meyers, Schleser, and their colleagues offer a potentially useful perspective on the perennial problem of generalization. In therapy with children, an absence of generalization may not necessarily be attributable to inadequate techniques alone. Instead, it may be that generalization requires cognitive/ conceptual capacities that are not in place until children have reached the concrete operational level of development. Although the findings presented here do suggest this possibility, we should note one significant limitation. These findings are based on research with nonreferred children, drawn from regular classrooms. It will be important to test the generalizability of the effects demonstrated here to samples of children whose behavioral problems lie within the clinical range.

4.4. Intelligence

Turning now from cognitive level to the possible role of *rate* of cognitive development, we consider studies in which intelligence was examined as a potential mediator of therapy outcomes with children. One rationale for such a mediating role flows directly from the nature of the IQ score. As originally construed, IQ was a measure of the extent to which information or skill (originally expressed in terms of mental age units) has been acquired relative to the time spent in acquisition (expressed in years and months of chronological age). Sometimes referred to as a measure of "lifetime learning rate," IQ might also be construed as a predictor of learning or acquisition rate over periods as brief as a training procedure or a therapeutic intervention (see Weisz, Yeates, & Zigler, 1982). We have found four studies that provide tests of this possibility.

In the earliest of these, Ridberg, Parke, and Hetherington (1971) studied effects of a film-mediated model on cognitive style in groups of impulsive and reflective 4th-grade boys. Both groups had IQs between 90 and 140; means were 118 for the reflective group, 115 for the impulsive group. Except for the control groups, all boys saw a filmed model responding to the Matching Familiar Figures Test using a cognitive style the opposite of their own (e.g., impulsive boys saw a reflective model). In each case, the model was successful on the test.

Because of the clinical emphasis of this chapter, we will focus only on the impulsive group (reflective behavior is generally not considered to be problematic). The impulsive children were divided into a no-treatment control group and four treatment conditions. In one treatment condition, the model merely waited a prescribed period of time (25–31 seconds) before responding to each item); in a *verbalizing* condition, the model also verbalized a response strategy (e.g., waiting, not choosing the first stimulus that seemed correct); in a *scanning* condition, the model revealed a strategy by pointing with his finger at the various stimuli as he considered them; finally, there was a *verbalizing and scanning* combination condition. Each treatment and control group contained boys above and below the sample IQ mean.

Film modeling produced a significant change in the response latencies of the impulsive boys. However, the type of modeling that made the biggest difference differed with IQ level. Low-IQ boys showed the greatest increase in reflectivity when exposed to the combined verbalizing and scanning procedure. High-IQ boys, by contrast, showed the most pronounced change with the verbalization-only and the scanning-only procedures. Under verbalization-only and scanning-only, high-IQ boys showed more change than low-IQ boys; in the combined condition, low-IQ boys showed more change than high-IQ boys; in the other treatment and control conditions, the two IQ groups did not differ.

When analyses focused on test errors rather than response latency, only one aspect of the latency findings with respect to IQ was replicated. Hi-IQ boys improved most with the verbalizing-only and the scanning-only procedures. Low-IQ boys improved similarly across the various treatment conditions. In the verbalizing-only and the scanning-only conditions, high-IQ boys showed greater improvement than low-IQ boys.

Ridberg et al. (1971) suggest that their findings may reveal different propensities in their high- and low-IQ groups. In particular, the investigators argue that high-IQ youngsters "may already be using effective attentional and covert verbal rehearsal processes with which the combined scanning-verbalizing condition interferes" (p. 377). One straightforward cue (e.g., verbalization or scanning alone) may be all the high-IQ youngsters need to get on track. By contrast, low-IQ children may require multiple cues as to what they should be doing (i.e., as in the verbalization-plus-scanning condition) to compensate for a more serious array of deficits in response monitoring and mediation.

In another study that included the IQ variable, Elliott and Pumfrey (1972) conducted nondirective group play therapy sessions with 7- to 9-year-old boys who were "socially maladjusted" and had low levels of reading achievement. The boys were of low–average intelligence, with mean IQs of 85 for both the therapy group and the no-treatment control group. The therapy group received nine weekly one-hour sessions based on approaches advocated by Carl Rogers and others.

Overall, there was no evidence that the therapy condition produced significant improvement in either social adjustment or reading performance. However, in the experimental group (and not the control group), the degree of posttreatment improvement shown in social adjustment was highly correlated ($r = 0.85$) with pretreatment IQ scores. The authors did not interpret this finding. We should emphasize the significance of the fact that IQ was related to improvement in the treated group but not in the untreated group. This, like the similar finding reported by Ridberg *et al.* (1971; see above), suggests that gains were not a function of high IQ alone, but of high IQ *in combination with treatment*.

A third study focusing on the role of IQ involved a rather different approach from the two discussed thus far. Levy and Hobbes (1982) reported results of a 30-month follow-up of 26 children who had been given DSM-III diagnoses of Attention Deficit Disorder with Hyperactivity. The children ranged in age from 4 years to 7 years, 8 months, with a mean of 6 years. WISC and WPPSI IQs ranged from 72 to 115, with a median of 95.5. Of particular interest in this follow-up was the extent to which medication had been needed to achieve self-control in addition to other treatments the youngsters had received.

Levy and Hobbes distinguished between three subgroups in their sample of 26: children never treated with methylphenidate, those treated initially but taken off medication by month 30, and those still on methylphenidate at 30 months; the implication is that the children in this latter group were less responsive to therapy. Children in the first two groups had median IQs of 100.0 and 101.0, respectively; children in the third group had significantly lower IQs, with a median of 85.0. The authors conclude that their follow-up result "confirms the importance of IQ in predicting prognosis of hyperkinesis in childhood . . ." (p. 245). They suggest, further, that previous studies in this area have often focused only on children with IQs above 80 or 85 and that "this may have masked the importance of initial IQ in determining outcome" (p. 246).

5. Research on Cognitions as Mediators of Therapy Effects

From research on cognitive capacity we now turn to research on the role of cognitions *per se*. As in the previous section, the available evidence is quite limited, but some of the findings are provocative.

5.1. Causal Attributions

The first type of cognition we shall consider is the venerable causal attribution, the subject of much research in social psychology and increasing research in the area of psychopathology but surprisingly little research in the area of treatment outcomes. One notable exception to this generalization is a thoughtfully designed study by Bugental, Whalen, and Henker (1977) in which the causal attributions of hyperactive boys were predicted to be mediators of the outcome of two intervention programs. Subjects, aged 7 to 12, were assigned to one of two treatment conditions: (1) a 6-week self-instructional training program patterned after Meichenbaum and Goodman's (1971) procedures, or (2) a 6-week social reinforcement program in which attention and praise were made contingent on appropriate attention to task. Two dependent measures were used: (1) qualitative errors on the Porteus Mazes, and (2) scores on the Conners Abbreviated Teacher Rating Scale.

Bugental et al. (1977) also assessed attributions for academic events and outcomes, using questions in which the children judged the extent to which their grades on tests were caused by (1) their own effort, (2) teacher bias, or (3) luck. The investigators predicted that children who attributed these academic outcomes to external causes such as teacher bias or luck would benefit more from a program in which external contingencies of reinforcement are "regularized" than a program that emphasizes children's personal (self-regulation) skill. By contrast, Bugental et al. predicted that the relative effectiveness of the two treatment approaches would be reversed for children who attributed academic outcomes to personal effort.

The actual findings did not reveal effects on Conners teacher ratings; however, there were effects on Porteus Maze errors that were rather consistent with the Bugental et al. predictions. Children in the two attribution–intervention congruent groups (i.e., self-attributions with self-instructional training and external attributions with reinforcement contingency program) showed significantly greater error reduction than children in the two attribution–intervention noncongruent groups.

These findings are provocative in their implications. They suggest that it may be a mistake to think that one particular pattern of attributions (or cognitions of any other sort) will necessarily be uniformly predictive of enhanced therapy effects. Instead, the task of the therapist may be to find an optimum match between the therapeutic approach employed and the child's cognitions that are relevant to the problem being treated. As Bugental et al. noted, intervention approaches may "have implicit attributional textures that interact with the attributional network of the individual to influence treatment impact" (p. 881).

In another study of attributional patterns, Kendall and Braswell (1984; see also Braswell, 1984) used a somewhat different approach. They assessed attributions made by impulsive 2nd through 5th graders at the *end* of a self-instructional training program. At posttreatment, all the children were told that they had done well in the training program and that things were going better for them in the classroom; the children were then asked to explain why they thought such changes had taken place. Children's spontaneous responses to this attributional question were recorded; then children were given forced-choice questions in which they were asked to choose from a list of causal attributions including child effort, child ability, good luck, or easy task.

In the open-ended assessment, Kendall and Braswell found that children who made effort attributions for their success were rated significantly higher by teachers than were other children on gains in self-control and reductions in hyperactivity. By contrast, those children who could not generate any spontaneous causal explanation were rated significantly lower than other children on the same two categories of improvement. In the forced-choice assessment, children who endorsed attributions to luck were significantly less likely than other children to be rated by teachers as improved in self-control at the end of treatment and at a 10-week follow-up and as improved in hyperactivity at follow-up.

As Kendall and Braswell noted, their findings are subject to certain interpretational problems. First, findings from the open-ended attributional inquiry did not match findings from the forced-choice items. Further, because the attributional assessments took place at the end of treatment, it is not clear whether the attributional patterns associated with favorable treatment outcomes were a cause or a consequence of improvement during treatment. As Braswell, Koehler, and Kendall (1985) later noted, it is not clear whether "a tendency to make effort-based attributions increase[s] the probability that a child will improve" or whether improvement during treatment makes it "more likely that the child will offer effort-based explanations" (p. 461).

5.2. Locus of Control

Closely related to attributional research is research on locus of control. We found three studies in which locus of control scores were studied as possible mediators of treatment effects with disturbed children. In one of these, Horn, Ialongo, Popovich, and Peradotto (1987) assessed treatment effects among 7- to 11-year-olds diagnosed ADD-H. Treatments included behavioral parent training, cognitive–behavioral self-instructional training for the children, and a combined intervention involving both types of training (no control group was included). Prior to treatment (and again, after treatment), children completed the Nowicki–Strickland Locus of Control Scale for Children (Nowicki & Strickland, 1973).

Several measures of outcome were employed, but there was little evidence of any outcome difference among the three treatments. The measure showing the most change was the Conners Parent Hyperactivity Index (with pretreatment Hyperactivity Index covaried). On this measure, improvement from pretest to follow-up (but evidently not from pretest to posttest) was positively related to pretest internality scores on the Nowicki–Strickland scale. Thus, the study yielded at least modest evidence that internal locus of control might mediate this particular treatment outcome. On the other hand, other measures from the Conners Questionnaire, as well as teacher questionnaires, child self-reports, and structured classroom behavior observations showed no evidence of a mediating role of locus of control.

A locus of control study by McMurray, Bell, Fusillo, Morgan, and Wright (1987) reached a similarly mixed conclusion. McMurray *et al.* worked with 9- to 12-year-olds suffering from moderate to severe dental anxiety. Half were assigned to a placebo condition, half to a coping condition in which they viewed a model learning to cope successfully, then practiced component coping skills (relaxing, use of self-statements, mental imagery, and self-reward). Prior to treatment, and again afterward, the children completed the McLucas Dental Locus of Control Scale (McMurray & Lucas, 1983); scores were used to divide the sample into internal and external locus of control groups. Locus of control and treatment versus control condition thus became factors in the experimental design (along with sex).

Change in dental anxiety was assessed with three measures: (1) self-reports of anxiety by the children; (2) physiological arousal, assessed via pulse rate meters; and (3) behavioral disturbance ratings completed by the dentists and dental assistants (who were blind to treatment condition). The self-report measure showed significant effects of treatment but no interaction involving locus of control. The physiological arousal measure showed no overall treatment effect but a significant main effect of locus of control; internal youngsters improved more than their external counterparts, regardless of treatment. The behavioral disturbance ratings showed no effects involving locus of control. Thus, in the primary analyses of the study, there was no evidence that locus of control mediated the effects of treatment.

However, reductions in self-reported anxiety from pretreatment to posttreatment were significantly correlated with increases in internality from pre to post. Of course, this finding may mean that increased internality caused reduced anxiety, that reduced anxiety led to increased internality, that both occurred, or that a third factor accounted for both changes.

In the third relevant study, Gundel (1981) reached a rather negative conclusion with regard to a mediating role of locus of control. Gundel

focused on boys from special classes for the "emotionally disturbed."
Three behavioral treatments were used in an attempt to modify socially
disruptive behavior (specifically, talking out, hitting, and out of seat).
The treatments included (1) *self-regulation* with self-monitoring and self-
reinforcement, (2) *teacher-regulation followed by self-regulation*, and (3)
contingency contracting. There was also a no-treatment condition. Prior to
the experiment, all youngsters filled in the Nowicki–Strickland Locus of
Control Scale; scores were divided into high, medium, and low thirds,
with subjects from each level randomly assigned to treatment and control conditions.

The interventions were effective, particularly the contingency contracting approach. However, contrary to Gundel's hypothesis, neither
multivariate nor univariate tests revealed any significant interactions
between locus of control and treatment. Evidently, locus of control, as
operationalized here, was not a mediator of treatment outcome.

5.3. Control-Related Beliefs

Findings of the three locus of control studies present relatively little
evidence of a mediating role for perceived internal control. One possible
explanation is simply that perceived internal control in fact has no mediating role. Another possible explanation, however, is that certain specific control-related beliefs may mediate response to therapy, whereas
such global beliefs as those measured by most locus of control questionnaires may not.

This possibility was explored in a recent study by Weisz (1986a).
The investigation was based on a two-dimensional model of control-
related cognition (discussed in Weisz, 1986b; Weisz & Stipek, 1982). In
this model, control is defined as the capacity to cause an intended outcome. Defined in this way, control is construed as a joint function of two
component factors: *outcome contingency* and *personal competence*. The contingency of a desired outcome, including amelioration of a personal
problem in therapy, is defined as the extent to which that outcome
depends on the behavior of individuals relevant to oneself—in the case
of a child, on "kids" in general, for example. Personal competence with
respect to a desired outcome is defined as the individual's capacity to
generate the behavior on which the outcome is contingent, to the extent
that contingency exists.

Working from this model, Weisz (1986a) developed a set of contingency, competence, and control probes to assess control-related beliefs among 8- to 18-year-old children who were just beginning the process of outpatient psychotherapy for a variety of problems at home and
at school. The probes, accordingly, were designed to assess control-

related beliefs specific to solving problems at home and at school. Four probes concerned perceived contingency (e.g., "When kids have problems at home, solving the problems depends on the kids and what they do."); four concerned perceived competence (e.g., "When I have problems at home, I am better than most kids at helping to solve the problems."); and four concerned perceived control (e.g., "When I have problems at school, I can solve them if I try.").

In addition to the probes, children answered the short form of Connell's (1980, 1985) Multidimensional Measure of Children's Perceptions of Control (MMCPC). This measure generates scores for perceived internal control, external control, and unknown control, over positive and negative outcomes.

Unlike the youngsters in other studies reviewed in this chapter, these children had been spontaneously referred for outpatient treatment in their communities. They had received therapy with clinic-assigned therapists uninfluenced by researchers. The purpose of the study was to assess whether the outcomes of such naturally occurring therapy might be predicted from children's control-related beliefs at the outset of therapy.

The children's problem behavior was assessed via the Child Behavior Checklist (CBCL) (Achenbach & Edelbrock, 1983) administered on the day therapy began and then again 6 months later, when therapy had ended for all the children. Improvement on the CBCL was correlated with two measures from the probes: contingency beliefs ($r = 0.48$) and control beliefs ($r = 0.41$). Only one measure from the MMCPC predicted improvement: the more strongly children endorsed the view that they did not know the cause(s) of their failures the less they improved over the course of therapy. To assess independent contributions of various predictors to improvement in therapy, a stepwise linear regression was carried out using these three significant correlates, plus age and sex, to predict CBCL regression residuals for total problems. The regression analysis showed that only two predictors—contingency and control beliefs—accounted for substantial variance. Together, these two belief dimensions accounted for 26% (adjusted R^2) of the variance in improvement in total problems. However, 23% of the variance was accounted for by contingency beliefs alone. The predictive power of control beliefs *independent of contingency beliefs* was thus quite modest.

Interpretation of these findings is subject to several limitations. First, because the focus was on naturally occurring therapy in real outpatient clinics, it was not possible to include a control group (publicly funded clinics cannot deny treatment to appropriate applicants solely for research purposes). Thus, the design makes it impossible to determine the extent to which improvement was a function of control-related beliefs *in combination with therapy*. Second, again because of the focus on therapy as it happened naturally, no control was exerted over what actually happened in the therapy sessions; thus, it is not possible to report which *type(s)* of therapy were associated with improvement in youngsters who held strong contingency and control beliefs.

Despite these limitations, the study may suggest useful hypotheses for future research. In particular, the findings suggest the possibility that some types of therapy may be particularly effective with youngsters who believe that "what kids do" determines whether their problems at home and school are solved. The findings also suggest that efforts to identify cognitive mediators of therapy effects may be most successful if they focus on cognitions about the problems areas to which the therapy is addressed.

6. Research on the Malleability of Child Cognitions

The research discussed thus far offers modest evidence that certain cognitions may mediate child behavior change for some forms of psychotherapy. As more information of this sort accumulates, it may assist us in understanding the process of psychotherapeutic change. Such information may also have practical implications: if cognitions mediate response to therapy, then perhaps we can enhance the effectiveness of therapy by modifying cognitions. Are the kinds of cognitions discussed here in fact modifiable in clinical samples of children? From decades of research we know that attempting to increase cognitive capacity (e.g., Piagetian level or IQ) is likely to yield very modest results, at best. As for cognitive content, on the other hand, there is more encouraging evidence of modifiability.

This evidence comes from several studies focused on the locus of control construct. In one of these, discussed earlier, McMurray *et al.* (1987) used a coping skills training program to reduce anxiety among 9- to 12-year-olds who had moderate to high dental anxiety. In addition to reducing self-reported anxiety, the training procedure resulted in a significant increase in internality on a Dental Locus of Control Scale (the training group showed more of an increase than the control group).

Working with a very different sample, incarcerated juvenile delinquent adolescent boys, Ollendick and Hersen (1979) found that a social skills training program led to more increased internality on the Nowicki–Strickland Locus of Control Scale than did discussion-only and control-group procedures.

Ostrom, Steele, Rosenblood, and Mirels (1971) obtained similar findings, but with the Rotter (1966) Internal–External Locus of Control

Scale. The study focused on effects of a small-group role play and discussion program for delinquent adolescent boys (only posttest scores were obtained and compared, however).

Williams, Omizo, and Abrams (1984) found that 9- to 12-year-old learning disabled children who took part in a parent–child program aimed at increasing "democratic parent–child interaction" showed greater increases in internality (on the Locus of Control Inventory for Three Achievement Domains; Bradley, Stuck, Coop, & White, 1977) than did control group youngsters. Other studies by Omizo and his colleagues have shown similar increases in children's internality as a function of (1) biofeedback-induced relaxation training with 13- to 16-year-old hyperactive boys (Omizo, 1980; the Nowicki–Strickland scale was used), (2) group relaxation training with parental involvement for 1st- and 2nd-grade hyperactive boys (Porter & Omizo, 1984; Nowicki–Strickland Scale), and (3) rational–emotive education groups for 8- to 11-year-old learning disabled children (Omizo, Cubberly, & Omizo, 1985; Nowicki–Strickland Scale).

The one exception we have found to this array of positive findings occurred in the study by Horn et al. (1987) discussed above. These investigators used behavioral parent training and cognitive–behavioral self-control therapy with 7- to 11-year-olds diagnosed as ADD-H. Internality on the Nowicki–Strickland Scale did not increase significantly as a function of the training programs.

Although the findings of these studies on malleability of locus of control are generally positive, it is important to bear in mind that locus of control is always assessed via self-reports. Thus, an inevitable interpretive question is whether increasing internality of children's scores reflects a true change in belief structure. In some cases, apparent increases in internality may actually represent increasing choices by children of the response options the training has implicitly encouraged them to endorse (see also a discussion by Ostrom et al., 1971).

7. Research on the Effects of Modifying Child Cognitions

Given this potential problem in interpretation, it is useful to identify studies in which efforts to modify child cognitions have led to changes in behavior. Two widely cited studies warrant brief discussion here, even though neither dealt with a clinical sample.

In one of these studies, Dweck (1975) identified 12 children, aged 8–13, who appeared to suffer from extreme learned helplessness—that is, they were "characterized by expectation of failure and deterioration of performance in the face of failure" (p. 676). Dweck's idea was that children would not be so debilitated by failures if they believed that the failures resulted from insufficient effort on their part; such a belief, she reasoned, would encourage children to exert special effort, rather than give up, in response to failure.

Half the children in Dweck's sample were given 25 daily sessions of *attribution retraining* in which they worked at math problems and were encouraged, when they failed, to take responsibility and to attribute their failures to lack of effort. Half were given a quasi-control procedure involving 25 daily sessions of *success-only* experiences with math problems. After training, youngsters in the attribution retraining group showed a significantly greater tendency to attribute failures to lack of effort. More important, these attributional changes were paralleled by performance differences between the groups. After training, youngsters in the success-only condition continued to show marked deterioration in performance following failure. By contrast, youngsters who received attribution retraining maintained or improved their performance on tasks following failure.

Following up on the Dweck (1975) findings, Andrews and Debus (1978) attempted to induce effort-oriented attributions in 6th graders who showed low levels of such attributions in a pretest. One third of the children served as a no-training control group; one third received social reinforcement for effort attributions on training problems (block designs), and another third received social reinforcement plus tokens. Following training, subjects in the two experimental groups showed significantly more effort attributions, for success as well as failure, than the control-group children. For the experimental groups, these attributional patterns were paralleled by increases from pretest to posttest in persistence following failure on a perceptual tracing task.

Taken together, the Dweck (1975) and Andrews and Debus (1978) studies indicate that cognitions related to beliefs about causality can be retrained and that certain changes in those cognitions may be associated with significant behavioral changes.

8. Summary and Critique of the Evidence

The studies reviewed in this chapter give at least preliminary evidence for a number of relationships that may merit further investigation. The evidence is thin enough to be summarized quite briefly. Some findings suggest that cognitive level—construed either as mental age or as Piagetian stage level—may be related to the outcomes of certain forms of therapy. The same can be said of cognitive developmental rate, indexed by IQ.

We have reviewed several findings suggesting that cognitions, *per se*, may relate to therapy outcomes. These cognitions include causal attributions and control-related beliefs, particularly perceived contingency. Evidence of a mediating role for general locus of control is less positive, though is does appear that locus of control may be malleable in clinical populations. We have also briefly noted two studies indicating that certain modifications in children's attributions may lead to beneficial changes in behavior, particularly increased persistence.

Turning a critical eye on the evidence reviewed here, we note significant limitations. Our first concern about the evidence is that there is so little of it—so little, in fact, that we would hesitate to conclude at this point that either cognitive capacity or cognitions, *per se*, really do mediate psychotherapy outcomes among children. More evidence is necessary. In what follows, we will offer suggestions as to the kinds of evidence that would be *most* helpful and ways in which such data can be efficiently generated.

Another concern regarding the evidence applies to the distinction between cognitive level and cognitive rate. Although this distinction strikes us as conceptually important, we are also struck by the fact that it is not convincingly drawn in any of the studies reviewed here. The Piagetian studies, for example, which use age-matched children of different stage levels, confound cognitive level and cognitive rate. This is true because when one compares preoperational and concrete operational children who are at the same age level, the concrete operational group is, by definition, developing at a faster rate than the preoperational group and would almost certainly display a higher mean IQ (and a higher mean MA).

A similar problem arises in studies examining the effects of IQ differences in age-matched or school grade-matched groups. In Ridberg, Parke, and Hetherington's (1971) study of impulsive boys, for example, the high-IQ and low-IQ groups being compared were both from the 4th grade. This being the case, the groups almost certainly differed not only in IQ, but also in MA and Piagetian cognitive level as well. If investigators wish to disentangle the effects of cognitive level and cognitive rate, they may need to consider leaving age free to vary and constructing experimental designs in which level or rate of cognitive development can be isolated for unconfounded attention (e.g., Weisz, 1981) or construed as orthogonal factors (see, e.g., Weisz, 1979).

Considering the studies of cognitions as mediators of therapy outcome, we note a dilemma. To be mediators, cognitions must interact with group (i.e., treatment versus control). Yet, a number of the studies (e.g., Weisz, 1986a) that gave evidence of a predictive relationship between cognitions and behavior change did not include a no-treatment control group. This absence creates interpretive problems, making it impossible to clearly establish that the cognitions were *mediators* of *therapy* outcomes, rather than direct causes of those outcomes. In the absence of a control group, one cannot rule out the possibility that the children who improved would have improved *without therapy*—perhaps because their cognitions promote development of adaptive behavior independently of any therapy they may receive.

The dilemma arises because those investigations that do include a control group often tend not to have great ecologically validity. Frequently, they focus on youngsters who are recruited for or assigned to treatments on the basis of a pretest score of some sort, and often they involve treatment packages delivered in standardized ways by trained assistants. Studies such as that of Weisz (1986a) may be useful because they focus on children who were actually referred to clinics and on therapy as practicing therapists provide it in real clinics of the type that serve most children in the United States. However, it is precisely this sort of ecological focus that rules out the possibility of a true control group, because clinics serving the public are not inclined to assign children randomly to no-treatment control conditions.

Perhaps the best way to resolve this dilemma is through a form of triangulation. By looking for a convergence of information from (1) well-designed studies that include control groups but that are less than ideal in terms of ecological validity, and (2) less-well-controlled studies on therapy with clinic-referred youngsters in naturally occurring situations, we may be able to assess more accurately whether cognitions mediate response to therapy in clinic-referred children.

Finally, the array of studies reviewed here can be faulted for its restricted range of types of therapy and types of children. With respect to therapies, the review is heavy on investigations involving cognitive–behavioral interventions, especially self-instructional training. With respect to subjects, the review is heavy on studies of preadolescents with self-control problems, especially attention deficits and overactivity. The studies we have identified tell us very little about treatment approaches outside the behavioral realm and very little about possible cognitive mediators of therapy effects among adolescents or among youngsters of any age whose problems do not fall into the externalizing, undercontrolled category. In fact, there is even a shortage of studies in which girls are treated. Clearly, there is a need for research on a broader array of children, problems, and therapeutic approaches than is evident in this chapter.

9. Recommendations for Future Research

This brings us to a set of recommendations for research. The recommendations with which most research reviews end almost always sound a call for more research. In the domain we have just surveyed, such a call appears unusually appropriate. Given the potential importance of knowledge in this area, both for understanding psychotherapeutic process and for increasing therapeutic efficacy, much more research attention is warranted.

Two types of studies may add significant new knowledge. First, researchers conducting child therapy outcome studies focusing primarily on issues *other than* cognitive mediation could make bountiful contributions to this area. We suggest that such researchers assess various cognitive characteristics at pretreatment and then test the interaction between these characteristics and group membership (i.e., treatment versus control subjects) with respect to outcome. Such a research strategy might provide a wealth of information, with relatively minor additional effort beyond that of the original outcome study.

For investigators who do follow such a strategy, it will be very important to report nonsignificant as well as significant findings. There may be a tendency on the part of researchers to avoid reporting null findings for variables of secondary interest. However, if the information that accumulates from such research efforts is to present a complete and valid picture, all findings, significant and otherwise, must be reported fully. Even the exact size of a nonsignificant correlation may provide necessary information for some future reviewer tackling the topic we have addressed in this chapter.

Of course, this particular research strategy will provide answers to only relatively simple questions. To answer the more complex questions, studies will be required that are designed specifically to investigate cognitive mediation. At present, though, our knowledge is at such a rudimentary level that finding answers to simple questions may be an appropriate step in the research agenda. Thus, we recommend the strategy of "piggybacking" tests of cognitive mediation onto broader studies of child psychotherapy outcome.

Next, we suggest a second variety of research: studies designed specifically to test whether certain cognitions mediate therapy outcomes. Such studies should address a broader range of problems, types of children and adolescents, and therapy approaches than has been sampled thus far (see our critique above). As a general approach, we see great potential merit in the kind of research represented by Bugental *et al.* (1977)—research aimed at identifying optimum matches of therapy type and child cognitions. A potentially important consideration in such research is the issue of the specificity of cognitions. The little available research suggests that control-related beliefs directly relevant to the issues addressed in therapy may mediate therapy effects, whereas more general control-related beliefs may not. At present, this is little more than a hypothesis, lightly supported; however, it may have heuristic potential.

A logical complement to the Bugental *et al.* approach is research aimed at optimizing the match between therapy type and children's cognitive capacity (e.g., Meyers & Cohen, 1984). It may also be useful to go beyond global cognitive capacity, to consider more specific cognitive abilities; one might test, for instance, whether some forms of therapy are particularly effective with children who show greater verbal than nonverbal ability.

Finally, we would point interested investigators to a type of research which the various studies in our review suggest might be quite productive. The studies we have reviewed suggest that certain cognitions may be associated with improvements during therapy. The studies we have reviewed bearing on the issue of malleability suggest that some of these cognitions may be modifiable given proper interventions. What both lines of research suggest is that it may be worthwhile to pair psychotherapy aimed at maladaptive child behavior with adjunct interventions aimed at modifying child cognitions so as to enhance the effects of the psychotherapy. Efforts of this sort may ultimately provide the most effective tests of whether there can be cognitive mediators of the outcomes of psychotherapy with children.

ACKNOWLEDGMENTS

Our research described in this chapter was supported by the National Institute of Mental Health [R01 MH 38240] and by the North Carolina Department of Human Resources, Division of Mental Health, Mental Retardation, and Substance Abuse Services.

10. References

Achenbach, T. M., & Edelbrock, C. S. (1983). *Manual for the Child Behavior Checklist and Revised Child Behavior Profile*. Burlington: University of Vermont, Department of Psychiatry.

Andrews, G. R., & Debus, R. L. (1978). Persistence and the causal perception of failure: Modifying cognitive attributions. *Journal of Educational Psychology, 70,* 154–166.

Bandura, A. (1982). Self-efficacy mechanism in human agency. *American Psychologist, 37,* 122–147.

Barkley, R. A., Copeland, A. P., & Sivage, C. (1980). A self-control classroom for hyperactive children. *Journal of Autism and Developmental Disorders, 10,* 75–89.

Bower, G. H. (1975). Cognitive psychology: An introduction. In W. H. Estes (Ed.), *Handbook of learning and cognitive processes* (Vol. 1). Hillsdale, NJ: Erlbaum.

Bradley, R., Stuck, G., Coop, R., & White, K. (1977). A new scale to assess locus of control in three achievement domains. *Psychological Reports, 41,* 656–661.

Braswell, L. (1984). *Cognitive-behavioral therapy with an inner city sample of nonself-controlled children.* Unpublished doctoral dissertation, University of Minnesota, Minneapolis.

Braswell, L., Koehler, C., & Kendall, P. C. (1985). Attributions and outcomes in child psychotherapy. *Journal of Social and Clinical Psychology, 3,* 458–465.

Bugental, D. B., Whalen, C. K., & Henker, B. (1977). Causal attributions of hyperactive children and motivational assumptions of two behavior change approaches: Evidence for an interactionist position. *Child Development, 48,* 874–884.

Casey, R. J., & Berman, J. S. (1985). The outcome of psychotherapy with children. *Psychological Bulletin, 98,* 388–400.

Chapman, M. (1984). Intentional action as a paradigm for developmental psychology: A symposium. *Human Development, 27,* 113–144.

Cohen, R., Meyers, A. W., Schleser, R., & Rodick, J. D. (1980). *The generalization of self-instructions as a function of cognitive level and delivery procedures.* Paper presented at the biennial meeting of the Southeastern Conference on Human Development, Alexandria, VA, April, 1980.

Connell, J. P. (1980). *A Multidimensional Measure of Children's Perceptions of Control: Manual.* Denver, CO: University of Denver.

Connell, J. P. (1985). A new multidimensional measure of children's perceptions of control. *Child Development, 56,* 1018–1041.

Dweck, C. S. (1975). The role of expectations and attributions in the alleviation of learned helplessness. *Journal of Personality and Social Psychology, 31,* 674–685.

Elliott, C. D., & Pumfrey, P. D. (1972). The effects of nondirective play therapy on some maladjusted boys. *Education Research, 14,* 157–161.

Flavell, J. H. (1977). *Cognitive development.* New York: Prentice-Hall.

Frese, M., & Sabini, J. (Eds.) (1985). *Goal-directed behavior: Psychological theory and research on action.* Hillsdale, NJ: Erlbaum.

Goodnight, J. A., Cohen, R., & Meyers, A. W. (April, 1983). *Generalization of self-instructions: The effect of strategy adaptation training.* Paper presented at the biennial meeting of the Society for Research in Child Development, Detroit, MI.

Gundel, R. C. (1981). The interaction of locus of control with three behavioral procedures in the modification of disruptive behavior in emotionally disturbed boys. *Multivariate Experimental Clinical Research, 5,* 99–108.

Hobbs, S. A., Moquin, L. E., Tyroler, M., & Lahey, B. B. (1980). Cognitive behavior therapy with children: Has clinical utility been demonstrated? *Psychological Bulletin, 87,* 147–165.

Horn, W. F., Ialongo, N., Popovich, S., & Peradotto, D. (1987). Behavioral parent training and cognitive-behavioral self-control therapy with ADD-H children: Comparative and combined effects. *Journal of Clinical Child Psychology, 16,* 57–68.

Kendall, P. C., & Braswell, L. (1984). *Cognitive-behavioral therapy for impulsive children.* New York: Guilford Press.

Kendall, P. C., Lerner, R. M., & Craighead, W. E. (1984). Human development and intervention in childhood psychopathology. *Child Development, 55,* 71–81.

Kendler, H. H., & Kendler, T. S. (1962). Vertical and horizontal processes in problem solving. *Psychological Review, 69,* 116.

Levy, F., & Hobbes, G. (1982). A 30-month follow-up of hyperactive children. *Journal of the American Academy of Child Psychiatry, 21,* 243–246.

McMurray, N. E., Bell, R. J., Fusillo, A. D., Morgan, M., & Wright, F. A. C. (1987).

Relationship between locus of control and effects of coping strategies on dental stress in children. *Child and Family Behavior Therapy, 8,* 117.

McMurray, N. E., & Lucas, J. O. (1983). *The McLucas Dental Locus of Control Scale: Experimental form.* Unpublished manuscript, Department of Psychology, University of Melbourne.

Meichenbaum, D. (1977). *Cognitive behavior modification.* New York: Plenum Press.

Meichenbaum, D., & Goodman, J. (1971). Training impulsive children to talk to themselves. *Journal of Abnormal Psychology, 77,* 115–126.

Meyers, A. W., & Cohen, R. (1984). Cognitive-behavioral interventions in educational settings. *Advances in Cognitive-Behavioral Research and Therapy, 3,* 131–166.

Neisser, U. (1976). *Cognition and reality.* San Francisco: Freeman.

Nichol, G., Cohen, R., Meyers, A. W., & Schleser, R. (1982). *Journal of Applied Developmental Psychology, 3,* 205–216.

Nowicki, S., Jr., & Strickland, B. R. (1973). A locus of control scale for children. *Journal of Consulting and Clinical Psychology, 40,* 148–154.

Ollendick, T. H., & Hersen, M. (1979). Social skills training for juvenile delinquents. *Behaviour Research and Therapy, 17,* 547–554.

Omizo, M. M. (1980). The effects of biofeedback-induced relaxation training in hyperactive adolescent boys. *The Journal of Psychology, 105,* 131–138.

Omizo, M. M., Cubberly, W. E., & Omizo, S. A. (1985). The effects of rational-emotive education groups on self-concept and locus of control among learning disabled children. *The Exceptional Child, 32,* 13–19.

Ostrom, T. M., Steele, C. M., Rosenblood, L. K., & Mirels, H. L. (1971). Modification of delinquent behavior. *Journal of Applied Social Psychology, 1,* 118–136.

Peterson, C., & Seligman, M. E. P. (1984). Causal explanations as a risk factor for depression: Theory and evidence. *Psychological Review, 91,* 347–374.

Piaget, J. (1970). Piaget's theory. In P. H. Mussen (Ed.), *Carmichael's manual of child psychology* (3d ed.; vol. 1). New York: Wiley.

Porter, S. S., & Omizo, M. M. (1984). The effects of group relaxation training/large muscle exercise, and parental involvement on attention to task, impulsivity, and locus of control among hyperactive boys. *The Exceptional Child, 31,* 54–64.

Ridberg, E. H., Parke, R. D., & Hetherington, E. M. (1971). Modification of impulsive and reflective cognitive styles through observation of film-mediated models. *Developmental Psychology, 5,* 369–377.

Rotter, J. A. (1966). Generalized expectancies for internal versus external control of reinforcement. *Psychological Monographs, 80* (Whole No. 1).

Schleser, R., Cohen, R., Meyers, A. W., & Rodick, J. D. (1984). The effects of cognitive level and training procedures on the generalization of self-instructions. *Cognitive Therapy and Research, 8,* 187–200.

Schleser, R., Meyers, A. W., & Cohen, R. (1981). Generalization of self-instructions: Effects of general versus specific content, active rehearsal, and cognitive level. *Child Development, 52,* 335–340.

Urbain, E. S., & Kendall, P. C. (1980). Review of social-cognitive problem solving interventions with children. *Psychological Bulletin, 88,* 109–143.

Weisz, J. R. (1979). Perceived control and learned helplessness in mentally retarded and nonretarded children: A developmental analysis. *Developmental Psychology, 15,* 311–319.

Weisz, J. R. (1981). Learned helplessness in black and white children identified by their schools as retarded and nonretarded: Performance deterioration in response to failure. *Developmental Psychology, 17,* 499–508.

Weisz, J. R. (1986a). Contingency and control beliefs as predictors of psychotherapy outcomes among children and adolescents. *Journal of Consulting and Clinical Psychology*, *54*, 789–795.

Weisz, J. R. (1986b). Understanding the developing understanding of control. In M. Perlmutter (Ed.), *Minnesota Symposia on Child Psychology* (Vol. 18). Hillsdale, NJ: Erlbaum.

Weisz, J. R., & Stipek, D. J. (1982). Competence, contingency, and the development of perceived control. *Human Development, 25*, 250–281.

Weisz, J. R., Weiss, B., Alicke, M. D., & Klotz, M. L. (1987). Effectiveness of psychotherapy with children and adolescents: A meta-analysis for clinicians. *Journal of Consulting and Clinical Psychology, 55*, 542–549.

Weisz, J. R., Yeates, K. O., & Zigler, E. (1982). Piagetian evidence and the developmental difference controversy. In E. Zigler & D. Balla (Eds.), *Mental retardation: The developmental difference controversy*. Hillsdale, NJ: Erlbaum.

Williams, R. E., Omizo, M. M., & Abrams, B. C. (1984). Effects of STEP on parental attitudes and locus of control on their learning disabled children. *The School Counselor, 2*, 126–133.

3

Improving the Peer Relationships of Rejected Children

Karen Linn Bierman

During the last decade, a number of studies have tested the effectiveness of school-based social skill training programs designed to promote positive peer relationships and peer acceptance. In the same time period, research on the characteristics of peer-rejected children has proliferated, as have conceptual models designed to delineate the maladaptive processes involved in the development of peer relation difficulties. It has become apparent that the behavior problems experienced by rejected children are multiple and diverse and that current interventions meet only some of the needs of these children.

In the following chapter, recent research characterizing the diverse problems experienced by rejected children illustrates the scope of intervention needs. Then a review of three general developmental models suggests three potential foci for intervention efforts. The components of recent social skill training programs for unpopular and rejected children are described in terms of both the theoretical framework upon which they are based and the empirical evidence of their efficacy. Finally, discussion focuses on the assessment and treatment of peer-rejected children in clinical settings.

1. Introduction

Accumulating evidence, gathered from retrospective and prospective studies on clinical and normative populations, leaves little doubt

Karen Linn Bierman • Department of Psychology, The Pennsylvania State University, University Park, Pennsylvania 16803.

that childhood peer rejection is an important "marker" of maladaptive social–emotional development and the risk for later maladjustment. Poor peer relations are prevalent in samples of emotionally disturbed and behaviorally disordered children and have diagnostic significance (Michael, Morris, & Soroker, 1957; Rinn & Markle, 1979; Whalen & Henker, 1985). For example, impaired peer relations are central features of several major child and adolescent disorders, including undersocialized conduct disorders, attention deficit disorder, several of the anxiety disorders, and schizoid disorder (American Psychiatric Association, 1980).

Furthermore, perhaps more than any other single symptom, impaired peer relations differentiate children with problematic social–emotional development from nonproblematic children. For example, Pelham and Bender (1982) found that teacher ratings of poor peer interactions had as much power to differentiate hyperactive from nonhyperactive boys as teacher ratings of inattention, impulsivity, and hyperactivity. Similarly, when Achenbach and Edelbrock (1981) entered parent ratings into a discriminant function analysis to differentiate clinic-referred from nonreferred children, they found that a single parent rating item, "poor peer relations," accounted for 11% of the variance in clinical status; parental reports of the amount and quality of their child's social interactions accounted for 28% of the variance in clinical status.

In addition to "marking" the existence of childhood adaptational difficulties, peer rejection indicates an increased risk for poor adult outcomes. Clinical interviews with seriously disturbed adults frequently reveal childhood histories of problematic social behavior and poor peer relations (Robins, 1972). Corresponding prospective studies corroborate the power of poor peer relations in childhood to predict later school adjustment and learning problems, juvenile delinquency, and referral for mental health services (cf. Parker & Asher, 1987).

Given the apparent clinical and developmental significance of poor peer relations, researchers have explored the characteristics of peer-rejected children, trying to understand how the social–emotional development of these children may have gone awry and hoping to illuminate directions for preventive and remedial interventions. In the next section, the highlights of recent research on the characteristics of peer-rejected children are reviewed.

2. The Characteristics of Peer-Rejected Children

2.1. Definition

The quintessential feature of the peer-rejected child is that he or she is actively disliked by peers. Usually, rejected children are identified as those who receive many negative (or "like least") nominations and few positive (or "like most") nominations. In other words, most of their classmates choose them when asked to select peers they don't like, and few classmates name them when asked to select peers they especially like. As illustrated later in this section, such actively rejected children typically have more concurrent problems and are more at risk for future maladjustment than other unaccepted or neglected children who may have few friends but who are not actively disliked.

Peer rejection tends to be quite stable over time, even across transitions into new peer groups (Coie & Kupersmidt, 1983). Indeed, 45% of rejected children remain rejected one year later and 30% are still rejected four years later. When rejected children do change their sociometric status, they are most likely to become neglected or, at best, average; rejected children rarely become popular (Coie & Dodge, 1983).

2.2. Correlates

In a number of studies, peer descriptions, teacher ratings, and naturalistic observations have been used to examine the correlates of peer rejection in school settings. Peers and teachers both describe rejected children as disruptive, aggressive, dependent, noncompliant, and uncooperative (Coie, Dodge, & Coppotelli, 1982). Peers would rather play or work with popular, average, or neglected classmates than with rejected children (French & Waas, 1985; Hymel & Rubin, 1985).

Naturalistic observations of rejected children in school settings, particularly free-play settings, tend to substantiate the peer descriptions and teacher ratings. Behavioral differences are not always evident when rejected, neglected, and unaccepted children are observed in structured classroom settings, although rejected children may engage in more task-inappropriate behavior and less task-appropriate behavior and may experience more teacher interaction and more peer rebuff than neglected or accepted children (Dodge, Coie, & Brakke, 1982; Foster & Ritchey, 1985). The social difficulties of rejected children are more obvious on the playground, however, where they engage in more unoccupied behavior, more aggressive acts (shoving, pushing, hitting, calling names, teasing, and insulting others), and less appropriate social interaction than children of average, popular, or neglected status (Dodge et al., 1982; Ladd, 1983). Compared with average and popular children, rejected children more frequently play in smaller groups, with younger and more unpopular children (Ladd, 1983).

Only a few investigators have examined children's social adjustment across both family and school settings, and they suggest that many rejected children have cross-situational problems. For example, parent ratings reveal that rejected children show more behavioral problems in their families than neglected, average, or popular children (French & Waas, 1985).

The problems of rejected children are not limited to conduct difficulties. Teachers also report higher-than-average levels of academic difficulties, anxiety, and hostile isolation for rejected children (Foster & Ritchey, 1985; French & Waas, 1985). Investigations including self-ratings suggest that rejected children are often aware of their social rejection and frequently experience loneliness and depression (Asher, Hymel, & Renshaw, 1984; Bierman & McCauley, 1987).

The multiple problems exhibited by rejected children make it difficult to select specific target areas for intervention. That is, one wonders which of these many problems are critical determinants of peer rejection and which are collateral problems that may warrant clinical attention in their own right but may have less direct impact on peer relations *per se*. Some guidance is provided by empirical investigations in which rejected children are compared with nonrejected children who show some common behavioral problems. For example, not all aggressive children are rejected; not all rejected children are aggressive. By comparing the *dissimilarities* between aggressive and aggressive–rejected children and the *similarities* between aggressive–rejected and rejected children, some investigators have tried to identify the critical and distinctive features associated with peer rejection.

2.3. Critical Features

Approximately one third of all aggressive boys do not experience social ostracism or peer rejection (cf. Bierman, 1986a). Across studies, boys who exhibit other behavioral problems (such as withdrawal or hyperactivity) as well as aggression, appear more at risk for social ostracism than boys who exhibit aggression without collateral behavioral problems.

For example, Ledingham (1981) found that, compared with aggressive or nonproblematic children, aggressive–withdrawn children were more withdrawn, inattentive, distractible, and less likable. Similarly, hyperactive–aggressive boys received lower peer acceptance scores than nonproblematic comparison children, whereas aggressive (nonhyperactive) boys did not (Landau & Milich, 1985). Pope, Bierman, and Mumma (in press) replicated the finding that hyperactivity was a more consistent predictor of sociometric status than was aggression in their general grade-school sample. However, they found that boys who were extremely aggressive were likely to have poor peer relations whether or not they exhibited collateral hyperactivity.

When Bierman, Smoot, and Aumiller (1987) asked peers to describe aggressive and aggressive–rejected boys in open-ended interviews, they found that aggressive–rejected boys were credited with more extensive and diverse aggressive behavior as well as with more hyperactivelike behaviors than were aggressive (nonrejected) boys. Specifically, peers described aggressive (nonrejected) boys as "mean fighters." They described aggressive–rejected boys as "mean fighters" who were also more likely to break rules, cheat, swear, and tattle, to engage in immature, insensitive, and obnoxious behaviors, and to be poor at their schoolwork.

Apparently, then, some aggressive behaviors, such as fighting or bullying, do not necessarily lead to peer rejection, unless they are exhibited at very extreme levels. Aggressive behavior appears more likely to contribute to rejection when it is more extensive and diverse (including rule violations or indirect and verbal aggression) and when it is accompanied by other insensitive, poorly regulated, and immature behaviors or academic difficulties.

Just as not all aggressive children are rejected, as many as one half of all rejected children do not exhibit overt aggressive behavior (French, 1988). Researchers are just beginning to explore the characteristics that can contribute to peer rejection when aggressive behavior problems are not evident. It is not yet clear whether aggressive and nonaggressive rejected children share similar problems and can be treated together or whether the similarity between these two groups ends with the common factor of their peer rejection.

Cluster analyses of rejected children conducted on two independent samples by French (1988) document the existence of two distinct clusters of rejected boys. In both samples, boys in one cluster exhibited high aggression, low self-control, behavioral problems, and withdrawn behavior. Boys in the other cluster exhibited only withdrawal (and were not higher than control children on measures of aggression, behavioral problems, or self-control). In both studies, almost 50% of the rejected group exhibited the nonaggressive behavioral profile. French (1988) and others (Rubin, LeMare, & Lollis, in press) suggest that social withdrawal may represent the primary disorder of this subgroup. They further postulate that these boys may be inhibited, anxious, easily stressed, and prone to depression.

However, nonaggressive rejected children are not necessarily free from undercontrolled behavioral problems. For example, when Bierman et al. (1987) asked peers to describe rejected (nonaggressive) boys in open-ended interviews, they described them as immature, bothersome, and obnoxious. In addition, peers ascribed to these children negative attributes, such as unattractiveness, disabilities, or non-normative characteristics. Previous researchers have demonstrated that hyperactive boys who are not aggressive are nonetheless very likely to suffer peer rejection (cf. Pelham & Bender, 1982).

Although rejected children, by definition, are all disliked and rebuffed by their peers, clearly, they vary in the type of maladaptive behavior they display and in the factors that contribute to their peer rejection. From one third to one half of all rejected boys display extensive and diverse forms of aggressive behavior. Many rejected boys (whether or not they display collateral aggression) exhibit immature and insensitive social behavior. A number of rejected children may be characterized as anxious, withdrawn, and depressed. In addition, a subgroup of children may be rejected for nonbehavioral characteristics, such as an unusual or unattractive appearance or for non-normative cultural differences.

2.4. Clinical Implications

The developmental and clinical significance of the diversity in the problem patterns exhibited by rejected children is an important but, as yet, unanswered empirical question. One might postulate that different etiological factors contribute to the emergence and maintenance of the various problem patterns associated with peer rejection. The cause–effect relations between peer rejection and other problems may likewise vary. In some cases, peer rejection may provide an index of the severity of other problems but may play a less active causal role in the etiology or maintenance of these other problems. In other cases, hostile treatment and ostracism or isolation from peers may contribute substantially to the emergence and maintenance of maladaptive social–emotional responses.

Different treatment components or approaches may be indicated depending upon the particular factors or processes contributing to the rejection of particular children. There may also be aspects of intervention that are suitable for all peer-rejected children. Although more empirical work is needed to answer these questions, certainly, the diversity of problems associated with peer rejection must be kept in mind as interventions for peer-rejected children are designed and evaluated.

Investigations about the characteristics of peer-rejected children address questions about who to treat. In addition, one must ask how to treat, an issue that depends largely on how one characterizes the factors linking child characteristics to peer rejection and on one's hypotheses about the mechanisms controlling the process of rejection. As discussed in the next sections, most of the interventions designed to improve children's peer relationships are based on one of three basic models concerning the postulated mechanisms controlling peer rejection (cf. Coie, in press; Coie & Koeppl, in press).

3. Models of Peer Rejection and Treatment Approaches

The approach one takes to the treatment of peer-relation difficulties depends largely on one's theoretical model concerning the factors responsible for (or contributing to) these difficulties. Simply put, how we go about fixing something depends on what we believe is wrong with it. Most current approaches to the treatment of peer rejection rest on one of three basic causal models: (1) a model emphasizing the critical role of the rejected child's social skills deficits in the etiology and maintenance of his or her peer-relation difficulties; (2) a model focusing on the rejected child's learned propensity to use coercive behaviors to control his or her interpersonal interactions; and (3) a model focusing on the role of social comparison processes, group dynamics, and reputational biases as central features of peer interactions that may contribute to the active ostracism of some children. The basic propositions and empirical support for each of these models are presented in the next sections, along with the treatment approaches based on each model.

3.1. Social Skills Deficits Model

3.1.1. The Model

Most interventions to enhance positive peer relationships are based on a cognitive–behavioral skills deficit model. In its simplest form, this model postulates that children who are unable to gain social acceptance are deficient in their ability to behave in ways that enable them to elicit positive and avoid negative responses from others.

Investigators have reasoned that infrequent positive peer interactions may directly precipitate or increase inadequacies in social adaptation (cf. Combs & Slaby, 1977). In naturalistic interactions, peers act as teachers, models, and sources of reinforcement and emotional support, facilitating the development of children's social competencies (such as cooperation and negotiation skills, aggression control, communication skills, and perspective-taking abilities) (cf. Hartup, 1983). Rejected children, deprived of the normal benefits of peer instruction and support, may fail to develop the knowledge and skills necessary to interact competently with peers.

Corroborating the model, investigators have found unpopular children to be less knowledgeable about peer-accepted ways of making friends, solving social conflicts, initiating social interactions, and communicating with peers than their more popular peers (Asher & Renshaw, 1981; Gottman, Gonso, & Rasmussen, 1975). Accordingly, investigators have suggested that coaching rejected children in positive interaction skills may enable them to use more peer-approved strategies in their peer interactions in place of aggressive or inappropriate interactional strategies.

Initial coaching models were somewhat "generic" in nature; they were based on the premise that most unpopular children could benefit from instructions in positive social skills, such as play skills or conversational skills (cf. Ladd & Asher, 1985). However, accumulating research suggested that deficits in positive behaviors might be more characteristic of children who have few friends than of children who are rejected (cf. Bierman, 1986a). Indeed, although rejected children almost always display higher-than-average rates of negative social behavior, they do not consistently show low rates of positive social behavior (Coie et al., 1982). Consequently, recent investigators have tried to expand and elucidate the basic social skills deficits model, hoping to identify more specific cognitive–behavioral deficits that might account for the poor peer relations of aggressive and rejected children (cf. Dodge, Pettit, McClaskey, & Brown, 1986).

In the expanded social skills deficits models, aggression and rejection reflect distortions or differences in social–cognitive information processing rather than deficits in positive interaction skills. For example, investigators have postulated that asocial goals, negatively biased social perceptions or interpretations, "preemptive" or impulsive direct-action response tendencies, or emotional overresponding may each contribute to the social difficulties of rejected children (cf. Dodge et al., 1986).

Considered in light of these expanded social skills models, coaching programs may benefit rejected children by teaching them to inhibit their initial responses and to think more carefully about the causes and effects of their social behavior. By building self-control skills, rejected children may become more successful at regulating their negative emotions, monitoring their social behavior, and selecting more adaptive interactional strategies. Interventions designed to foster self-control and thoughtful interpersonal problem solving have been tested on impulsive and aggressive children; the effects of such programs on peer rejection per se have not been evaluated systematically.

A selective review of empirical studies evaluating the effectiveness of various social skills training interventions is presented in the next section. Only studies that incorporated group comparisons and appropriate control conditions are included. A number of other studies using case-study methodologies or inadequate control procedures (e.g., no control groups or raters who were not blind to the treatment condition of the children) often provide a more positive but somewhat misleading picture of the potentially beneficial effects of these treatments for behaviorally disordered, peer-rejected children than do well-controlled studies.

3.1.2. The Treatment

Social skill training programs designed to teach positive interaction strategies include three basic instructional components. First, verbal instructions, demonstrations, and guided discussions are presented to enable children to form a concept of a basic interactional skill or strategy and to help them generate a series of specific behavioral examples of that strategy. Next, children are given an opportunity to practice the skill in peer interactions. Finally, children receive feedback on their performance designed to help them to modify and adjust their conceptualization and performance of the skill (Ladd, 1985).

The specific skills selected for training have varied across investigations. Some programs have targeted a few specific skills, such as conversational skills (Bierman & Furman, 1984; Ladd, 1981) or game-playing skills (Oden & Asher, 1977). Other programs have been less focused, subsuming a wide diversity of behaviors. LaGreca and Santogrossi (1980), for example, targeted eight behaviors including smiling, greeting, joining, inviting, conversing, sharing and cooperating, complimenting and grooming; Gresham and Nagle (1980) spent two coaching sessions on each of three areas of social behavior: game playing, friendship making, and peer interaction.

Initial programs had mixed effects on children's social behavior and peer acceptance. For example, the program designed by LaGreca and Santogrossi (1980) produced increased rates of social initiations but not of positive social behaviors; the program developed by Gresham and Nagle (1980) resulted in decreased negative social behavior but no increases in positive behaviors initiated by coached children. In another short-term coaching program, Oden and Asher (1977) observed no behavioral changes. In terms of sociometric effects, LaGreca and Santogrossi (1980) observed no increase in peer acceptance, whereas both Gresham and Nagle (1980) and Oden and Asher (1977) documented improved peer ratings for treated children as compared with nontreated children at a follow-up assessment.

As basic research proliferated documenting the heterogeneity among unpopular children, investigators became more selective in identifying appropriate target children for particular interventions. For example, Ladd (1981) and Bierman and Furman (1984) used both sociometric status and a pretreatment behavioral screening to identify unpopular children who displayed deficits in the skills to be taught. In both of these studies, coached children exhibited posttreatment gains in target skills and some improvements in peer acceptance. Furthermore, the changes observed in these low-interacting unpopular children matched the predictions of a social skills deficits model. That is, the low levels of conversational skills exhibited by target children in early treatment sessions gradually increased with coaching, and the skill gains during treatment predicted both behavioral and sociometric improvements (Bierman, 1986b).

The success of coaching documented for unpopular children who interact with peers infrequently, however, may have little relevance for the majority of peer-rejected children, who are more aversive in their interactional style. In fact, in the two published studies in which social skills training has been applied specifically to rejected children, the results have not been as encouraging. For example, Coie and Krehbiel (1984) compared the effectiveness of academic training and social skills training on a subgroup of 40 rejected children who also had academic problems. Social skills training alone produced only transitory improvements in sociometric ratings and no changes in classroom behavior. Academic training, in contrast, produced improvements in achievement scores, classroom behavior, and sociometric ratings. Coie and Krehbiel (1984) suggest that, for low-achieving rejected children, academic training may be necessary to reduce classroom disruptiveness and increase attentive classroom behavior—improvements that may be critical for enhancing peer evaluations. On the other hand, the traditional social skills training program alone seemed to provide few short-term and no long-term benefits for this subgroup of rejected children.

Bierman, Miller, and Stabb (1987) selected rejected children who showed high pretreatment rates of negative social behavior. They suggested that, in order to be effective with socially negative children, social skills training programs might need to include prohibitions and behavioral control strategies to reduce negative behavior, as well as instructions to increase positive social behavior. They assigned children to treatments that included instructions for positive behavior, prohibitions for negative behavior, or both instructions and prohibitions (in addition to a no-treatment control group). Prohibitions with response cost for negative behaviors resulted in immediate and stable declines in negative behavior and led to temporary increases in positive responses received from peers, whereas instructions and reinforcement of specific social skills promoted sustained positive peer interactions six weeks after treatment. Only the combination of instructions and prohibitions led to improved sociometric ratings, and these were limited to reductions in the rejection ratings given to target boys by their nontarget treatment partners. None of the treatment conditions produced changes in classroom teacher or peer behavioral or sociometric ratings.

Because only two large-scale group comparison studies have tested the effectiveness of coaching rejected children in positive interactional strategies, no firm conclusions can be drawn about the appropriateness of the skills deficit model or the effects of skill training on the peer relations of these children. It does appear, however, that in their traditional format, coaching programs promoting positive interaction strategies are not sufficient to meet the needs of most rejected children.

One aspect of traditional coaching programs that could conceivably be tailored more specifically to the needs of aggressive–rejected children is the focus of training. That is, just as social skills deficit models for rejected children have been expanded to include distortions in social perception and interpretation processes and inadequacies in interpersonal response generation and evaluation, conceivably skill training programs could be expanded to include instruction in self-control and thoughtful interpersonal problem solving. Anger-control and interpersonal problem-solving interventions have been designed specifically for impulsive and aggressive children, although their impact on peer relations *per se* has not been evaluated. Like the social skills training programs, carefully controlled evaluations reveal limitations in the effectiveness of anger control and interpersonal problem-solving programs for aggressive children.

For example, in a fairly comprehensive program developed by Lochman and his colleagues (Lochman, Burch, Curry, & Lampron, 1984), aggressive boys participated in a 12-session program including instruction in self-control procedures, anger-coping strategies, and interpersonal problem solving. In addition, these boys had behavioral contracts during the 12 weeks of treatment, which were monitored daily and reinforced contingently by their classroom teachers. Compared to aggressive boys who received no treatment, boys in this combined treatment condition engaged in less disruptive/aggressive off-task classroom behavior at posttreatment. No significant differences between these two groups, however, emerged for teacher, peer nor parent aggression ratings, nor for problem solving abilities.

Similarly, Saylor, Benson, and Einhaus (1985) carefully evaluated the effects of an 18-session, individually tailored "stress-innoculation" program for aggressive boys in an inpatient psychiatric facility. Compared with boys who received a control treatment, boys who received the stress inoculation program (which included discussions about anger, training in relaxation, rehearsal of adaptive self-statements, and role playing anger-provoking situations) improved on self-ratings but not on teacher or staff ratings, or on behavioral observations. The effects of these programs on peer relations were not examined. It should be remembered that most of the skill training programs reviewed in this section were school based and fairly time limited (usually lasting 4 to 12 weeks). Yet, as discussed previously, rejected children represent a multiproblematic, heterogeneous, and often severely dysfunctional group. Hence, the limited outcomes produced by skill training for peer-rejected children may reflect the limited time and scope of these programs. Alternatively, these programs may fail to adequately address some critical factors contributing to the peer problems of rejected children.

For example, the nature of behavioral changes observed in one coaching program with rejected, aggressive boys (Bierman, Miller, & Stabb, 1987) suggested that, over time, negative social behavior suppressed the display of positive social skills. Specifically, at the beginning of the school year when pretreatment observations were conducted, rejected target boys did not show lower-than-average levels of positive peer interactions. Over time, however, positive behaviors were observed less frequently in noncoached boys, so that these boys appeared to have prosocial skill deficits by the posttreatment and follow-up observations. Coaching did not increase the prosocial behaviors of coached boys, but it did protect boys against the decline in positive interactions that characterized noncoached boys. Apparently, negative social behavior may sometimes lead to (rather than result from) social skills deficits.

Two other recent studies similarly suggest that negative behaviors may be the most common "driving force" leading to peer rejection (Coie & Kupersmidt, 1983; Dodge, 1983). In both studies, the boys who became rejected in newly formed groups were those who showed initial high rates of aggression, hostile verbalizations, disruptive attention-getting behavior, and behavior designed to exclude peers. In the next section, models emphasizing a causal role for aggressive and negative social behavior in the development of peer rejection are discussed, along with corresponding treatment approaches.

3.2. Negative Behavior Model

3.2.1. The Model

Aggressive and negative social behavior have been studied frequently as indicators of maladaptive social–emotional development and risk for poor adult outcomes. Such behaviors are quite stable during middle childhood, perhaps as stable as IQ (Olweus, 1979), and are predictors for many negative adult outcomes, such as juvenile delinquency, adult antisocial personality disorders, poor interpersonal and marital relations, alcoholism, and other psychiatric disorders (Kohlberg, La-Crosse, & Ricks, 1972; Robins, 1972). Developmental models linking negative social behavior to peer rejection begin with the initial emergence of high rates of aggressive and negative interpersonal behavior within the family (Patterson, 1982, 1986). Patterson (1986) describes the postulated developmental sequence as follows:

> . . . disrupted family management skills lead to the development of anti-social child behavior. The noncompliant and coercive features of the child's behavior place him or her directly at risk for both rejection by normal peers and for academic failure. The same pattern of behavior in the home leads to parental rejection and, in turn, causes the child to develop low self-esteem. Academic failure, rejection by peers, and possibly low self-esteem are thought to place the child at greater risk for remaining in the process. (p. 432)

By "disrupted family management skills" Patterson refers to the failure by parents to effectively monitor and control a broad range of noncompliant and negative interpersonal behavior displayed by children. Instead, parents of aggressive children frequently admonish their children but fail to follow through with their threats. Their responses to both positive and negative child behavior are inconsistent. Although they may often ignore negative child behavior, they may sometimes react with extremely harsh or violent punishments. Children may respond by learning to escalate their negative behaviors in order to avoid or escape parental demands or criticism. Indeed, Patterson (1986) estimates that one third of the negative behaviors shown by aggressive children within the family context involve a reaction to aversive intrusions by other family members; furthermore, 70% of the aggressive counterattacks launched by these children are "successful" and lead to the withdrawal of the intruder. In this model described by Patterson and his colleagues (Patterson, 1982, 1986), family members essentially train each other to become increasingly aversive in their interactions—a process labeled "coercion."

Patterson and his colleagues have tested causal models linking inept parental discipline and negative family interactions to high rates of child fighting and then to poor peer relations (Patterson, 1986). In one such model, tested with 91 aggressive boys in 4th, 7th, and 10th grades, an adequate fit of the data was obtained, accounting for 58% of the variance (Patterson, Dishion, & Banks, 1984).

Coercive interpersonal strategies, learned in the home and generalized to school settings and peer interactions, may be further strengthened by positive peer reinforcement (Patterson, Littman, & Bricker,

1967). Indeed, Klein and Young (1979) observed that 20% to 70% of all classroom disruptions were reinforced by peers.

3.2.2. The Treatment

In order to reduce a child's negative ineractions within this model, it becomes critical to gain control of and change the interpersonal antecedents and consequences that are eliciting and maintaining the negative behaviors. Two types of treatment strategies characterize most attempts made in school settings to reduce or eliminate peer reinforcement of negative behavior: (1) the use of contingency management procedures to consequate the behaviors of the target children, and (2) direct attempts to manipulate peer responses to target children.

The most commonly used contingency management procedures are time-out and differential reinforcement. Although there are a variety of ways in which time-out may be operationalized, the basic procedure is to remove children who exhibit a negative behavior briefly from the peer interaction situation in order to decrease any opportunity they may have to receive peer reinforcement for the negative behavior. A response-cost or punishment procedure may be used alone or in conjunction with time-out in which children's negative behavior also results in the loss of privileges or rewards or in which children's negative behavior is consequated by some form of demerit or other negative consequences.

Typically, when they are used consistently and prudently in school settings, negative consequences, time-out, or response-cost procedures can produce fairly quick and predictable reductions in specific negative behaviors in the "controlled" setting (Rosen, O'Leary, Joyce, Conway, & Pfiffner, in press). Unfortunately, many naturalistic peer interactions take place in "uncontrolled" school settings that are not well monitored by adults. For example, although most contingency management programs focus on improving classroom behavior, rejected children are more likely to behave aggressively during recess when peer interactions involve more "rough-and-tumble" play and when adult supervision and structure are at a minimum.

A second approach to intervention, designed to affect peer interactions even in unstructured situations when teachers are unable to monitor closely, is to teach peers to respond differentially to negative behavior displayed by target classmates. Empirical evaluations have shown that peers can be taught effectively to elicit and reward positive peer interactions in their developmentally delayed and withdrawn classmates (Strain & Kerr, 1981). Research also suggests that peers may be trained to act as monitors in peer interaction situations such as group work or recess and thus contribute the information necessary for a teacher to follow through with positive or negative consequences (Carden-Smith & Fowler, 1984; Dougherty, Fowler, & Paine, 1985). In addition, Solomon and Wahler (1973) demonstrated that peers could be trained directly to act as positive behavior modifiers. Having taught peers to attend selectively to the appropriate social behaviors and to ignore the disruptive behaviors exhibited by particular target children, they documented reductions in the inappropriate classroom behaviors of the target children.

Apparently, the design and administration of contingency management programs that effectively control negative behavior in naturalistic peer interactions is not an easy task. However, when adequate monitoring of negative child behavior is obtained and interpersonal consequences are controlled (by teacher intervention or direct peer training), negative peer interactions can be reduced effectively.

Unfortunately, the reduction of negative behavior alone may not improve the peer ratings given to many rejected children. For example, although Drabman, Spitalnik, and Spitalnik (1974) found that four different token economies effectively reduced the disruptive behavior of identified problem children, only one of the systems—a system in which the poorly behaved student was able to earn reinforcement for his or her whole group by improving his or her behavior—also led other group members to rate this student as more "responsible." Despite behavioral improvements, none of the programs led to improved friendship ratings for target children.

Resistance to change in sociometric ratings—even in the face of observed behavioral changes induced by skill training or contingency management techniques—is not uncommon (Bierman & Furman, 1984; LaGreca & Santogrossi, 1980). Although behavioral observations documented the fact that the rejected children changed in these studies, peers continued to treat them as if they were acting "the way they always did," apparently responding to these children more on the basis of their negative expectancies than the children's actual behavior. The proposition that negative reputations and stereotypes may lead peers to treat some children aversively is explored in the next section. Treatments designed to improve peer attitudes and mitigate negative peer reputations are then described.

3.3. Reputation Model

3.3.1. The Model

Interview and observation studies supply evidence that peers hold rigid negative stereotypes characterizing some rejected children. For example, peers tend to underestimate the competencies of unpopular children on dimensions ranging from intelligence to physical prowess; they even underestimate them in judgments of physical height (Koslin, Haarlow, Karlins, & Pargament, 1968). Peers may also make differential and more negative interpretations about the behavior of disliked children. For example, Dodge (1980) told boys hypothetical stories in which particular classmates treated others in a negative fashion. When the boy named as the perpetrator of the hypothetical negative act was a classmate with a reputation for aggressive behavior, his peers were likely to assume the act was intentionally harmful. If, on the other hand, the boy was a nonaggressive classmate, his peers were likely to assume that the negative act was accidental and that no harm was intended.

In another study, Hymel (1986) examined attributional biases in children's interpretations of hypothetical stories involving positive and negative behaviors displayed by either liked or disliked peers. When told stories about liked peers, children attributed the positive behaviors to more stable, internal causes and negative behaviors to less stable causes, minimizing the responsibility of the liked peers for negative acts. In contrast, when interpreting stories about disliked peers, children tended to view the causes of negative behaviors as more stable than the causes of positive behaviors, and they felt that the disliked peers were equally responsible for both.

Negatively biased expectations and attributions may lead classmates to treat rejected children differently (and more aversively) than they treat their well-accepted peers. That is, when peers expect inappropriate social behavior from a particular child, they may become selectively attentive to such behavior and unresponsive to that child's prosocial behavior (Hymel, Wagner, & Butler, in press). Indeed, observations suggest that peers do respond more negatively to rejected than to accepted children, even when the two groups show no apparent differences in the quality of their social initiations. For example, although Foster and Ritchey (1985) observed no differences in rates of positive or negative behaviors initiated by rejected children and their peer-accepted classmates, rejected children received fewer positive peer responses. Similarly, Solomon and Wahler (1973) observed classroom interactions and noted that peers ignored the prosocial behaviors of identified problem children and attended almost exclusively to the deviant actions of these children.

Thus, children who behave in an aversive fashion and become rejected may then be exposed to more negative social interactions and to a more stressful and hostile socializing environment than well-behaved children. As Patterson (1976) described them, these children may be both victims and architects of coercive interpersonal systems.

3.3.2. The Treatment

Changing the expectations, attitudes, and behaviors of nonrejected peers is perhaps the least-studied intervention technique for rejected children. However, several studies suggest that peers can be included in treatment and that changing the responsivity of peers to the rejected child may be crucial to the long-term success of many programs.

Perhaps the most well-known attempt to modify hostile peer attitudes is that described by Sherif, Harvey, White, Hood, and Sherif (1961) in their classic Robber's Cave experiment. In this study, two initially unfamiliar groups of grade-school boys were formed and allowed to interact in a series of frustrating team competitions, which fostered the growth of substantial intergroup hostility. Unstructured group contacts served only to exacerbate acts of intergroup aggression, which were accompanied by increasing intergroup animosity. The investigators then presented the groups with problem situations that all had one essential feature—they involved superordinate goals. That is, they involved goals that could not be attained by the efforts and energies of one group alone and required intergroup cooperation for successful completion. Under these conditions, group friction began to decrease and intergroup cooperation and friendship emerged. Other investigators have likewise documented that children behave more cooperatively and like each other better after working together toward a superordinate goal (Bryan, 1975; Kagan & Madsen, 1971).

In the study by Bierman and Furman (1984), the effects of providing unpopular children with opportunities to engage in positive interactions with more popular classmates under the conditions of a superordinate goal were tested directly. Unpopular target children, randomly assigned to "peer involvement" treatment conditions, were paired with nontarget partners. Triads were told that there help was needed to make instructional video-films for college students, showing the students the kinds of things that grade-school friends talked about and did together. In a series of ten half-hour sessions, the triads engaged in cooperative activities designed to help them get to know one another better and then planned and rehearsed a series of videotapes. In the final session, they produced together a finished instructional videotape. Half of the triads received coaching in conversational skills as part of their planning and rehearsal sessions; the other triads engaged in the activities and videotaping without any specific social skills training. At the posttreatment assessment, unpopular children who experienced peer involvement under superordinate goals received higher sociometric ratings and gave themselves higher ratings on the social subscale of the Perceived Competence Scale for Children (Harter, 1982) than did children who received individual coaching or no treatment.

Several factors may account for the positive effects of peer involvement under superordinate goals. In these close interactions with socially competent peers, peer-approved social behavior is clearly modeled and reinforced for unpopular target children. In addition, the unpopular children may have a chance to break through previously unpenetrable negative peer attitudes. That is, whereas the peer partners' negative expectations may have led them to avoid the disliked child before treatment, the series of close rewarding interactions may have fostered a positive reassessment of the unpopular child's potential as a playmate. Indeed, as popular children watched themselves behaving in a warm and friendly fashion with the unpopular children in the videotapes, they may well have been faced with attributional cues stimulating a positive reevaluation of their professed attitudes toward the unpopular children—for example, "we're behaving like good friends, perhaps we are friends" (Bem, 1965).

However, in this study as in others, positive peer involvement and superordinate goals alone did not produce sustained improvements in children's peer acceptance. Apparently, one can create environments to foster positive peer attitudes toward unpopular children, but these gains may rescind quickly after the termination of the environmental manipulation unless the characteristics that initially fostered rejection are addressed directly (Rucker & Vincenzo, 1970). For example, the children who received coaching and experienced positive peer involvement in the Bierman and Furman (1984) study did show sustained positive behavioral and sociometric gains at the follow-up evaluation 6 weeks after treatment.

Perhaps peers would be more positively responsive to the behavior changes made by rejected children in skill training or contingency management programs if they had more frequent opportunities for cooperative interactions with the more well-behaved target children. Indeed, cooperative learning programs, such as Teams-Games-Tournaments or Jigsaw Classroom, which have been designed to facilitate more positive peer interactions in general within classrooms, may be particularly useful for increasing peer interaction opportunities and enhancing positive peer attitude change for rejected children after skill training or contingency management treatments (Blaney, Stephan, Rosenfield, Aronson, & Sikes, 1977; DeVries & Slavin, 1976). In these programs, academic studies are organized around interdependent tasks. Group achievements or group reward structures provide superordinate goals to foster cooperation and positive peer relationships as an integral part of classroom interaction.

It is important to note, however, that it is not always easy to structure cooperative activities for rejected children that will be mutually rewarding for all of the children involved. Interdependent tasks, which demand cooperative interaction, require more interpersonal negotiation and communication skills for their successful completion than do individualistic tasks. Not all rejected children have the requisite interpersonal skills to manage cooperative interactions without careful structure, supervision, and support. If peers are depending upon each other to attain a superordinate goal or achieve a group reward and the rejected child is unable to contribute to the group goal and is responsible for the group's failure, the experience may actually increase his or her rejection by peers and exacerbate feelings or incompetence. Clearly, cooperative peer involvement and superordinate goals may provide a powerful and positive influence, but these opportunities must be engineered and administered with care.

3.4. Integrated Model

Although each of the three models of peer rejection described thus far presents a distinct set of hypotheses concerning the causes of peer rejection and prescribes a correspondingly different approach to intervention, the models are by no means mutually exclusive. Instead, they might be considered three sources of influence that, for various children, contribute more or less to the genesis and maintenance of peer difficulties.

Several different developmental trajectories may lead to the common outcome of rejection. For example, one trajectory is described in Patterson's (1986) model, in which children's difficulties begin when family factors foster the learning of coercive interpersonal response patterns. The child's resulting negativism and noncompliance interferes with his or her "openness" to positive socializing experiences, precipitating failures to learn and use positive social interaction skills. Peer rejection follows, along with other negative outcomes, such as academic difficulties and low self-esteem.

Other children may achieve peer rejection via somewhat different pathways. For example, children who display initial anxious avoidance or immature dependence in their peer interactions may be excluded by peers. Negative treatment from peers may then exacerbate the social anxieties and isolative tendencies of these children (Rubin, LeMare, & Lollis, in press).

Coie (in press) argues compellingly that negative peer treatment will rarely be the primary source of a child's rejection, but it may often contribute to the maintenance of rejected status. That is, a child is unlikely to achieve sustained peer rejection unless he or she is behaving in some way that displeases or antagonizes peers. Once rejected, however, negative peer expectations, continuing or increasing social skills deficits, and disruptive or insensitive social behavior may all contribute to continuing social difficulties.

Although it may not always be possible to identify the particular trajectory by which any one child arrived at his or her rejected status, it is important to consider the multiple factors contributing to his or her current rejection in order to plan effective treatments. The three types of treatment approaches described in this chapter appear to target specific aspects of peer difficulties; combined approaches are indicated for children whose rejected status reflects multiple causes.

The differential and additive nature of the three major approaches to treatment are illustrated in two studies. In one, Bierman, Miller, and Stabb (1987) contrasted the effects of coaching cooperative play skills with the effects of punishing (with response cost) negative social behavior. The response cost for negative behaviors resulted in immediate and stable declines in negative behavior. Coaching, in contrast, promoted sustained positive peer interactions. In another study, Bierman and Furman (1984) compared the effects of social skills training with the effects of providing opportunities for positive peer interaction under superordinate goals. Whereas coaching in conversation skills had a major impact on increasing children's conversational skills, peer involvement produced significant, though temporary, improvements in peer acceptance and feelings of social efficacy. In each of these studies, combined treatment approaches showed additive advantages, facilitating improvements across multiple domains.

Not all treatments, however, are compatible. Indeed, some programs designed to modify negative behaviors may include components that unwittingly increase negative peer reputations. For example, in a procedure designed by Goodwin and Mahoney (1975) to facilitate children's anger-control skills, peers are recruited to surround a target aggressive child and try to taunt, tease, and provoke that child's anger and distress. Peers receive a reward if they can successfully upset the target child. Ostensibly, the purpose of this procedure is to teach the aggressive child to "cope" by engaging in inaction and showing no overt distress when harassed unfairly by peers. One can only imagine, however, that by instructing and rewarding peers for behaving repeatedly in a hostile fashion toward a specific classmate—up to 10 repeated sessions in one school-based program designed by Blue, Madsen, and Heimberg (1981)—one is reinforcing their already negative attitudes toward the target child and "teaching" them that active ostracism of that child is not only acceptable, but even desirable.

In summarizing the empirical research presented in this chapter, one might conclude that rejected children represent a very heterogeneous group, many of whom show multiple areas of maladjustment, including conduct problems, attention deficits, learning difficulties, or depression. No treatment has produced long-term improvements in the behavioral adjustment and peer status of rejected children, although various treatment approaches have led to specific gains in some children. Clearly, a great deal more research is needed. Meanwhile, where does the clinician go from here?

In the last section of this chapter, a few general considerations are offered as guidelines to facilitate the design of interventions for rejected children in clinical settings.

4. Clinical Issues

In three important domains, the clinician who is designing interventions for individual rejected children is at a disadvantage relative to the researcher: (1) frequently, the clinician does not have access to sociometric or peer ratings upon which to base assessment and treatment planning; (2) the clinician's access may be limited to naturalistic peer groups and to the adults who control the locations in which interventions may be conducted; and (3) whereas researchers typically select children at a particular developmental level appropriate to their intervention, the clinician must adapt his or her intervention to the developmental levels of the presenting clients.

4.1. Assessing Peer Relations without Sociometrics

Typically, a clinician is able to use standardized parental ratings, teacher ratings, and behavioral observations to attain a reasonable picture of a child's behavioral presentation in home and school settings and to assess the quality and severity of particular behavior problems in each of these settings. Assessing the quality of a child's peer relations in clinic settings, however, is a more difficult task. The methods of choice for evaluating a child's sociometric status (e.g., peer nominations and ratings) are often unavailable clinically. Such measures may be impractical to gather on a case-by-case basis, and ethical concerns may limit their desirability in individual cases. That is, one cannot go into a classroom and ask for peer ratings on a particular child without drawing undue attention to that child; on the other hand, one cannot collect sociometrics on the whole group without informed consent from the school system and parents of participating children, a formidable tasks for the assessment of a single child.

One approach taken by Lahey and his colleagues (Carlson, Lahey, Frame, Walker, & Hynd, 1987; Strauss, Lahey, Frick, Frame, & Hynd, 1988) is designed to provide sociometric ratings for individual children while minimizing these potential risks. They ask teachers to administer sociometric nominations to their entire class (thus avoiding the singling out of particular children); however, teachers report to them only the scores received by the target child (thus avoiding the collection of data for children who have not received informed parental consent). In their use of this procedure for several years, Lahey and his colleagues have found the school districts and teachers in their area cooperative and have had no reports of negative effects from teachers or parents. In other school districts, however, clinicians may find regulations or policies that limit the extent to which school personnel are allowed to elicit information about the children's personal thoughts and feelings without prior parental permission. In these cases, the clinician must rely on information gathered from parents, teachers, and children themselves to estimate the level of a child's peer acceptance and rejection.

Of these informants, teachers provide descriptions of peer interactions and ratings of peer popularity that correspond most closely to observed social behavior and peer-rated sociometric status (Glow & Glow, 1980). For example, reported correlations are fairly high between teacher and peer ratings of popularity ($r = 0.55$ for preschool children; Connelly & Doyle, 1981) and between teacher ratings and peer-positive and peer-negative nominations ($r = 0.50$ and -0.59, respectively, for kindergarten children; Landau, Milich, & Whitten, 1984). Similarly, teacher ratings of grade-school children's likability using the Pupil Evaluation Inventory (e.g., helping others, being nice, having many friends) are moderately correlated with peer-play ratings ($r = 0.47$), whereas teacher ratings of peer aggression and social withdrawal/ostracism on the same scale are inversely correlated with peer-play ratings ($r = -0.33$ and -0.51, respectively; LaGreca, 1981). Although teacher ratings are not as effective as peer ratings in predicting children's social behavior with peers (Landau et al., 1984), they still provide a "second-best" estimate of peer relations when direct sociometric evaluations are unavailable.

Parents, in contrast, are typically poor judges of the quality of their children's peer relations (Graham & Rutter, 1968). However, parents can provide useful information concerning their children's extracurricular activities and peer involvement. For example, parental reports on the social competence scale of the Child Behavior Checklist, which includes information about a child's activities, social involvement, and school success, have proven valid clinically (Achenbach & Edelbrock, 1981).

Finally, the clinician may consider including children's self-reports of their peer relations in an evaluation. Although self-ratings are typically only mildly related to peer and teacher ratings (Ledingham, Younger, Schwartzman, & Bergeron, 1982), they may provide unique information concerning the child's awareness of and reaction to his or her peer relations. Cairns and Cairns (1984) have documented a high degree of stability in children's self-evaluations of their peer relations across a 1-year period and stress the importance of collecting measures of "private" experiences and perceptions regarding children's social adjustment, along with the "public" measures of teacher and peer ratings. Standardized questionnaires are available, that are designed to assess grade-school children's descriptions of their peer interactions (Bierman & McCauley, 1987), feelings of loneliness (Asher, Hymel, & Renshaw, 1984), and perceived social competence (Harter, 1982).

4.2. Gaining Access to Peer Groups

Information about the nature and extent of the child's behavioral problems and social difficulties enables a clinician to construct a list of treatment goals. Selecting optimal intervention strategies to meet those goals, however, must also depend on a determination of the interpersonal support and environmental opportunities available for a particular child. Of the three intervention strategies described in preceding sections, only one (skill training) can be conducted without environmental mediation or support. In the other two types of strategies, contingency management and peer involvement, adults or peers in the child's naturalistic environment must be available for some level of inclusion in the treatment plan. Even skill training, although it theoretically can be conducted in an individual setting with a child, is unlikely to effectively change a child's peer status without naturalistic practice and extended attempts to garner peer support (Bierman & Furman, 1984; Ladd, 1983).

No standardized guide is available to help the clinician evaluate the optimal peer interaction opportunities or potential social supports available in a child's environment. Several factors need to be considered: (1) the types of peer interaction opportunities available to children in a particular community and the "difficulty level" of each of these opportunities, (2) the potential benefits for a particular child of different social experiences, and (3) the likelihood that a particular child has the needed skills or could be provided with the support necessary to be successful in a particular social placement.

In considering potential peer interaction contexts for the initial treatment and eventual naturalistic integration of a rejected child, the clinician needs to know what is available in his or her community and

what the "difficulty level" is for competent social interaction in each
potential peer context. In general, the "difficulty level" of various contexts is controlled by the size of the group, the characteristics and skills
of others in the group, the amount of task structure within the group,
and the extent and type of available adult support and supervision.

Relatively few rejected children will have difficulty interacting in a
dyadic situation with a kind and agreeable peer on a structured task that
involves limited negotiation when an adult is available for help as
needed. Most rejected children, on the other hand, will become disruptive, anxious, or isolative when they are faced with a large group of
boisterous peers who are negotiating the use of a limited set of resources
or are playing in a rough-and-tumble fashion under the conditions of
little task structure and unavailable adult support. Competitive games
with complicated rules, although "structured," may also increase the
difficulty level of an interactive task for many rejected children because
of the heightened arousal engendered by such games and the corresponding emotional regulation required.

The clinician will want to begin treatment in a setting in which
mastery or success in the peer interaction task is within the grasp of the
rejected child. In many cases, this requires setting up an "analogue"
peer interaction opportunity in which the size, structure, and available
adult monitoring for the group interaction is considerably greater than
in most naturalistic settings. Often, a small therapy group experience
will serve this purpose. Because research suggests that rejected children
who show aggressive or immature social behavior respond variably and
with some difficulty even to peer group therapy, it is particularly desirable to be able to add controls and vary the size and structure of the
group as needed to maintain a therapeutically positive peer support
context.

Under improper conditions, the danger exists that the intense level
of peer interaction stimulated by social skills training in a peer-group
context will exacerbate negative peer reactions toward target children
and can even contribute to the victimization of some target children. For
some rejected children, therefore, it may be necessary to design long-
term skill training programs that include only limited peer contact initially and then gradually increase the level of peer interaction contingent
upon the target child's behavioral improvements, thus avoiding social
interaction challenges that overwhelm the target children's positive interaction capabilities. The composition of initial therapy groups may also
be quite important. When two or more children in a group are highly
reactive and easily aroused to physical aggression, it may be difficult to
maintain positive enough group interactions to foster mutual friendships among group members.

One cannot expect even the most successful and supportive therapy group experience alone, however, to prepare a rejected child adequately for the "plunge" into naturalistic peer interactions of high difficulty (such as the large, unstructured, and unsupervised recess interactions). To foster the child's integration into naturalistic interactions, the clinician may consider placing the child in a peer group setting of low-level difficulty and working, via consultation, to decrease the difficulty level of naturalistically occurring peer experience.

For example, a typical sequence of peer experiences for rejected children treated in our clinic might include (1) an initial experience in a structured therapy group, of a duration dependent on the child's rate of progress; (2) an initial naturalistic placement in a highly structured peer experience, such as swimming lessons or (available in our community) a music therapy group (which involves a small group organized around musical activities); (3) fostering closer interactions in dyadic situations with adult monitoring (either at home or school); (4) placement in a naturalistic peer group of intermediate difficulty, such as a time-limited day-camp experience organized around crafts or outdoor activities; (5) placement in a peer group of greater difficulty, such as a Boy Scout or Girl Scout group, a 4-H group, or another club. For some children, team sports activities may be attractive and may be attainable at a later stage in treatment—depending upon the level of competition and support fostered by adult leaders in a particular community sport. The difficulty level and potential "match" between any particular child and the available peer experiences (including those described above or other common groups, such as church youth groups, recreational class groups, school interest clubs, musical or drama groups) must often be based on the clinician's knowledge of the actual organization, type of adult supervision, and type of peer interaction in any particular community group.

As Furman (1984) has pointed out, integration into peer-group activities may be only one of the goals of a socialization treatment program for a rejected child. For some children, who have had severely dysfunctional early relationships, it may be desirable to supplement peer-group-oriented treatment with the provision of more basic interpersonal experiences. For example, a positive relationship with an adult (via Big Brothers or Sisters or via a close tutoring relationship) may contribute to the development of some children's interpersonal skills. Such experiences are not likely to lead directly to improved peer interactions for most rejected children, but they may make important therapeutic contributions in their own right. Furman (1984) makes the additional point that some rejected children are rather unlikely to ever achieve popularity or general group acceptance in school settings. Helping these children to form at least one dyadic friendship even outside of school, to strengthen bonds with family members or adult friends, or to find some social niche in which they can experience nonconflictual social interactions may be more realistic therapy goals.

Although clinicians are more apt to emphasize their initial contributions toward skill training and behavioral management in a therapy group, our clinical experiences suggest that taking the additional step to identify potential naturalistic peer experiences for rejected children, monitoring the success of these experiences, and providing direct consultation to the adults supervising these experiences is critical for the eventual integration of many rejected children into more "normal" peer interactions. Parents and teachers may, of course, be instrumental in the identification and monitoring of such peer experiences, but rarely do they have the skills themselves to plan, evaluate, and troubleshoot systematically a course of social integration for a socially inept rejected child.

4.3. Developmental Considerations

Most of the research and discussion covered in this chapter has focused on grade-school children, primarily grade-school boys. Yet developmental level and sex may have an impact both on the type of interpersonal behaviors approved by peers and on the structure and organization of peer relations. For example, with age, peer interactions and friendships become more interactive, verbal, reciprocal, and complex. During the preschool years, most peer interactions are focused around shared play activities. Play skills including sharing, smiling, looking, giving, along with neutral task-oriented communications characterize positive interactions. In the course of elementary school, two notable changes take place in peer interactions. First, play becomes more organized and more elaborate. Rather than engaging in the manipulative object play or dyadic dramatic play that characterizes preschool interactions, grade-school children select more complex, rule-bound games that often involve multiple players and multiple roles, such as kickball or board games (Hartup, 1983). Second, stable best friendships or chumships begin to emerge (Sullivan, 1953). These relationships are marked by a unique sense of intimacy with and commitment toward each other. By the end of grade school with the coming of preadolescence, communication (including talking at recess, sending notes in class, and calling friends on the phone) surfaces as a new major focus of peer relationships (Hartup, 1983). Throughout these years, then, as peer relationships become more interactive, reciprocal, and complex, the skills needed for and learned during positive peer contacts become more plentiful and more complex.

In addition, developmental studies suggest that, during preadolescence and adolescence, peer-group norms begin to crystallize. During these years, children become more peer oriented and they increasingly seek to associate with peers and use peer standards to evaluate their own and others' social behavior (O'Brien & Bierman, in press). There is greater group consensus about the reputations of various peers, and sociometric status shows less fluctuation (Horrocks & Buker, 1951). Hence, negative peer stereotypes may have a more critical impact on social adjustment and self-concept after preadolescence than they do for younger children.

Systematic studies comparing the effects of various treatment interventions on the social adjustment of rejected children across different developmental levels are not yet available. Hence, no specific guidelines exist to help clinicians tailor their interventions to the developmental level of their clients. However, the developmental lines described briefly in this section suggest that the specification of skills to be taught, the type of peer interaction to foster, and the extent to which a child's own self-concept and the attitudes of peers must be considered in treatment may all vary depending on the developmental level of the children involved.

5. Conclusions

To be actively rejected, perhaps mistreated or teased by peers, can be a provoking, frightening, and intensely painful childhood experience. We can probably each reach back into our childhood memories and touch one or two still tender memories of times when peers turned against us. For those children who are regularly excluded, the experience may be unbearable, as the following excerpt from an aggressive rejected 11-year-old boy illustrates:

> They don't like me. They won't leave me alone. They follow me wherever I go, they tell everybody about me. Like if a new kid comes to school I think maybe this once I'll finally have one friend. But no. As soon as they tell him about me, then he'll have nothing to do with me. And they follow me wherever I go. Once they came after me when I was going home and they tried to take my coat. I'd fight them too—I didn't care. But there were four of them. They threw rocks at my house and my mom and sister were in there too. They hate me and I hate them back.

At the same time, we can probably each also generate childhood memories of one or two rejected children we knew who really were incredibly unlikable—disruptive or bossy or whiny or selfish. As two classmates of the above 11-year-old testified:

He's nasty and mean and he stinks. No one wants him here. He's always doing weird things, like he thinks he's so cool. He beats up on the little kids, too.

Once he stole my lunch money. I know it was him. He said he didn't but he's a liar. He's always taking people's stuff or messing it up. I think they should kick him out of this school.

Clearly, this boy's rejection is a critical index as well as a cause of significant social and emotional difficulties. As with many rejected children, if treatment is to be effective, it will need to be multifaceted and extensive.

Although current research provides some directions for intervention efforts, further intervention development and evaluation is clearly needed. The past decade has seen extensive gains in the area of understanding and treating peer rejection; effective comprehensive remedial and preventive programs remain a future goal.

6. References

Achenbach, T. M., & Edelbrock, C. S. (1981). Behavior problems and competencies reported by parents of normal and disturbed children 4-16. *Monographs of the Society for Research in Child Development, 46* (1, Serial #188).

American Psychiatric Association. (1980). *Diagnostic and statistical manual of mental disorders* (3d ed.). Washington, DC: Author.

Asher, S. R., Hymel, S., & Renshaw, P. D. (1984). Loneliness in children. *Child Development, 55,* 1456–1464.

Asher, S. R., & Renshaw, P. D. (1981). Children without friends, social knowledge and social skill training. In S. R. Asher & J. M. Gottman (Eds.), *The development of children's friendships.* Cambridge: Cambridge University Press.

Bem, D. J. (1965). An experimental analysis of self persuasion. *Journal of Experimental Social Psychology, 1,* 199–218.

Bierman, K. L. (1986a). The relationship between social aggression and peer rejection in middle childhood. In R. Prinz (Ed.), *Advances in behavioral assessment of children and families* (Vol. 2, pp. 151–178). Greenwich, CT: JAI Press.

Bierman, K. L. (1986b). Process of change during social skills training with preadolescents and its relation to treatment outcome. *Child Development, 57,* 230–240.

Bierman, K. L., & Furman, W. (1984). The effects of social skills training and peer involvement on the social adjustment of preadolescents. *Child Development, 55,* 151–162.

Bierman, K. L., & McCauley, E. (1987). Children's descriptions of their peer interactions: Useful information for clinical child assessment. *Journal of Clinical Child Psychology, 16,* 9–18.

Bierman, K. L., Miller, C. M., & Stabb, S. (1987). Improving the social behavior and peer acceptance of rejected boys: Effects of social skill training with instructions and prohibitions. *Journal of Consulting and Clinical Psychology, 55,* 194–200.

Bierman, K. L., Smoot, D. L., & Aumiller, K. A. (1987). Distinguishing characteristics of aggressive-rejected, aggressive (non-rejected) and rejected (non-aggressive) boys. Paper presented at the biennial meeting of the Society for Child Development, Baltimore, MD, April.

Blaney, N. T., Stephan, S., Rosenfield, D., Aronson, E., & Sikes, J. (1977). Interdependence in the classroom: A field study. *Journal of Educational Psychology, 69,* 121–128.

Blue, S. W., Madsen, C. H., & Heimberg, R. G. (1981). Increasing coping behavior in children with aggressive behavior: Evaluation of the relative efficacy of the components of a treatment package. *Child Behavior Therapy, 3,* 51–60.

Bryan, J. H. (1975). Children's cooperation and helping behavior. In M. Hetherington (Ed.), *Review of child development research* (Vol. 5, pp. 127–181). Chicago: University of Chicago Press.

Cairns, R. B., & Cairns, B. D. (1984). Predicting aggressive patterns in girls and boys: A developmental study. *Aggressive Behavior, 1,* 227–242.

Carden-Smith, L., & Fowler, S. A. (1984). Positive peer pressure: The effects of peer monitoring on children's disruptive behavior. *Journal of Applied Behavior Analysis, 17,* 213–227.

Carlson, C. L., Lahey, B. B., Frame, C. L., Walker, J., & Hynd, G. W. (1987). Sociometric status of clinic referred children with attention deficit disorders with and without hyperactivity. *Journal of Abnormal Child Psychology, 15,* 537–548.

Coie, J. D. (in press). Toward a theory of peer rejection. In S. R. Asher & J. D. Coie (Eds.), *Peer rejection in childhood.* New York: Cambridge University Press.

Coie, J. D., & Dodge, K. A. (1983). Continuities and changes in children's social status: A five-year longitudinal study. *Merrill-Palmer Quarterly, 29,* 261–282.

Coie, J. D., Dodge, K. A., & Coppotelli, H. (1982). Dimensions and types of social status: A cross-age perspective. *Developmental Psychology, 18,* 557–570.

Coie, J. D., & Koeppl, G. K. (in press). Adapting intervention to the problems of aggressive and disruptive rejected children. In S. R. Asher & J. D. Coie (Eds.), *Peer rejection in childhood.* New York: Cambridge University Press.

Coie, J. D., & Krehbiel, G. (1984). Effects of academic tutoring on the social status of low-achieving, socially rejected children. *Child Development, 55,* 1465–1478.

Coie, J. D., & Kupersmidt, J. B. (1983). A behavioral analysis of emerging social status. *Child Development, 54,* 1400–1416.

Combs, M. L., & Slaby, D. A. (1977). Social skills training with children. In B. Lahey & A. Kazdin (Eds.), *Advances in clinical child psychology* (Vol. 1, pp. 161–201). New York: Plenum Press.

Connolly, J., & Doyle, A. (1981). Assessment of social competence in preschoolers: Teachers versus peers. *Developmental Psychology, 17,* 454–462.

DeVries, D. L., & Slavin, R. E. (1976). *Teames-Games-Tournament: A final report on the research.* Center for Social Organization of the School. The Johns Hopkins University, Report #217.

Dodge, K. A. (1980). Social cognition and children's aggressive behavior. *Child Development, 51,* 162–170.

Dodge, K. A. (1983). Behavioral antecedents of peer social status. *Child Development, 54,* 1386–1399.

Dodge, K. A., Coie, J. D., & Brakke, N. P. (1982). Behavior patterns of socially rejected and neglected preadolescents: The roles of social approach and aggression. *Journal of Abnormal Child Psychology, 10,* 389–409.

Dodge, K. A., Pettit, G. S., McClaskey, C. L., & Brown, M. M. (1986). Social competence in children. *Monographs of the Society for Research in Child Development, 51* (2, Serial No. 213).

Dougherty, B. S., Fowler, S. A., & Paine, S. C. (1985). The use of peer monitors to reduce negative interactions during recess. *Journal of Applied Behavior Analysis, 18,* 141–153.

Drabman, R., Spitalnik, R., & Spitalnik, K. (1974). Sociometric and disruptive behavior as a function of four types of token reinforcement programs. *Journal of Applied Behavior Analysis, 7,* 93–101.

Foster, S. L., & Ritchey, W. L. (1985). Behavioral correlates of sociometric status of fourth-, fifth-, and sixth-grade children in two classroom situations. *Behavioral Assessment, 7,* 79–93.

Furman, W. (1984). Enhancing peer relations. In S. Duck (Ed.), *Personal relationships 5: Repairing personal relationships*. New York: Academic Press.

French, D. C. (1988). Heterogeneity of peer-rejected boys: Aggressive and non-aggressive subtypes. *Child Development, 59*, 976–985.

French, D. L., & Waas, G. A. (1985). Behavior problems of peer-neglected and peer-rejected elementary-age children: Parent and teacher perspectives. *Child Development, 56*, 246–252.

Glow, R. A., & Glow, P. H. (1980). Peer and self-rating: Children's perception of behavior relevant to hyperkinetic impulse disorder. *Journal of Abnormal Child Psychology, 8*, 397–404.

Goodwin, S., & Mahoney, M. (1975). Modification of aggression through modeling: An experimental problem. *Journal of Behavior Therapy and Experimental Psychiatry, 6*, 200–202.

Gottman, J., Gonso, J., & Rasmussen, B. (1975). Social interaction, social competence and friendship in children. *Child Development*, 709–718.

Graham, P., & Rutter, M. (1968). The reliability and validity of the psychiatric assessment of the child: II. Interview with the parent. *British Journal of Psychiatry, 114*, 581–592.

Gresham, F. M., & Nagle, R. J. (1980). Social skill training with children: Responsiveness to modeling and coaching as a function of peer orientation. *Journal of Consulting and Clinical Psychology, 84*, 718–729.

Harter, S. (1982). The perceived competence scale for children. *Child Development, 53*, 87–97.

Hartup, W. W. (1983). Peer relations. In E. M. Hetherington (Ed.), P. H. Mussen (Series Ed.), *Handbook of child psychology: Vol. 4. Socialization, personality, and social development* (pp. 103–196). New York: Wiley.

Horrocks, J. E., & Buker, M. E. (1951). A study of the friendship fluctuations of preadolescents. *The Journal of Genetic Psychology, 1951, 78*, 131–144.

Hymel, S. (1986). Interpretations of peer behavior: Affective bias in childhood and adolescence. *Child Development, 57*, 431–445.

Hymel, S., & Rubin, K. H. (1985). Children with peer relationships and social skills problems: Conceptual, methodological, and developmental issues. In G. J. Whitehurst (Ed.), *Annals of child development* (Vol. 2). Greenwich, CT: JAI Press.

Hymel, S., Wagner, E., & Butler, L. J. (in press). Reputational bias: View from the peer group. In S. R. Asher & J. D. Coie (Eds.), *Peer rejection in childhood*. Cambridge: Cambridge University Press.

Kagan, J., & Madsen, M. C. (1971). Cooperation and competition of Mexican, Mexican-American, and Angloamerican children of two ages under four instructional sets. *Developmental Psychology, 5*, 32–38.

Klein, A. R., & Young, R. D. (1979). Hyperactive boys in their classroom: Assessment of teacher and peer perceptions, interactions, and classroom behaviors. *Journal of Abnormal Child Psychology, 7*, 425–442.

Kohlberg, L. A., LaCross, J., & Ricks, D. (1972). The predictability of adult mental health from childhood behavior. In B. Wolman (Ed.), *Manual of child psychopathology* (pp. 1217–1283). New York: McGraw-Hill.

Koslin, B. L., Haarlow, R. N., Karlins, M., & Pargament, R. (1968). Predicting group status from members' cognitions. *Sociometry, 31*, 64–75.

Ladd, G. (1981). Effectiveness of a social learning method for enhancing children's social interaction and peer acceptance. *Child Development, 52*, 171–178.

Ladd, G. (1983). Social networks of popular, average, and rejected children in school settings. *Merrill-Palmer Quarterly, 29*, 282–307.

Ladd, G. W. (1985). Documenting the effects of social skill training with children: Process and outcome assessment. In B. Schneider, K. Rubin, & J. Ledingham (Eds.), *Children's peer relations: Issues in assessment and intervention* (pp. 243–269). New York; Springer-Verlag.

Ladd, G. W., & Asher, S. R. (1985). Social skill training and children's peer relations: Current issues in research and practice. In L. L'Abate & M. Milan (Eds.), *Handbook of social skill training* (pp. 219–244). New York: Wiley.

LaGreca, A. (1981). Peer acceptance: The correspondence between children's sociometric scores and teacher's ratings of peer interactions. *Journal of Abnormal Psychology, 9,* 167–178.

LaGreca, A. M., & Santogrossi, D. A. (1980). Social skills training with elementary school students: A behavioral group approach. *Journal of Consulting and Clinical Psychology, 48,* 220–227.

Landau, S., & Milich, R. (1985). Social status of aggressive and aggressive/withdrawn boys: A replication across age and method. *Journal of Consulting and Clinical Psychology, 53,* 141.

Landau, S., Milich, R., & Whitten, P. (1984). A comparison of teacher and peer assessment of social status. *Journal of Clinical Child Psychiatry, 13,* 44–49.

Ledingham, J. E. (1981). Developmental patterns of aggressive and withdrawn behavior in childhood: A possible method of identifying preschizophrenics. *Journal of Abnormal Child Psychology, 9,* 1–22.

Ledingham, J., Younger, A., Schwartzman, A., & Bergeron, G. (1982). Agreement among teacher, peer and self-ratings of children's aggression, withdrawal and likeability. *Journal of Abnormal Child Psychology, 10,* 363–372.

Lochman, J. E., Burch, P. R., Curry, J. F., & Lampron, L. B. (1984). Treatment and generalization effects of cognitive-behavioral and goal-setting interventions with aggressive boys. *Journal of Consulting and Clinical Psychology, 52,* 915–916.

Michael, C. M., Morris, D. P., & Soroker, E. (1957). Follow-up studies of shy, withdrawn children II: Relative incidence of schizophrenia. *American Journal of Orthopsychiatry, 27,* 331–337.

O'Brien, S. B., & Bierman, K. L. (in press). Conceptions and perceived influence of peer groups: Interviews with preadolescents and adolescents. *Child Development.*

Oden, S., & Asher, S. R. (1977). Coaching children in social skills. *Child Development, 48,* 495–506.

Olweus, D. (1979). Stability of aggressive reaction patterns in males: A review. *Psychological Bulletin, 86,* 852–857.

Parker, J. G., & Asher, S. R. (1987). Peer relations and later personal adjustment: Are low-accepted children at risk? *Psychological Bulletin, 102,* 357–389.

Patterson, G. R. (1976). The aggressive child: Victim and architect of a coercive system. In E. J. Mash, L. A. Hamerlynck, & L. C. Handy (Eds.), *Behavior modification and families.* New York: Brunner/Mazel.

Patterson, G. R. (1982). *Coercive family processes.* Eugene, OR: Castalia Press.

Patterson, G. R. (1986). Performance models for antisocial boys. *American Psychologist, 41,* 432–444.

Patterson, G. R., Dishion, T., & Banks, L. (1984). Family interaction: A process model of deviancy training. *Aggressive Behavior, 10,* 253–267.

Patterson, G. R., Littman, R. A., & Bricker, W. (1967). Assertive behavior in children. *Monographs of the Society for Research in Child Development, 32,* 1–43.

Pelham, W. E., & Bender, M. E. (1982). Peer relationships in hyperactive children: Description and treatment. *Advances in learning and Behavioral Disabilities* (Vol. 1, pp. 365–436). Greenwich, CT: JAI Press.

Pope, A. W., Bierman, K. L., & Mumma, G. H. (in press). Relations between hyperactive and aggressive behaviors and peer relations at three elementary grade levels. *Journal of Abnormal Child Psychology*.

Rinn, R. C., & Markle, A. (1979). Modification of social skill deficits in children. In A. S. Bellack & M. Hersen (Eds.), *Research and practice in social skill training*. New York: Plenum Press.

Robins, L. N. (1972). Follow-up studies. In H. C. Quay & J. S. Werry (Eds.), *Psychopathological disorders of childhood*. New York: Wiley.

Rosen, L. A., O'Leary, S. G., Joyce, S. A., Conway, G., & Pfiffner, L. J. (in press). The importance of prudent negative consequences for maintaining the appropriate behavior of hyperactive students. *Journal of Abnormal Child Psychology*.

Rubin, K. H., LeMare, L., & Lollis, S. (in press). Social withdrawal in childhood: Developmental pathways to peer rejection. In S. R. Asher & J. D. Coie (Eds.), *Peer rejection in childhood*. New York: Cambridge University Press.

Rucker, C. N., & Vincenzo, F. M. (1970). Maintaining social acceptance gains made by mentally retarded children. *Exceptional Children, 36*, 679–680.

Saylor, C. F., Benson, B., & Einhaus, L. (1985). Evaluation of an anger management program for aggressive boys in inpatient treatment. *Journal of Child and Adolescent Psychotherapy, 2*, 5–15.

Sherif, M., Harvey, O. J., White, B. J., Hood, W. R., & Sherif, C. W. (1961). *Intergroup conflict and cooperation: The Robber's Cave Experiment*. Norman: University of Oklahoma.

Solomon, R. W., & Wahler, R. G. (1973). Peer reinforcement control of classroom problem behavior. *Journal of Applied Behavior Analysis, 6*, 49–56.

Strain, P. S., & Kerr, M. M. (1981). Modifying children's social withdrawal: Issues in assessment and clinical intervention. In M. Hersen, R. M. Eisler, & P. M. Miller (Eds.), *Progress in behavior modification*, Vol. 11. New York: Academic Press.

Strauss, C. C., Lahey, B. B., Frick, P., Frame, C. L., & Hynd, G. W. (1988). Peer social status of children with anxiety disorders. *Journal of Consulting and Clinical Psychology, 56*, 137–141.

Sullivan, H. S. (1953). *The interpersonal theory of psychiatry*. New York: W. W. Norton.

Whalen, C. K., & Henker, B. (1985). The social worlds of hyperactive (ADDH) children. *Clinical Psychology Review, 5*, 447–478.

4 Diversion from the Juvenile Justice System

Research Evidence and a Discussion of Issues

WILLIAM S. DAVIDSON II AND JOANNA BASTA

1. Background Considerations

Concern over adult crime and juvenile delinquency is prominent in American society. In annual surveys conducted from 1972 through 1984, U.S. citizens were asked "Is there more crime in this area than there was a year ago, or less?" In each year save one, the most frequent response was "More Crime," indicating the belief that crime has been increasing (Gallup, 1984). In similar surveys from 1965 through 1984, respondents were asked "Is there any area right around here—that is, within a mile—where you would be afraid to walk alone at night?" Over the last 17 years, the proportion of respondents indicating fear in their own neighborhood has steadily increased from one third to nearly one half (Roper, 1985).

Although the rising concern over crime is not debatable, contemporary approaches to aiding troubled youth have been characterized by disagreements over where and when to direct ameliorative efforts. There has been a continuing tension between a desire to *prevent* crime and the need to protect society from convicted offenders (Elliot, Huizinga, & Ageton, 1985; Empey, 1982; Krisberg & Austin, 1978). As early as the 1800s, social reformers suggested houses of refuge as an alternative to adult prisons. More recently, there has been debate between those who support early identification of potential offenders as a basis for prevention interventions (e.g., Hawkins & Lishner, 1985; Loeber, Dishion, & Patterson, 1984) and those who support selectively incapacitating career criminals (e.g., Greenberg, 1977).

WILLIAM S. DAVIDSON II AND JOANNA BASTA • Department of Psychology, Michigan State University, East Lansing, Michigan 48824.

Another factor in the debate has been ineffectual traditional treatment with criminal populations. This lack of demonstrated ability to rehabilitate is cited as a primary justification for alternative intervention models, as well as an argument *against* implementing widespread preventive interventions (e.g., Lipton, Martinson, & Wilks, 1975; Trojanowicz & Morash, 1987).

The search for valid intervention models has led to discussion of effective implementation issues. What should be included in an intervention? Major juvenile delinquency theories have been drawn upon in response to this question (Elliot *et al.*, 1985). One rich source of ideas has been the concept of individual differences, reflected in the early work of Glueck and Glueck (1951). Their classic study compared 500 institutionalized delinquent youth with 500 noninstitutionalized "normal" youth on over 400 characteristics including a variety of personal, physical, and social variables. From the large number of observed statistically significant differences, prediction schemes were developed to identify delinquents. Subsequent studies consistently reported differences between delinquents and nondelinquents (Andrew, 1981; Waldo & Dinitz, 1967). Similar comparisons have been made in terms of socialization (Smith & Ausnew, 1974), moral development (Prentice, 1972), family communication patterns (Alexander & Parsons, 1973), learning disabilities (Broder, Dunivant, Smith, & Sutton, 1981), social skills (Gaffney & McFall, 1981), interpersonal contingencies (Stuart, 1971), intelligence (Mednick & Christiansen, 1977), and problem-solving skills (Spivack & Shure, 1982). Not surprisingly, most of this research has documented differences between delinquents and nondelinquents.

This paradigm has been very influential with most intervention attempts drawing heavily on established differences between delinquents and nondelinquents. The specific forms of intervention programs have varied widely and have focused on psychological, educational, medical, vocational, recreational, or other presumed deficits present in predelinquents (Mayer, Gensheimer, Davidson, & Gottschalk, 1987).

Theories focusing on environmental variables as the source of delinquent behavior have also been used as a basis for prevention programs. Cultures, social structures, social opportunities, social control mechanisms, and social institutions have all been cited as causally related to delinquency. In the reverse sense, Viniaminov, for example, reported *no* cases of murder in the 20 years he spent living among the Aleutian people (Pelto & Pelto, 1976). This observation, that some societies are remarkably lacking in aggression, led to the recognition of cultural factors as the source of antisocial behavior. In contrast, it has been suggested that the social conflict inherent in complex materialistic societies, such as that of the United States, fosters crime as a result of anomie (Cloward & Ohlin, 1960; Merton, 1957). Anomie, or normlessness, is thought to be produced by social disorganization and differential opportunity for achievement. To oversimplify, if a youth cannot earn enough money to buy a car legitimately, then the pressure to steal a car is increased. Social control theory specified the processes through which macrolevel theoretical variables affect delinquent behavior—that is, a variety of conditions lead to the weakening of the youth's ties to the conventional order, thus producing delinquent behavior (Hirschi, 1969).

A final theoretical position, social labeling theory, suggests that delinquency can be understood only in the context of individual behavior *and* society's response to that behavior. This theory assumes that society defines deviant behavior and that environmental labeling, in response to a perceived deviant act, makes "deviants" deviant (Becker, 1963). Also, people's reaction to an act helps to create deviance and hence delinquency (Glaser, 1975; Matza, 1969). Certain behaviors were "designated as crimes when they were repugnant to persons with sufficient political power to have the law impose their standards of conduct on others" (Glaser, 1975). Typically, both the actor and the act are labeled deviant.

A variety of alternative intervention programs are based on environmental theories of criminal behavior. One example would be the community-based interventions that seek to alter the opportunity structure for youthful offenders (Empey, 1971). These various therapeutic models seek to capitalize on the social-control aspects of behavioral contingencies, families, or peer groups (Emshoff, Davis, & Davidson, 1981). Further, the rise in diversion programs for juvenile offenders can be attributed directly to the influence of social labeling theory (Davidson, Gensheimer, Mayer, & Gottschalk, 1987).

1.1. The Specific Context of the Adolescent Diversion Project

In addition to the social influences and theoretical developments described, the impetus for the diversion program was the result of a series of unfolding events. Two factors in particular highlighted our need to consider programmatic alternatives. The first was ineffectual traditional treatments for adjudicated delinquents (Davidson, Gensheimer, Mayer, & Gottschalk, 1987; Lipton et al., 1975; Romig, 1978) leading to the hope that alternatives could have constructive impact on juvenile delinquency and ultimately on adult crime. Providing alternatives to the traditional juvenile justice system can avoid the stigmatizing effects of legally ordered treatment.

Second, even if traditional approaches were effective, they tended to be prohibitively expensive. Current cost estimates of institutional treatment for youthful offenders consistently run over $40,000 per year per offender, and existing institutions are bulging at the seams (Davidson et al., 1987; National Institutes of Justice, 1987). Given the expense of the traditional approaches, lower-cost alternatives are very appealing.

The decision to design a juvenile delinquency diversion program raised several issues. The first was when to intervene—*before* delinquent behavior was formally labeled (primary prevention) or *after* such formal labeling (secondary or tertiary prevention)? We decided to intervene at a midpoint along this continuum, that is, after the appearance of official juvenile delinquency but before the point of formal adjudication. The intervention targeted youth who had been formally apprehended by the police and referred to juvenile court but who had not yet been found guilty or innocent by a juvenile court judge.

We selected this intervention point for two reasons: (1) to minimize the potential negative labeling effects of court adjudication, and (2) notwithstanding the appeal of intervening as soon as possible with troubled youth, the delinquency literature offered no support for choosing an earlier intervention point. There was no evidence of primary prevention efforts affecting later delinquent behavior. Identification of high-risk groups or individuals was espoused in the prevention literature, but the inability to accurately predict delinquent behavior made the feasibility of a demonstrably successful intervention seem doubtful (Kahn, 1965; Loeber & Loeber-Stouthamer, 1987). Indeed, the best available evidence suggested that programs based on predictors of delinquency would identify two youngsters inaccurately for every accurately identified youth. For these reasons, we decided to provide the intervention to youth in immediate risk of formal juvenile justice system involvement.

The second major decision had to do with who should deliver the preventive intervention. Strong arguments were being made for the use of nonprofessional change agents because of their effectiveness and low cost (Durlak, 1973; Rappaport, Chinsky, & Cowen, 1971). The recent evidence was even more convincing for the effectiveness of nonprofessionals (Berman & Norton, 1985; Durlak, 1979). The decision to use college students as service providers in our program also meant the change agents would be developmentally close to the adolescent youth. We hypothesized that their developmental similarity would enhance their effectiveness.

The third important implementation decision concerned the content of the intervention. At the time the project was being developed, there were no unequivocal research findings on which to base a specific juvenile delinquency intervention (e.g., Davidson & Seidman, 1974). Therefore, we selected and compared the most promising models during the project. Generally, relatively intense, time-restricted intervention models based on social learning theory were implemented. The one-on-one interventions were carried out in the youths' natural environments: family, school, and employment. The interventions were relatively brief (16 to 18 weeks) and included structured implementation steps to ensure the attainment of specific program goals. The intervention models and their content are described more fully below.

A final important aspect of the Adolescent Diversion Project (ADP) was the action-research concept that guided its progress. The ADP model, outlined in detail elsewhere (Fairweather & Davidson, 1986), went through four systematic studies. Briefly stated, the concept involves four phases: program development, evaluation, replication and, if warranted, dissemination. The ADP went through the stages of development, evaluation, and replication from 1974 to 1986. That work is the focus of the rest of this chapter. More detail is available in a recent volume by Davidson, Redner, Amdur, and Mitchell (1988).

2. Developing the Original Model

The first developmental phase of the ADP took place during 1973–1975 in Champaign-Urbana, Illinois. The original research on the effectiveness of the ADP was done as part of a larger project studying the effectiveness of nonprofessional change agents (Seidman & Rappaport, 1974).

Because the ADP targeted youth in legal jeopardy, we made arrangements for referrals with the juvenile divisions of the two local police departments. Youths participated in the project *prior* to their formal involvement with the juvenile justice system. Administrative agreements were made with the police, who, to our surprise, also sought an alternative to the juvenile court and its treatment.

Annually, the two police departments (Champaign and Urbana) were in contact with 1,200 to 1,500 youthful law violators. The vast majority of violations involved minor legal infractions that were typically disposed of by talking with the youth. Approximately 10% of those contacted or arrested were considered for petition to the local circuit court. Project referrals were drawn from this latter 10%.

Following initial planning activities with the two police departments, considerable effort was devoted to implementation of the ADP model. Plans were discussed for referral procedures, intake and termination assessment, random-assignment procedures, the assurance of the participant's *voluntary* involvement, protection of the youth's constitutional rights, and specification of the intervention methods. After a period of negotiation, we agreed that the referral decision should be left to the discretion of individual juvenile officers in the two participating cities. Referral decisions were based on the following guidelines:

> Since the project does not want to become involved with youth who have been charged with only a single minor offense and are not likely to find themselves in further legal difficulty, only refer youth for whom court referral is being seriously considered.

During the ADP's first two years, only Fall referrals were accepted since the change agents were college students and the program had to be coordinated with the academic calendar. A total of 73 youths were referred during these two years. Following formal referral, an interview was held with the offender and one parent. At that time, an ADP staff member explained the program and reviewed participants' rights both from a legal perspective and as voluntary participants in a prevention project. Participation and confidentiality agreements were signed at this time.

After intake assessment, the delinquent youth and his or her parents were informed of the random-assignment outcome. Participants were assigned to the ADP or a control group. This control group completed the preassessment and a termination assessment four months later but had no other contact with the project. All preassessment was done with participants naive as to experimental or control-group assignment. The ADP's first phase compared participants with no-treatment control subjects. Police and court records were followed on all 73 youths during their time in the ADP and for a 2-year follow-up.

2.1. Participant Youth

The 73 Phase One youths (61 male, 12 female) averaged 14.3 years of age; 49 were white and 24 black. On average, they had completed eight years of school. In the year prior to referral to the ADP, they had been arrested an average of 2.16 times, for a variety of offenses, of which the two most common were larceny and breaking and entering.

2.2. Student Volunteers

Undergraduate student volunteers—most of whom majored in psychology, sociology, and related social sciences—were assigned to participating youths within 48 hours of intake. Every effort was made to match students and youths on the basis of mutual interests, race, and sex. Students received academic credit for their participation.

2.3. Intervention Model

The ADP operated on the educational pyramid model (Seidman & Rappaport, 1974). Volunteers received 6 weeks of training based on a six-unit training manual that included reading assignments, homework assignments, and practice role plays. Advanced graduate students trained students weekly in groups of six to eight. After training, there were weekly supervisory meetings. Graduate student trainers in turn were supervised weekly by two faculty members, who were doctoral-level psychologists.

Each volunteer worked with an assigned youth 6 to 8 hours a week for the 18 weeks. Intervention techniques included developing a good relationship with the youths (Goodman, 1971), behavioral contracting (Stuart, 1971), and child advocacy (Davidson & Rapp, 1976). The contracting component involved the assessment and modification of the interpersonal contingencies in the lives of the youths (i.e., modifying relationships between the youths and their parents or teachers). This technique was based on written interpersonal agreements between the youths and significant others.

In addition, most youths required access to community resources. Resource mobilization maximized the durability of desired changes and provided legitimate avenues for youths to attain their goals. The model of child advocacy used in the ADP involved specifying areas of need, identifying individuals or organizations with needed resources, selecting and using strategies to access the needed resources, and transferring advocacy skills to the youth (Davidson & Rapp, 1976).

2.4. Results

Davidson et al. (1977) describe the diverse findings that emerged from the ADP's first developmental phase. Of major concern here was the model's effectiveness in preventing delinquency. Table 1 presents

TABLE 1
Phase One Project—Simple Recidivism Cumulative 2-Year Follow-Up

Condition	N	No petitions	One or more petitions
Behavioral contracting/child advocacy	49	27	22
Control	24	1	23

Note. χ^2 (1, N = 73) = 17.68; $p < .001$.

the simple recidivism rates for the ADP's first phase of operation. The table includes the simple recidivism rates (defined as one or more police contacts) for the cumulative "during-project," 1-year follow-up, and 2-year follow-up. As can be seen, the ADP model produced significantly lower recidivism rates than the control group, whose participants were released with no further intervention. In summary, the ADP project services were effective in reducing delinquency.

2.5. Conclusions from the Phase One Project

Relative to the literature on interventions with delinquents, the ADP produced positive results. The observed impact on official delinquency was unusually strong and the durability of the results over a 2-year follow-up period was encouraging. The positive nature of these early findings highlighted the needs for replication and more careful examination of the model's components to identify the specific factors responsible for delinquency reduction. Two major questions emerged form Phase One model development. First, how much did the *type* of intervention contribute to the results? Second, how much did the *type* of service provider (i.e., college students) contribute to the results? These questions were examined in Phases Two and Three.

3. Phase Two of ADP Development

The ADP's second phase replicated and extended the initial work and addressed the questions raised by Phase One findings. To examine the effectiveness of intervention content, we constructed variations on the original model. The original model was labeled the Action Condition. To separate its components and examine their relative contributions to reducing delinquency, four separate components were compared with the prototypical model. First, we developed a specific intervention and training model around a family-focused behavioral program (e.g., Alexander & Parsons, 1973; Gross, Brigham, Hopper, & Bologna, 1980; Stuart, Jayaratne, & Tripodi, 1976). This variation was labeled the Action Condition Family Focus. Second, because the original ADP involved relationship development, we constructed a relationship therapy intervention and training model (e.g., Goodman, 1971; Robin & Foster, 1984; Shelley, 1971). The relationship component of the model was named the Relationship Condition. Third, administrative setting (i.e., within versus outside the setting; Kushler & Davidson, 1981), rather than treatment content, was studied in relation to program outcomes. To that end we administered the intervention within the juvenile court setting. This group was named the Action Condition Court Setting Condition. A fourth, and final component, examined whether the Phase One findings were due to nonspecific attention. This group was labeled the Attention Placebo Condition. Isolating the effects of nonspecific attention or differential recordkeeping is not often done in outcome studies, yet it is critical to the process of making causal inferences about effects (Smith, Glass, & Miller, 1980). Accordingly, student volunteers were given brief, nonspecific training in relying on their "natural helping skills" as the basis for intervention. In Phase Two of the ADP development we compared these delinquency intervention models.

3.1. Youths Involved in Phase Two

Phase Two took place in Lansing, Michigan. From the fall of 1976 through the spring of 1980, a total of 228 youths were referred to the project; eight refused to participate. 83% were male; 26% were minorities; and the mean age was 14.2 years. In the year prior to referral, the 220 participants had been arrested an average of 1.46 times and petitioned to court an average of 1.54 times. Youths had been charged with a wide variety of crimes including person, property, and status offenses; however, the two most common crimes again were larceny (34%) and breaking and entering (24%). No other crime category reached a frequency of 10%.

Youths were referred from the local juvenile court following a preliminary hearing. The referral criteria excluded youths the court would otherwise release, youths charged with serious person crimes, or youths already on probation.

The court's intake referee provided the youths and parents with a brief description of the diversion alternative. Youths and parents interested in participating met with project staff, who explained the project and obtained permission for participation. Youths were then randomly assigned to one of the alternative ADP models described below. Randomization was stratified for sex, race, court referee, and order of referral. Seven youths dropped as a result of various conditions (no more than two youths dropped from any one condition), resulting in a final sample of 213 youths.

3.2. Project Operation in Phase Two

Because of administrative and pragmatic considerations, not all intervention conditions were implemented during each year of Phase

Two's 5-year period. This resulted in a different number of youth being assigned to each condition. The specific years in which each condition was operated are detailed below. Each ADP model, however, involved college students working one-on-one in the community with youth. Eight weeks of training were followed by the 18-week intervention period, during which students worked 6 to 8 hours a week under supervision. Specifically, all youth and volunteer interventions took place in the youth's home, at recreational locations, or in any other mutually agreed-upon community setting.

There were important variations in training and supervision across conditions. Training groups for the Action, Action–Family Focus, Action–Court Setting, and Relationship Groups consisted of 6 to 8 volunteers trained and supervised by two individuals 2 hours per week for 26 weeks. The Attention Placebo Group by contrast had 8 to 15 volunteers supervised by two individuals 2 hours per month for 26 weeks. Notwithstanding the structural similarity of the several models, their training and supervision differed, as described in the following sections.

The *Action Group* ($n = 76$), essentially a replication of Phase One, was implemented each year for 5 years. This condition used the techniques of behavioral contracting (Douds, Engelsgjerd, & Collingwood, 1977; Stuart, 1971) and child advocacy (Davidson & Rapp, 1976; Melton, 1983) to intervene in problem areas of the youth's life. Behavioral contracting was based primarily on social learning theory, and child advocacy was based on the propositions of differential opportunity theory.

Student training in this condition for a total of 80 hours was guided by an eight-unit manual consisting of written material, homework assignments, and role plays. Ten psychology graduate students worked in pairs as volunteer supervisors. They in turn received 2 days of training and 2 hours of supervision per week throughout the entire intervention by Ph.D. psychologists. All supervisors served in multiple conditions to avoid confounding supervisor and treatment effects.

The intervention model involved four phases: assessment of desired behavior change and needed community resources, initiation of behavioral contracts and advocacy efforts, assessment and revision of intervention efforts, and preparation for the end of service. Throughout the intervention, the volunteer's responsibility was to use advocacy and contracting techniques to meet the youth's individual needs. Youths and parents were also trained in these techniques to facilitate their use after the project ended.

The *Action–Family Focus Group* ($n = 24$) was implemented during the fourth ($n = 12$) and fifth ($n = 12$) years of the project. In this condition, principles of advocacy and contracting were applied exclusively with family members. During the 80 hours of volunteer training, an eight-unit manual similar to that of the Action model was used; however, the importance of family relationships as determinants of delinquency was emphasized (Patterson, 1985). Five senior graduate students in psychology worked in pairs as supervisors. They received 2 days of training with 2 hours of supervision per week by doctoral-level psychologists. As with the Action Condition, the emphasis was on a behavioral approach rather than any form of psychotherapy. The advocacy and contracting efforts were applicable to parents or siblings depending upon specific circumstances.

The *Action–Court Setting Group* (n = 12) was implemented during the fifth year as a preliminary attempt to assess the contribution of supervisor and supervision setting to treatment effectiveness. The key question was the extent to which the program's efficacy depended on its independence from the court system (Rappaport, Seidman, & Davidson, 1979; Vincent & Trickett, 1983).

The Action–Court Setting Group differed from the other Action model interventions on two components: (1) use of a juvenile court member as a trainer/supervisor, and (2) use of the court setting for volunteer supervision. Student volunteers were trained in the Action model of intervention by an advanced psychology graduate student and a caseworker from the juvenile court, selected to be representative of juvenile court staff. The court caseworker had a master's degree in Criminal Justice and 17 years of juvenile justice experience. Both the court caseworker and psychology graduate student conducted the 8 weeks of training in classrooms at the University (as in all other groups). As in the other conditions, the doctoral-level staff provided 2 days of training to both the graduate student and court caseworker. At the end of training, the weekly supervision sessions were moved to the caseworker's office and he assumed sole supervision responsibility.

The *Relationship Group* (n = 12) was implemented during the third year. Intervention procedures were derived from the interpersonal theory of human behavior (e.g., Goodman, 1971; Robin & Foster, 1984; Rogers, 1957; Sullivan, 1953; Truax & Carkhuff, 1967) emphasizing the importance of interpersonal relationships as determinants of delinquency. Therefore, Relationship Group training focused on the development of empathy, unconditional positive regard, communication skills, and genuineness (Egan, 1975). Student volunteers were trained with an eight-unit manual for a total of 80 hours. Four different senior graduate students in psychology worked in pairs as supervisors. The graduate student supervisors received 2 days of training with intervention supervision 2 hours per week from the doctoral-level staff.

The Relationship Group condition thus emphasized the development of a strong relationship between the youths and volunteers. It was distinctly different from all other conditions because it did *not* involve significant others in the intervention and did not use either behavioral contracting or advocacy techniques.

The *Attention Placebo Group* ($n = 29$) was implemented during the third year of Phase Two. Because this group represented an attempt to control for the effects of nonspecific attention, it provided minimal training and supervision and emphasized the volunteers' natural skills (Durlak, 1979; Korchin, 1976). Student volunteer training consisted of three 2-hour lectures covering the history of the juvenile court, prominent theories of delinquency, and the importance of the helping relationship. The two lecturers, members of a University-run volunteer organization, had experience as human service workers and as volunteer supervisors for various projects; both had completed college credits in psychology and social work. The lecturers received 2 days of training and 2 hours of monthly supervision. The intervention consisted primarily of recreational activities such as athletics and was intentionally atheoretical.

There was a separate *Control Group* ($n = 62$) for each project year. Participants in this group were returned to the local juvenile court for normal processing. It should be recalled that youth were randomly assigned to conditions using a stratification procedure that controlled for sex, race, court referee, and order of referral. In contrast to Phase One, which involved a comparison between treatment and on treatment or legal intervention, the comparison in Phase Two was between treatment and typical court processing.

3.3. Results from Phase Two

Phase Two program effectiveness findings, based on a complex set of process and outcome measures, are reported in detail in Davidson *et al.* (1987). The present discussion concerns only the impact of the several models of the ADP on future delinquency. Table 2 shows the results of the cumulative 2-year follow-up in terms of recidivism. There were a number of interesting results. First, there were no differences in recidivism among the Action Group, the Action–Family Focus Group, and the Relationship Group. Together, the results for these three treatment groups were superior to those of the combined Action–Court Setting Group, the Attention Placebo Group, and the Control Group. Second, taken individually, the Action Group had results that were superior to those of the Attention Placebo Group in a statistically reliable sense. Although the Relationship Group and Action–Family Focus Groups also demonstrated average recidivism rates lower than those of the Attention Placebo Condition, when they were individually compared with those of the Attention Placebo Condition, the differences were not statistically

TABLE 2
Phase Two Project—Simple Recidivism: Cumulative

Condition	N	No petitions	One or more petitions
AC	76	47	29
ACFF	24	13	11
ACCS	12	4	8
RC	12	8	4
APC	29	14	15
CC	60	23	37

Note. AC = action condition; ACFF = action condition-family focus; ACCS = Action condition-court setting; RC = relationship condition; APC = attention placebo condition; CC = control condition. χ^2 (5, N = 213) = 10.29; $p < .07$.

reliable. Finally, the Action–Court Setting was the least effective in reducing delinquency. Although not statistically different from the Control Group, the Action–Court Setting Group was different from all other groups in a statistically reliable way.

These results led to the following conclusions. First, the Phase One results were replicated, thus supporting the conclusion that the program helped prevent delinquency. Second, it appeared that the intervention may need a well-specified model in order to be effective. The several specific intervention models we compared were not differentially effective in reducing delinquency. Unstructured attention was not as effective in reducing delinquency as any of the systematic interventions. These conclusions led to the design of the Phase Three study, which examined the differential effectiveness of three volunteer types.

4. Phase Three of ADP Development

This study addressed a major question arising from Phase One: how much did the *type* of service provider (or change agent) contribute to the effect of reduced delinquency? Clearly, the interventions were effective when university student volunteers were the change agents; however, many prevention programs use nonuniversity community members as change agents. The research literature on the effectiveness of nonprofessionals provides evidence that college students may be particularly successful as service providers (Durlak, 1979). First, the academic credit that college students often receive for their participation serves to sustain motivation and commitment. Second, college students often have the enthusiasm and idealism needed to develop special rapport with their clients. This rapport then can increase the chances of success with difficult populations. Third, the demographics and social status of college students are frequently more similar to their clients than are the demographics of professional change agents. This role similarity has been proposed as a mechanism for the greater success of indigenous nonprofessionals with their clients (Durlak, 1979). In light of the above evidence, it seemed reasonable to experimentally examine the generalizability of the ADP when noncollege students were utilized as service providers.

Because there were few differences in the efficacy of Phase Two's three structured intervention groups, the decision was made to use the Action Group model in Phase Three. In Phase Two, Kantrowitz (1979) had found that Action Group volunteers reported greater enjoyment of, and satisfaction with, the intervention than either the Action-Family Focus or Relationship volunteers. This finding, in combination with the greater role flexibility that the Action Group model allows, resulted in a decision to implement the behavioral contracting and advocacy model.

In summary, Phase Three of ADP development experimentally evaluated the Action intervention model implemented with university college students, community college students, or community members as change agents. The control group again consisted of youths who received typical court processing.

4.1. Youths Involved in Phase Three

Phase Three took place in Lansing, Michigan, from the fall of 1979 to the spring of 1981. A total of 134 youths were referred to the project following the same procedures used in Phase Two. All agreed to participate. Criteria for youth selection and random assignment to groups were also identical to those of Phase Two. Five youths were dropped for various conditions resulting in a final sample of 129 youths. The mean age of the youths was 14.10 years; 83.9% were males and 29.8% were minorities. In the year prior to referral, the 129 juveniles had been arrested an average of 1.5 times and petitioned to court an average of 1.32 times. As in the previous study, youths had been charged with diverse crimes, but the two most common were larceny and breaking and entering.

4.2. Project Operation in Phase Three

The three intervention groups all involved volunteers working individually with their assigned youth. Each intervention group used the behavioral contracting and child advocacy techniques described for the

Action Group in Phase Two. Training and supervision procedures were similar to those used in the prior programs. The difference between Phase Three intervention groups was the type of volunteer used to implement the model. The new project operated on the same schedule as the earlier ones, that is, 8 weeks of volunteer training and 18 weeks of intervention with case supervision.

The *University Volunteer Group* ($n = 47$) consisted of students recruited from a large midwestern university. Volunteers were randomly selected from a large pool of interested students and allowed to enroll in a psychology course for credit. The students' average age was 21; 52% were female, 91% were single, 4% had children, 91% were white, 44% were Catholic, and 70% had some previous human service experience.

The *Community College Group* ($n = 35$) volunteers were recruited from a midwestern community college in the same city as the prevention program. Similar to the University Volunteer Group, these volunteers were allowed to enroll in a psychology course for which they received course credit and grades. Their average age was 26; 70% were female, 67% were single, 33% had children, 91% were white, 70% were Protestant, and 67% had some previous human service experience.

The *Community Volunteer Group* ($n = 18$) differed from the other two. Although their training, supervision, and intervention models were identical to those of the other conditions, volunteers in this group did not receive course credits or grades for their participation.

It was difficult to recruit and retain community members. They were recruited through a variety of methods including presentations to service clubs, public service announcements in the electronic media, newspaper ads, posters, and word of mouth. Over 200 potential volunteers made contact with the project. All but 18 dropped out prior to the completion of training. The vast majority in fact dropped out before training started. Because the volunteer pool was small, the project could not select volunteers randomly; rather, each person who volunteered was allowed to participate. The average age of community volunteers was 35; 67% were female, 36% were single, 43% were married, 21% were divorced or separated, 40% had children, 100% were white, 60% were Protestant, and 93% had some human service experience.

The *Control Group* ($n = 25$) consisted of delinquent youths who, as in Phase Two, were returned to the juvenile justice system for normal court processing.

4.3. Results from Phase Three

Table 3 presents the results of the analysis of simple recidivism for the Phase Three groups. Recidivism rates are again presented cumula-

TABLE 3
Phase Three Project—Simple Recidivism: Cumulative 2-Year Follow-Up

Condition	N	No petitions	One or more petitions
University volunteers	47	30	17
Community college volunteers	35	26	9
Community volunteers	17	13	4
Control	25	8	17

Note. Chi-square = 13.38; *df* = 3; *p* < .01.

tively from the point of intake through two years of follow-up. Collectively, the three groups that had interventions involving a volunteer (regardless of type of volunteer) had significantly lower recidivism rates than the control group. There were, however, no statistically dependable differences among the three volunteer intervention programs. The results from Phase Three demonstrated that the Action model (behavioral contracting and child advocacy), implemented by the several different volunteer groups, was far more effective in reducing delinquency than traditional court processing.

Phase Three thus provided another replication of the Action model's effectiveness. In addition, it allayed suspicions that the program's effectiveness was due in large part to the characteristics of the university volunteers. Although there were numerous reasons to believe that college students contributed something special to the program, Phase Three indicated that somewhat older, more experienced individuals could also be effective change agents.

5. Phase Four of ADP Development

The fourth phase of ADP development involved a more extensive replication of the model program than had occurred in Phases Two and Three. The goal was to replicate the ADP action model in a large urban setting and assess its generalizability using paid staff as service providers. In many respects, the fourth phase was a preliminary examination of the model's potential for dissemination. Phase Four also involved an experimental comparison of the ADP action model with an outright-release group and a court-processed group.

5.1. Youths Involved in Phase Four

Phase Four took place in Detroit, Michigan. During its 25 months of operation (1982–1983), 521 eligible youths were referred by the juvenile divisions of four precincts of the Detroit metropolitan police department. The eligibility criteria specified that the youths had to be between 12 and 16 years of age, residents of one of the four precincts, charged with an offense that would normally have been referred to court. Additional restrictive criteria stated that youths could not be on probation, receiving services from a juvenile court program, or involved in pending juvenile court cases.

Of the 521 referrals, 395 agreed to participate in the project. We randomly assigned youths to one of three alternatives: participation in the diversion program (ADP Group), release to parents with no further intervention (Release to Parents Group), and traditional court processing (Court Processed Group). The group averaged 14 years of age; 84% were male, 91% were black, 58% came from a single-parent household. They had completed an average of 7.4 years of formal education at the time of referral. Most (65%) were referred for property-related offenses such as breaking and entering, larceny, and auto theft.

5.2. Project Operation in Phase Four

Fifteen youth officers from four separate Detroit city precincts made the referrals. All were given a written copy of the referral procedures and a brief overview of the project. After reviewing the initial complaint, usually made by a street officer, youth officers determined eligibility and made referrals. The intake worker at a local agency contacted the parents of youth who met initial criteria via phone or house call to arrange for the intake interview.

The intake interview occurred within 2 days of the referral. The youth and one or both parents met with the intake worker. The interviewer consisted of a description of the project, the voluntary nature of participation, the random-assignment procedures for the three dispositional alternatives, and the responsibilities of both the family and the project. After the completion of the intake interview, the youths were randomly assigned (stratified for sex) to the ADP Group, the Release to Parents Group, or the Court Processed Group.

Project staff was hired after screening approximately 400 resumes and conducting 16 interviews. The screening and interviewing was conducted by the research staff and an employee of the local agency. The project was staffed by a project director, an assistant project director, two family workers, and an intake worker.

Project staff participated in an intensive 2-week training program that included an introduction to the project, an overview of local and national juvenile justice issues, and eight training units presenting the conceptual framework for the ADP intervention model. Each unit included specifics in assessment, behavioral contracting and advocacy techniques, methods to monitor the intervention, and case termination procedures. Also included were individual case planning exercises, role playing of intervention situations, and exercises on assessment procedures.

After intake, ADP group members ($n = 137$) were contacted by a family worker within 48 hours of random assignment. The ADP intervention combined child advocacy (Davidson & Rappaport, 1978) and behavioral contracting techniques (Karoly & Steffen, 1984; Patterson, 1982; Stuart, 1971). The goal was to develop participating families' advocacy and behavioral contracting skills. Initially, the family worker provided training and experience in behavioral contracting and advocacy. Subsequently, the family worker encouraged the parents and youth to pursue advocacy and contracting activities on their own. The family worker's initial responsibility assessment of behavioral changes desired by youth and parent(s) and surveying the family's unmet needs. Once the assessment process was completed, the family worker and family agreed upon a "plan of action" using the techniques of advocacy and contracting. These sessions occurred either in the home or in another mutually agreeable setting other than the worker's office. During the first 12 weeks, the family worker was involved with each family 3 hours per week. During the final four weeks, the family worker acted as a consultant to the family for 1½ hours per week. Contracting and advocacy efforts by the family were encouraged during this stage to facilitate transfer of these skills.

After intake, youths in the release to parents group ($n = 134$) were sent home without further intervention for the referring offense by the police or the court. All referring (instant) charges were therefore dismissed.

After intake, the court processed group ($n = 124$) youths were returned to the police for petitioning to Juvenile Court. During the intake meeting, the intake worker explained that the youth would have normally been petitioned to court and had, as a result of random assignment, a one-in-three chance of still being petitioned to court. The intake worker submitted a form to the referring police officer identifying the youths who needed formal handling by the juvenile justice system.

5.3. Results from Phase Four

The complex process and outcome measures used to evaluate Phase Four of the ADP, as well as program findings, have been reported in detail in Davidson and Johnson (1987). Table 4 shows the impact of the project on delinquent behavior through 1-year follow-up on simple re-

TABLE 4
Phase Four Project—Simple Recidivism: Cumulative 1-Year Follow-Up

Condition	N	No petitions	One or more petitions
Juvenile court	124	82	42
A.D.P.	136	107	29
Release to parents	135	92	43

Note. Chi-square = 5.87; *df* = 2; *p* < .06.

cidivism. The results in terms of recidivism indicated that the Action model was superior to either the Release to Parents Group or the Court Processed Group. The difference between the Action Group and the two other conditions were statistically dependable. Thus, it seems the Action model can be used effectively by paid professional staff in a major urban setting. It is also important to note that there was no statistical difference in the recidivism rates of the Release to Parents Group and the Court Processed Group.

6. Critical Issues in the Operation of Diversion Programs

The major purpose of this chapter is to provide information about effective treatment programs. This program of research and intervention-model development has shed some light on key issues in the field. We consider the original question posed in the literature of whether diversion works to be inappropriate. This research goes a long way toward confirming the conclusion previously drawn in the major reviews of this body of research that all diversion programs are not created equal (e.g., Romig, 1978).

This research also adds to the mounting evidence concerning the ineffectiveness of traditional interventions with delinquents (e.g., Martinson et al., 1971; Levitt, 1971; Davidson & Seidman, 1974; Romig, 1979; Greenwood, 1977; Davidson, Gensheimer, Mayer, & Gottschalk, 1987; Schur, 1973). Phase Four directly compared traditional court processing with nonintervention and found no effect on future delinquency. The consistency of these findings with the literature means that the efficacy of traditional approaches must still be questioned.

The positive effects demonstrated by the ADP model remain a relatively rare finding in the diversion literature. The ADP focuses on variables seen as critical in the delinquency causation chain. Its focus on family variables and environmental resources is drawn from prominent theoretical work in the field (e.g., Elliot et al., 1979; Patterson, 1982). Yet the model is not unique, and other interventions, including those studied here, share some of the same components but do not produce positive results (i.e., Action–Court Setting Condition).

That different conclusions could be reached about the effectiveness of the ADP on the basis of self-reported delinquency and official recidivism also deserves comment. Although this study does not provide definitive answers, it is becoming clear that self-report delinquency and official delinquency are not merely two independent indicators of an underlying construct of delinquency. In a series of studies, these two measures perform as relatively uncorrelated variables (Amdur & Davidson, 1988), which would not be expected if they were both indicators of the same construct. Future research will have to unravel this complexity.

6.1. Clinical and Administrative Issues

It has often been assumed that the operation of innovative programs is easily understood and their core ingredients clearly articulated by their demonstration of effectiveness. However, at a more practical level, there are many issues that impinge on the successful operation of alternative treatment programs. We shall speculate on some of these variables here.

The articulation of the critical ingredients of an innovative program has become a major field of study known as dissemination process research (e.g., Blakely et al., 1987; Tornatzky, Fergus, Avellar, Fairweather, & Fleischer, 1981). The general research finding is that the dissemination process is complex. In fact, this line of research finds that replications of effective programs sometimes bear little resemblance to the original model (e.g., Blakely et al., 1987; Hall & Loucks, 1978; Rappaport, Seidman, & Davidson, 1979). These findings are particularly troublesome given the positive relationship between the integrity of programs replications and their efficacy (Blakely et al., 1986; Tornatzky et al., 1981).

In this section, we comment on the "key ingredients" of the ADP model and include suggestions for its successful adoption. To accomplish this, we draw on a broader dissemination literature as well as our specific experiences in conducting the ADP over a 15-year period.

At the level of social systems, each phase of the ADP model required intense involvement with local juvenile justice institutions. Typically, ADP staff spent the better part of 2 days per week working directly with juvenile justice system staff. In the Phase Four project, for example, the intake worker spent one morning per week in each of the four precinct stations. During this time, the intake worker was available for referrals, attended roll call, met with precinct leadership, and checked on future referrals. Similarly, in Phases Two and Three, ADP staff spent 2 half days per week with the intake staff of the local juvenile court. A critical aspect of this time was the social contact between project and juvenile justice staff. The shared cups of coffee were as important as the required staff meetings. It has been our experience that an active approach to interagency relationships is vital to ensure successful project adoption and replication.

Convincing the local justice officials that the project will not be "here today and gone tomorrow" is just as important as forming an informal relationship. A critical ingredient in the success of the ADP was the view on the part of local officials that the project was a continuing dispositional alternative. In the past, programs involved juvenile courts in alternative treatment efforts for a year or two and then were denied funding and disappeared. Such unstable commitments were particularly common during the era of prolific federal seed money; they created suspicion of promises from alternative programs. In the case of the ADP, there were two positive side effects of our long-term commitment to the court. First, local officials who were opposed to dispositional alternatives couldn't ignore us and wait for the project to "die on the vine." The ADP became a relatively stable entity that could not be denied by its opponents. Second, our continuing commitment during times of few referrals or court administrative turmoils demonstrated that we were as sincerely concerned with juvenile delinquency as the police, the juvenile court staff, or the community.

Another critical ingredient in the ADP's success was the intervention setting (i.e., the youth's natural environments). For years, it has been argued that an understanding of environmental variables was crucial to understanding juvenile delinquency. Adolescents' involvement with families, schools, and peers are core factors in most contemporary explanations of juvenile delinquency. All of the ADP's structured interventions involved change agents participating in the youths' natural environments as opposed to the change agents' offices or centers. This was also a critical issue in selecting change agents. Overprofessionalized staff or those trained in restrictive professional roles often express ambivalence about entering the environments of delinquent youths. It is essential to select change agents who are willing to work in the youths' natural settings. Only then can the major causes of delinquency be addressed.

Other issues relate more directly to the intervention model itself. First, both experience and the dissemination literature (Rappaport et al., 1979) indicate that close adherence to the original ADP model is necessary in order for the results to be replicated. Second, the ADP model emphasizes youths' strengths rather than their weaknesses. Various theoretical positions use different language to describe this perspective. The behaviorists refer to "behavioral accelerators," advocates refer to "youth rights," community psychologists refer to "empowerment," and so on. These perspectives share a view of youths as individuals with assets and abilities rather than repositories of environmental and personal pathologies. Third, the ADP model had specifiable components and a limited intervention period. Our experience was that both of these ingredients were important for successful intervention. A detailed "plan of action" maximizes the chances of accurate replication, and a limited intervention period does not foster the youth's dependency on the change agent.

The ADP's underlying philosophy was that it be a "true alternative" to justice system processing for all appropriate youths. Accordingly, our administrative agreements with the juvenile court stated that we would *not* return difficult youths to the police or court system. This decision produced positive effects for the program's operation. Change agents and supervisors were completely aware that their task was to make the intervention "work" for both easy and difficult cases. None of this is to imply that the ADP is a panacea for *all* adolescents in trouble. Rather, what we learned is that the program made it possible to deal successfully with cases that would otherwise have been identified as "impossible." This was due to the original decision *not* to return difficult cases to the legal system. We believe that this decision is an important operating principle that must be incorporated in dissemination efforts.

Our experience, confirmed by the Phase Two research, was that change agents required close supervision. Weekly case supervision was important for at least two reasons. First, it kept change agents faithful to the intervention model. There is a tendency for all change agents to drift from intervention models in the face of real-world frustrations. Our experience and the research literature indicate that this tendency degrades the integrity of the intervention model (Sechrest & Redner, 1979). Second, we found that weekly supervision required less time than monthly supervision. In Phase Two research, Kantrowitz (1979) found that supervisors who met monthly with their change agents actually spent more total time supervising than those supervisors who met weekly with their change agents. This was due to frequent contacts that were needed outside of supervisory sessions.

7. Concluding Comments

We have several final thoughts about potentially important components of the ADP model. First, alternative intervention programs often compete with existing agencies for clients. More important, successful alternative intervention programs can make existing agencies superfluous. Although the hope is that effective prevention efforts will allow existing systems to deal more effectively with youth who are not suited for such programs, one immediate result of an effective program may be to reduce an agency's client flow. Such potential "competition for cases" needs to be anticipated, especially in the case of the justice system, which is very sensitive to caseload issues. In the case of the ADP, the agency responsible for our referrals was the agency most likely to be threatened by the program's success. Our experience proved that this situation is a tightrope necessitating constant balancing.

Second, change agents are often reluctant to work in their clients' natural environments. Creating a change-agent role that demanded close involvement with youths and maintaining close supervision were effective strategies to deal with these issues. In our intervention, professional staff were more difficult to train than nonprofessional volunteers because of the restrictive role behaviors they had adopted.

Third, replicating the ADP model required intense community activity to initiate and maintain the source of referrals. Mental health professionals often use relatively passive referral modes. Our early experiences with the ADP demonstrated the futility of a passive approach to the juvenile justice system. If one waits in the office for referrals, one will spend a lot of time waiting. An active mode of interacting with the juvenile justice system is necessary.

A final major issue is funding. The original ADP projects (Phases One through Three) were supported by federal research grants. In all phases, the ADP was committed to continuation of the project contingent upon positive results. To keep this commitment, we sought nonfederal sources of support. Our experience has been that state and local sources offer excellent opportunities for funding alternative interventions. Local and state officials are particularly interested in any potential fiscal savings offered by alternative programs. They also will understand the chronically overloaded situations facing many criminal justice and mental health systems.

The task of creating and maintaining alternative treatment programs is neither simple nor quick. These programs require long-term commitments from program developers, researchers, community agencies, and funding sources. This commitment must be firm at the initial stages of the program because definitive results take time, reasonable numbers of clients, and continued funding. Finally, replication and dissemination programs must operate systematically; they must be developed with a specifiable set of operations and clearly defined goals. Only when all these conditions have been met will there be some hope of success.

8. References

Alexander, J. F., & Parsons, B. V. (1973). Short term behavioral intervention with delinquent families. *Journal of Abnormal Psychology, 81,* 219–225.

Andrew, J. M. (1981). Delinquency: Correlating variables. *Journal of Child Clinical Psychology, 10,* 136–140.

Becker, H. S. (1963). *Outsiders: Studies in the sociology of deviance.* New York: Free Press.

Berman, J. S., & Norton, N. C. (1985). Does professional training make a therapist more effective? *Psychological Bulletin, 98,* 401–407.

Blakely, C. H., Mayer, J. P., Gottschalk, R. G., Roitman, D., Schmitt, N., Davidson, W. S., & Emshoff, J. G. (1986). *Salient processes in the dissemination of social technologies.* Washington, DC: National Science Foundation.

Blakely, C. H., Mayer, J. P., Gottschalk, R. G., Schmitt, N., Davidson, W. S., Roitman, D., & Emshoff, J. G. (1987). The fidelity-adaptation debate: Implications for the implementation of public sector social programs. *American Journal of Community Psychology, 15,* 253–268.

Broder, P. K., Dunivant, N., Smith, E. C., & Sutton, L. P. (1981). Further observations on the link between learning disabilities and juvenile delinquency. *Journal of Education Psychology, 73,* 838–850.

Cloward, R., & Ohlin, L. (1960). *Delinquency and opportunity.* Glencoe, IL: Free Press.

Davidson, W. S., Gensheimer, L. K., Mayer, J. P., & Gottschalk, R. G. (1987). Current status of rehabilitation programs for juvenile offenders. In C. Hampton (Ed.), *Antisocial behavior and substance abuse* (pp. 254–297). Washington, DC: U.S. Government Printing Office.

Davidson, W. S., & Johnson, C. (1987). *Diversion in Michigan.* Lansing, MI: Department of Social Services, Office of Children and Youth Services.

Davidson, W. S., & Rapp, C. (1976). A multiple strategy model of child advocacy. *Social Work, 21,* 225–232.

Davidson, W. S., & Rappaport, J. (1978). Towards a model of advocacy. In G. Weber and G. McCall (Eds.), *Advocacy and the disciplines* (pp. 67–98). New York: Sage.

Davidson, W. S., Redner, R., Amdur, R., & Mitchell, C. (1988). *Alternative treatments for troubled youth.* New York: Plenum Press.

Davidson, W. S., Redner, R., Blakely, C. H., Mitchell, C. M., & Emshoff, J. G. (1987). Diversion of juvenile offenders: An experimental comparison. *Journal of Consulting and Clinical Psychology, 55,* 68–75.

Davidson, W. S., & Seidman, E. (1974). Studies of behavior modification and juvenile delinquency. *Psychological Bulletin, 81,* 998–1011.

Davidson, W. S., Seidman, E., Rappaport, J., Berck, P., Rapp, N., Rhodes, W., & Herring, J. (1977). Diversion programs for juvenile offenders. *Social Work Research and Abstracts, 13,* 40–49.

Douds, A. F., Engelsgjerd, M., & Collingwood, T. R. (1977). Behavior contracting with youthful offenders and their parents. *Child Welfare, 56,* 409–417.

Durlak, J. A. (1973). Myths concerning the nonprofessional therapist. *Professional Psychology, 4,* 300–304.

Durlak, J. A. (1979). Comparative effectiveness of paraprofessional and professional helpers. *Psychological Bulletin, 86,* 80–92.

Egan, G. (1975). *The skilled helper.* Belmont, CA: Brooks/Cole.

Elliot, D. S., Huizinga, D., & Ageton, S. S. (1985). *Explaining delinquency and drug abuse.* Beverly Hills, CA: Sage.

Empey, L. T. (1971). *Explaining delinquency.* Lexington, MA: D. C. Heath.

Empey, L. T. (1982). *American delinquency: Its meaning and construction.* Homewood, IL: Dorsey.

Emshoff, J. G., Davis, D. D., & Davidson, W. S. (1981). Social support and aggression. In A. P. Goldstein, E. G. Carr, W. S. Davidson, & P. Wehr (Eds.), *In response to aggression: Methods of control and prosocial alternatives.* New York: Pergamon Press.

Fairweather, G. W., & Davidson, W. S. (1986). *An introduction to community experimentation.* New York: McGraw-Hill.

Gaffney, L. R., & McFall, R. M. (1981). A comparison of the social skills in delinquent and nondelinquent adolescent girls using behavioral role-playing inventory. *Journal of Consulting and Clinical Psychology, 49,* 959–967.

Gallup, G. (1984). *The Gallup report.* Princeton, NJ: Gallup.

Glaser, D. (1975). *Strategic criminal justice planning.* Washington, DC: U.S. Government Printing Office.

Glueck, S., & Glueck, E. (1951). *Unraveling juvenile delinquency.* Cambridge, MA: Harvard University Press.

Goodman, G. (1971). *Companionship therapy.* San Francisco, CA: Jossey-Bass.

Greenberg, D. (1977). The incapacitative effects of imprisonment: Some estimates. *Law and Society Review, 9,* 541–580.

Gross, A. M., Brigham, T., Hopper, C., & Bologna, W. (1980). Self-management and social skills training: A study with predelinquent and delinquent youths. *Criminal Justice and Behavior, 7,* 161–183.

Hall, G. E., & Loucks, S. F. (1978, March). Innovation configurations: Analyzing the adaptation of innovations. Paper presented at the annual meeting of the American Educational Research Association, Toronto, Ontario, Canada.

Hawkins, J. D., & Lishner, D. M. (1985). Childhood predictors and the prevention of adolescent substance abuse. In C. L. Jones & R. D. Battjes (Eds.), *Etiology of drug abuse: Implications for prevention* (pp. 1–23). Washington, DC: NIDA ADM85-1385.

Hirschi, T. (1969). *Causes of delinquency.* Los Angeles: University of California Press.

Kahn, A. J. (1965). A case of premature claims. *Crime and Delinquency, 20,* 233–240.

Kantrowitz, R. E. (1979). *Training nonprofessionals to work with delinquents: Differential impact of varying training/supervision/intervention strategies.* Unpublished doctoral dissertation, Michigan State University, East Lansing, MI.

Karoly, P., & Steffen, J. J. (1984). *Adolescent behavior disorders: Foundations and contemporary concerns.* Lexington, MA: Lexington Books.

Korchin, S. (1976). *Modern clinical psychology.* New York: Basic Books.

Krisberg, B., & Austin, J. (1978). *The children of Ishmael.* Palo Alto, CA: Mayfield Press.

Kushler, M., & Davidson, W. S. (1981). Community and organizational level change. In A. P. Goldstein, E. G. Carr, W. S. Davidson, & P. Wehr (Eds.), *In response to aggression.* New York: Pergamon Press.

Lipton, D., Martinson, R., & Wilks, J. (1975). *The effectiveness of correctional treatment.* New York: Praeger.

Loeber, R., Dishion, T. J., & Patterson, G. R. (1984). Multiple gating: A multistage assessment procedure for identifying youths at risk for delinquency. *Journal of Research in Crime and Delinquency, 21,* 7–32.

Loeber, R., & Loeber-Stouthamer, M. (1987). Prediction. In H. C. Quay (Ed.), *Handbook of juvenile delinquency.* New York: Wiley.

Matza, D. (1969). *Becoming deviant.* Englewood Cliffs, NJ: Prentice-Hall.

Mayer, J. P., Gensheimer, L. K., Davidson, W. S., & Gottschalk, R. G. (1987). Social learning treatment within juvenile justice: A meta-analysis of impact in the natural environment. In A. Goldstein & S. Apter (Eds.), *Youth violence.* New York: Pergamon Press.

Mednick, S., & Christiansen, S. O. (1977). *Biosocial basis of criminal behavior.* New York: Gardner Press.

Melton, G. B. (1983). *Child advocacy.* New York: Plenum Press.

Merton, R. K. (1957). *Social theory and social structure* (2nd ed.). New York: Free Press.

National Institutes of Justice. (1987). Juveniles in institutions. *NIJ Reports.* Washington, DC: U.S. Department of Justice.

Patterson, G. R. (1982). *Coercive family interactions.* Eugene, OR: Castalia Press.

Patterson, G. R. (1985, August). *Performance models for antisocial boys.* Paper presented at the annual meeting of the American Psychological Association, Los Angeles, CA.

Pelto, G. H., & Pelto, P. J. (1976). *The human adventure.* New York: Macmillan.

Prentice, N. M. (1972). The influence of live and symbolic modeling on prompting moral judgement of adolescent delinquents. *Journal of Abnormal Psychology, 80,* 159–211.

Rappaport, J., Chinsky, J. M., & Cowen, E. L. (1971). *Innovation in helping chronic patients: College students in a mental institution.* New York: Academic Press.

Rappaport, J., Seidman, E., & Davidson, W. S. (1979). Demonstration research and manifest versus true adoption: The natural history of a research project to divert adolescents from the legal system. In J. Kelly, L. Snowden, & R. Munoz (Eds.), *Social and community interventions* (pp. 101–144). San Francisco, CA: Jossey-Bass.

Robin, A. L., & Foster, S. L. (1984). Problem-solving communication training: A behavioral-family systems approach to parent-adolescent conflict. In P. Karoly & J. J. Steffen (Eds.), *Adolescent behavior disorders: Foundations and contemporary concerns* (pp. 195–240). Lexington, MA: Lexington Books.

Rogers, C. R. (1957). The necessary and sufficient conditions of therapeutic personality changes. *Journal of Consulting Psychology, 21,* 95–103.

Romig, D. A. (1978). *Justice for our children.* Lexington, MA: Lexington Books.

Roper Organization. (1985). Opinion roundup. *Public Opinion, 5,* 12.

Sechrest, L. B. & Redner, R. (1979). Strength and integrity of treatments. In *Review of criminal evaluation results* (pp. 19–62). Washington, DC: National Criminal Justice Reference Service, U.S. Department of Justice.

Seidman, E., & Rappaport, J. (1974). The educational pyramid: A paradigm for research, training, and manpower. *American Journal of Community Psychology, 2,* 119–130.

Shelley, E. (1971). *Volunteers in probation.* Boulder, CO: National Center for Volunteers in Juvenile Court.

Smith, M. L., Glass, G. V., & Miller, T. I. (1980). *The benefits of psychotherapy.* Baltimore, MD: Johns Hopkins University Press.

Smith, P. M., & Ausnew, H. R. (1974). Socialization as related to delinquency classification. *Psychological Reports, 34,* 677–678.

Spivack, G., & Shure, M. B. (1982). The cognition of social adjustment. In B. B. Lahey & A. E. Kazdin (Eds.), *Advances in child clinical psychology* (pp. 139–164). New York: Plenum Press.

Stuart, R. B. (1971). Behavioral contracting within the families of delinquents. *Journal of Behavior Therapy and Experimental Psychiatry, 2,* 1–11.

Stuart, R. B., Jayaratne, S., & Tripodi, T. (1976). Changing adolescent deviant behaviour through reprogramming the behaviour of parents and teachers: An experimental evaluation. *Canadian Journal of Behavioural Science, 8,* 132–144.

Sullivan, H. S. (1953). *The interpersonal theory of psychiatry.* New York: W. W. Norton.

Tornatzky, L. G., Fergus, E. O., Avellar, J. W., Fairweather, G. W., & Fleischer, M. (1981). *Innovation and social process: A national experiment in implementing social technology.* New York: Pergamon Press.

Trojanowicz, R. C., & Morash, M. (1987). *Juvenile delinquency: Concepts and control* (4th ed.). Englewood Cliffs, NJ: Prentice-Hall.

Truax, C. B., & Carkhuff, R. (1967). *Toward effective counseling and psychotherapy*. Chicago: Aldine.

Vincent, T. A., & Trickett, E. J. (1983). Preventive interventions and the human context. In R. D. Felner, L. A. Jason, J. N. Moritsugu, & S. S. Farber (Eds.), *Preventive psychology* (pp. 67–86). New York: Pergamon Press.

Waldo, G. P., & Dinitz, S. (1967). Personality attributes of the criminal: Analysis of research studies from 1950–1965. *Journal of Research in Crime and Delinquency, 4*, 185–202.

5   *Parental Child Abduction*

The Problem and Possible Solution

REX FOREHAND, NICHOLAS LONG, AND
CAROLYN ZOGG

1. Introduction

Although many of the issues associated with parental divorce that can impact upon children have been well documented, there has been one notable exception: parental child abduction or child stealing. According to Agopian (1981), "Parental child-stealing is the act of a parent abducting or detaining a child from the custodial parent in violation of a custody decree" (p. 1). Other authors give a broader definition to include all incidents that occur prior to an official custody decree.

1.1. Epidemiology of Child Abduction

Unofficial estimates suggest that between 25,000 and 100,000 children are abducted by a noncustodial parent each year in the United States (Agopian, 1984; McCoy, 1978). However, the results of a national survey (Gelles, 1984) indicate that the incidence of this problem may be much higher. Gelles (1984) used the following definition: "Parental child snatching is when a parent physically takes, restrains, or does not return a child under the age of 14 after a visit, and keeps the child concealed so that the other parent does not know where the child is" (pp. 735–736). Parents could be married, separated, or divorced (a legal custody decree was not required), and the definition did not discriminate between brief (e.g., 1 day) and long-term abduction. Using this definition, Louis Harris and Associates conducted a national survey of 3,745 adults. Results

REX FOREHAND • Department of Psychology, University of Georgia, Athens, Georgia 30602.   NICHOLAS LONG • Department of Pediatrics, University of Arkansas for Medical Sciences, Little Rock, Arkansas 72202.   CAROLYN ZOGG • Child Find of America, Inc., 7 Innis Avenue, New Paltz, New York 12561.

of this survey suggest that there are 459,000 to 751,000 incidents of such child abduction annually. However, until the National Study of the Incidence of Missing Children, currently being conducted by the Family Violence Research Program at the University of New Hampshire in conjunction with Westat, Inc., of Rockville, Maryland, is completed, there are no accurate estimates of the prevalence of parental abduction. Nevertheless, it does appear to be a problem of significant magnitude.

In spite of the large number of children and parents exposed to this stressful event, there has been an extreme paucity of research in this area. Systematically collected data on parental child abduction have rarely occurred. One project that has involved such data collection was conducted by Agopian (1980, 1981). He examined the files of the 91 cases of parental child stealing screened by the District Attorney's office in Los Angeles during a one-year period in the late 1970s. As Agopian (1981) has noted, because of the limitations of his sampling procedures, caution must be used when interpreting his data. In spite of these limitations, Agopian's work remains important as it reports previously unknown characteristics concerning the crime of parental child abduction.

Agopian's data provide an initial insight into who tends to commit this crime, who tends to be the victims, and under what circumstances the crime is usually committed. Because of their significance Agopian's findings will be presented in some detail. In all 91 of the cases reviewed by Agopian (1981), the parents were either divorced (76%) or separated (24%). For those cases involving divorced parents, 55% of the abductions occurred within 18 months of the custody order or divorce action and 37% of the cases occurred at least two years following such actions. In regard to which parent did the abducting, fathers (71%) were much more likely to be the abductors than mothers (29%). This finding is not surprising because mothers usually retain custody in 90% of divorce cases (Agopian, 1981). In fact, given the fact that only 10% of fathers typically have custody, the finding that 29% of cases involved mothers abducting the children is significant. This tends to suggest that children in the custody of their father may be at greater risk for parental child abduction.

In regard to race, 69% of the parents were Caucasian, 13% were Black, 15% were Mexican-American, and 3% were Oriental. Unfortunately, Agopian does not state how representative this racial breakdown is of the general population of Los Angeles. He does, however, postulate that Caucasians may be overrepresented because other racial groups tend to more readily accept the notion that mothers should be the primary parent in regard to daily child rearing (Agopian, 1981). Therefore, non-Caucasian fathers would be less likely to want custody of their children and thus be less likely to engage in parental child abduction, In regard to age, the majority (75%) of parents were less than 37 years old. For those parents whose employment status was indicated (122 of 182), most were employed (69%).

The 91 cases of parental child abduction involved 130 children. In 64% of the cases, only one child was abducted, whereas two children were abducted in 30% of the cases. An even number of boys (51%) and girls (49%) was involved. The majority of children abducted were 3 to 11 years old. The actual breakdown of the children's ages was as follows: 5% were under 3 years old, 34% were 3 to 5 years old, 22% were 6 to 8 years old, 26% were 9 to 11 years old, and 13% were at least 12 years old.

Agopian (1981) also reports data on temporal patterns of parental child abduction. Abductions occurred throughout the year with a somewhat higher incidence in the summer and fall. In regard to days of the week, abductions tended to occur more frequently around weekends. The higher incidence of abductions at these times corresponds with the higher frequency of visitation during weekends and the finding that abductions were incorporated into regular visitation privileges in 55% of the cases. That is, a parent picks up his or here child for regular visitation but does not plan on returning the child to the custodial parent after the scheduled visitation period. The use of force in parental child abduction was infrequent. Physical force, usually just restraint, was used in 14% of the cases; threats of force were used in an additional 8% of the cases.

In 47% of the cases, the parent who abducted the child or children contacted the custodial parent after the abduction. Agopian (1981) states that these contacts had one of three purposes: (1) announcement of safety and intention, (2) mechanism to influence the relationship, or (3) communication to rationalize the crime. These communications usually occurred by telephone (72%); mail (16%) and in-person contacts (12%) were much less common.

As a result of the complex dynamics involved in parental child abduction, it is impossible to easily understand and explain. It is usually preceded by a long and often conflictual series of events that typically surround separation and divorce. Unfortunately, child custody is often viewed as the "Grand Prize" in contested divorces. Agopian (1984) was able to identify four common motivating factors for parental child abduction. He states:

> Typical motivations of offenders include: (1) the belief that the child is, or is apt to be, neglected by the custodial parent; (2) the desire to continue a full-time parenting role; (3) the desire to punish the other parent who may be

blamed for the marital failure; or (4) the effort to induce the withdrawal of a
divorce action or initiate a reconciliation. (p. 511)

1.2. Effects on the Child

Although parental child abduction is obviously a very stressful
event for all concerned, its short- and long-term effect on children is
basically unknown. However, there is a theoretical basis and there are
empirical findings to suggest that the effects of abduction are detrimental for a child. Bowlby (1973) has proposed a separation theory that can
be applied to child abduction. This theory states that separation from the
primary attachment figure results in offspring maladjustment, which is
characterized by acute upset and apathy. In the case of child abduction,
the maladjustment would likely be exacerbated by the suddenness of
the separation, the lack of explanation or erroneous explanation (e.g.,
parental rejection, parental death) for the change, and the ongoing
stressful life events with the abduction (a new name, frequent moves,
loss of friends, reduced economic resources, isolation from a peer
group, etc.). Many of these same events (e.g., loss of friends, frequent
moves, reduced economic resources) have been implicated as important
influences in child maladjustment following divorce (Atkeson, Forehand, & Richard, 1982) and would be expected to be even more stressful
in cases involving abduction.

The data regarding the effects of parental abduction on children are
relatively sparse. Several clinical reports indicate that children usually
show posttraumatic emotional consequences (Agopian, 1984; Senior,
Gladstone, & Nurcombe, 1982; Terr, 1983). These problems were reported to include depression, grief, mental indoctrination, and parental
rejection. One recent better-controlled investigation (Forehand, Long,
Zogg, & Parrish, 1988) found that, after their return, abducted children
demonstrated a short-term increase in behavior problems.

1.3. Possible Solutions

In view of the estimates of the frequency of child abduction and the
detrimental effects on children of such an event, the need for effective
procedures to have the stolen child returned is obvious. Unfortunately,
legal problems often hinder or prevent the locating of these children and
the successful disposition of the cases when the children are located.
Although there have been legal steps taken in the right direction (i.e.,
the Federal Parental Kidnapping Prevention Act of 1980 and the Uniform Child Custody Jurisdiction Act), the legal system has not typically
handled this crime effectively (Agopian, 1981). In response to this inef-

fectiveness, private organizations have been established. According to figures from Child Find of America, Inc., one third of the abducted children are returned through present efforts, which consist of investigative work, circulating photographs of missing children to schools, and exposing the general public to pictures of missing children by way of television and photographs on various consumable products (e.g., milk cartons, paper bags, cereal boxes). Clearly, additional procedures are needed to increase this percentage.

The methods utilized by both the legal system and private organizations at this time have not involved soliciting the abducting parent's cooperation. That is, only "search and find" procedures have been employed rather than appealing to the abducting parent to begin a process whereby the child will be returned. Considering the motivational factors reviewed earlier, an approach involving a direct appeal to abducting parents and subsequent mediation of an effective solution to the situation would appear to be a promising intervention for many cases of child abduction. Furthermore, such a procedure may be more effective for the long-term satisfaction of the parents and the adjustment of the child than "search and find procedures" (e.g., hiring a detective to find the child).

Agopian (1981) has noted that in the majority of cases where the child was successfully returned, the parents had communicated with each other by telephone after the abduction. In commenting on this finding, Agopian (1981) states:

> The eventual return of the child that included direct communication between the ex-spouses may indicate a sincere concern for the care of the child or even the use of the crime situation as a forum to discuss the ruptured marital relationship. (p. 67)

If the abducting parent later decides that the abduction is not in the child's best interest, if the need to continually elude authorities becomes too stressful, or if the parent is using the abduction as a means of addressing the parental relationship, then providing the abducting parent with an opportunity to mediate a solution would likely be perceived as a positive technique to help resolve the situation. Such postabduction communication could be facilitated by professional mediators who could promote productive communication between the parents toward the successful resolution of the situation.

In mediation, a neutral professional attempts to promote communication, clarify communication, assist in generating potential solutions, and help solidify workable and mutually acceptable agreements (Deutsch, 1973). The general use of mediation in disputes related to divorce is becoming a common alternative to litigation. Emery and Wyer (1987) have pointed out three ways that mediation differs from litigation:

(a) In mediation communication takes place with a single professional; (b) mediation is based on an assumption of cooperation rather than competition; and (c) the parties make their own decisions in mediation. (p. 472)

Because the use of mediation in divorce disputes is a relatively new phenomenon, there have been only a few studies examining its effectiveness. At the present time, the best data in this area come from two large-scale research projects (Irving, Benjamin, Boham, & McDonald, 1981; Pearson & Thoennes, 1982). As in any new area of research, caution should be used when interpreting the finding of these projects (see Levy, 1984). However, the results of the studies suggest that individuals involved in divorce proceedings report more general satisfaction with the process and outcome of mediation than with litigation (Irving *et al.*, 1981; Pearson & Thoennes, 1982).

Another outcome measure that tends to support the effectiveness of mediation is the rate of relitigation among parties whose divorces were mediated as opposed to litigated. Pearson and Thoennes (1982) found that individuals whose original divorce was litigated were more than twice as likely to become involved in later court proceedings concerning the divorce (e.g., visitation disputes, child support) than those individuals whose divorce was mediated. Therefore, mediation may have greater long-term effectiveness than litigation.

A common issue that is mediated in divorce proceedings is child custody. Emery and Wyer (1987) state that child custody is one of the areas especially appropriate for mediation. There are, in fact, some official data that tend to support the use of mediation for settling child custody disputes. Since 1981, California law requires all divorcing parents to mediate child custody and visitation before a custody hearing is held. Approximately 55% of these parents reach an agreement in mediation (McIsaac, 1982). Drastic decreases in child custody hearings have been reported in California since the enactment of the mediation law (King, 1982).

Therefore, mediation does appear to be an effective process for handling child custody disputes. Based on its apparent effectiveness in the area of child custody disputes, mediation may hold potential as an intervention in the area of parental child abduction. Such a procedure may provide an effective alternative or addition to traditional "search and find" procedures. Furthermore, the cooperative nature of mediation may be beneficial for the long-term adjustment of a child by reducing subsequent interparental conflict and reabduction. Exploring this potential, Child Find of America, Inc., undertook a project to facilitate the return of parental-abducted children through mediation. The purpose of this chapter is to describe this unique intervention effort and provide some initial data regarding its effectiveness. In addition, the project also provides the opportunity to expand on Agopian's (1981) work by examining the characteristics of those who abduct children as well as those who are contemplating such abductions.

2. The Florida Project

In early 1986, Child Find of America, Inc., undertook an alternative to the usual "search and find" procedures utilized to locate missing children abducted by one parent. After various alternatives had been considered for setting up such a program, the following procedures were developed and tested in one state from August 21, 1986, through December 7, 1986.

2.1. Procedures

Public service advertisements consisting of television, radio, and newspaper ads were developed and distributed in the state of Florida announcing that parents who had abducted a child could contact a specified toll-free number in order to receive information on a way out of the current situation. Calls were received on a 24-hour basis by a telephone answering service that screened those that were not appropriate (e.g., wrong number, prank calls). Meaningful phone calls were then forwarded to one of six professionally trained mediators from a mediation institute. A total of 71 phone calls were received that involved an initial contact between a caller and a mediator.

2.2. Outcome

Table 1 presents information on the reason for each of these phone calls. As is evident, 25 of the 71 phone calls were from a parent who was in flight with an abducted child. Twenty-three additional phone calls came from parents who were contemplating taking a child. These calls were made primarily to find out the consequences of child abduction and/or to seek an alternative to abduction. Other reasons for calling (e.g., searching for an abducted child, wanting visitation rights enforced) occurred substantially less often.

Table 2 presents an overview of what occurred with the 71 callers. As is obvious, mediation or resolution of the dispute regarding the child(ren) occurred successfully in four cases. For the 40 cases in which mediation was attempted or at least considered appropriate (the first and fourth categories in Table 2), there was some contact with both

TABLE 1
Reason for Call

Parent	Number
In flight	25
Contemplating abduction	23
Searching	6
Attempting to prevent abduction	6
Wants visitation rights enforced	4
Wants information regarding custody/guardianship	4
Wants change in visitation or custody	2
Seeking emergency shelter information	1
Total	71

parents, which is a first requirement for mediation, in the seven cases. Of the seven, two of these occurred when a parent was in flight, three occurred when a parent was contemplating abducting a child, one was from a parent who wanted a visitation right enforced, and one was from a searching parent. Of these seven cases, two reached a final resolution. One additional call involved some mediation between the caller (who

TABLE 2
Outcome of Phone Calls

Categories	Number of calls
Some mediation/resolution occurred	4
Some other positive action resulted[a]	9
Referred[b]	5
Mediation thwarted[c]	36
Not warranted/crank call	2
Outcome not ascertained	15
Total	71

[a]Agreed to return child without mediation occurring, developed alternative to abduction, or decided to pursue action through courts.
[b]Referred to a social or legal agency.
[c]Agreed to mediate but terminated, one of the two parents refused to mediate, no way to recontact parent who called, no way to contact parent from whom child abducted, incorrect information given for other parent, or parent hung up.

had fled with her children while she was being prosecuted in court) and the court judge (through the caller's legal counsel). In this case, a resolution was reached as the caller negotiated to return to the original jurisdiction with the children and respond to the original charges lodged against her. Another additional case also reached a resolution as the caller, with the advice and guidance of the mediator, negotiated directly with the other parent.

As is also indicated in Table 2, some type of positive action other than successful mediation (see footnote *a* in Table 2) occurred in nine cases and in five cases the most appropriate action was to refer a case elsewhere for services. In one half of the total calls, mediation was thwarted by one of the parents or by logistical procedures (see footnote *c* in Table 2).

In terms of characteristics of the 71 callers, 49 were fathers, 21 were mothers, and one was a grandparent. Of particular interest is the fact that, of the 25 phone calls from an in-flight parent, 10 (40%) were from mothers. Additional information concerns characteristics of the children who had been taken by a parent. For the children taken for which information on sex was available, 13 were males and 16 were females. The age range of the children abducted was 8 months to 14 years. Of the 15 in-flight parents, fifteen, six, and one had abducted one, two, and three children, respectively. (Information on number of children abducted was not obtained for three parents.)

The results of the Florida Project were interesting and surprising in many ways. First, the majority of calls were not from parents who were in flight with a child. Second, mediation occurred or was attempted not only with cases in which parents were in flight but with parents who had other child dispute issues, such as contemplating abduction and wanting visitation rights enforced. Third, successful mediation was much more difficult than was originally expected. Hindsight suggests that this should not have been surprising as only one parent was initially expressing an interest in mediation and that parent was in a precarious situation (e.g., being sought by legal authorities). Finally, of the sample of families who contacted the service, mothers constituted 40% of the parents who were in flight, a percentage higher than that (29%) reported by Agopian (1981).

3. The National Project

The Florida Project was viewed as informative and, although not as positive as expected in terms of actual cases mediated, at least promising. As a result, after its completion, a gradually expanding national project was planned and implemented. The project was designed to continue in Florida, to be implemented in New York, followed by initiation in three western states and then in five southern states, and, subsequently, gradually expanding throughout the nation. The television, radio, and newspaper ads for the national project were formally begun in April, 1987, in New York, although some calls continued to be received from the Florida project in January through March, 1987. In October, 1987, the ads were begun in California, New Mexico, and Arizona, and they were initiated in Texas in November and Georgia, Mississippi, Louisiana, and Alabama in February, 1988. The present report is based on the calls received from January 1, 1987, through March 31, 1988. Phases 2 and 3 of the project will involve implementation of the program in 24 and 16 additional states, respectively.

3.1. Changes in Procedures

Based on the pilot project in Florida, a number of changes were deemed necessary and thus made in the operating procedures employed. First, as a result of the number of calls received that did not directly involve mediation, it was decided to have a counselor, rather than a mediator, receive calls. This individual, who possessed general counseling skills as well as knowledge about the legal system and various referral resources, then would make an assessment of the most appropriate referral for a caller. If mediation was determined to be the best course of action, a referral was made to one of eight professionally trained mediators, who agreed to work *pro bono* with Child Find of America, Inc. Second, because of expenses, the Child Find mediation service was reduced to a business work week, Monday through Friday, with initial screening continuing on a 24-hour, seven-day basis. Third, as will be noted subsequently, some of the categories in which data were collected and tabulated were changed. Furthermore, some additional information was collected from each caller.

3.2. Outcome

During this assessment of the program, 526 meaningful phone calls were received. Of these, 286 were documented case files involving a child. The remaining 240 calls involved calls not concerning children but some other type of problem (e.g., alcohol abuse, drug abuse, AIDS) or general information. The number of calls received from each state is indicated in Table 3.

Table 4 provides information on the type of call (in-flight, searching,

Table 3
State from Which Each Phone Call Was Placed

State	Number of calls
New York	82
Florida	62
California	30
Texas	26
New Jersey	12
Washington	7
Maryland	6
New Mexico	4
Arizona	3
Georgia	3
Michigan	3
Oklahoma	2
Pennsylvania	2
South Carolina	2
Vermont	2
Alabama	1
Arkansas	1
Colorado	1
Connecticut	1
Illinois	1
Kentucky	1
North Carolina	1
Oregon	1
Tennessee	1
Utah	1
Virginia	1
Virgin Islands	1
Philippines	1
Not ascertained	15
Total	286

contemplating abduction, etc.) by the service provided (legal referral, counseling, mediation, etc.).* As in the pilot project, those calls from a parent in flight with a child and from a parent contemplating abduction of a child were by far most common.

Five types of services were provided. The service provided depended upon the assessment of the problem by the individual receiving the call. Legal referral and counseling were the most common with an

*Multiple types of services were often provided. For classification purposes we assigned each call to the primary type of service provided.

TABLE 4

Type of Call by Service Provided

Service provided	In flight	Searching	Contemplating abduction	Preventing abduction	Visitation enforced/changed	Custody information/change	General information	Other	Total
Legal referral[a]	19	6	52	4	6	18	5	—	110
Counseling[b]	40	5	31	5	1	2	3	—	87
Mediation	23	1	1	0	5	1	1	—	32
Information[c]	3	0	1	1	0	1	6	—	12
Social service referral[d]	6	7	6	0	3	1	1	—	24
None[e]	3	0	2	0	0	0	1	15	21
Total	94	19	93	10	15	23	17	15	286

[a]Caller referred to American or state Bar Association, court, or legal aid society in order to have questions addressed or services provided.
[b]Person receiving phone call primarily provided support, encouragement, and alternatives for handling issue presented.
[c]General information (e.g., about custody) primarily provided.
[d]Referred to a therapist, social service agency or, in seven cases, to a local mediator.
[e]Caller hung up, did not call back, called only to report information, or, in the case of the "Other" category, the call was a prank or was irrelevant.

additional 32 cases being referred to a Child Find mediator. (As noted in footnote *d* of Table 4, seven additional cases were deemed more appropriate to be handled by a mediator in the vicinity of the caller rather than one of Child Find's nationally based mediators. The subsequent outcome of these cases was not ascertained.) Some trends in regard to type of call by service provided are also apparent in the figures presented in Table 4. Counseling, followed by mediation, was most frequently provided to in-flight parents, whereas a legal referral was primarily provided to those contemplating abduction and those wishing to have their visitation privileges enforced or custody changed.

As the two primary types of calls were from parents contemplating abduction and parents in flight, detailed background information is provided for these two groups in Table 5. For those contemplating abduction, fathers were the callers in about two thirds of the cases and in two thirds of the cases, the caller was either divorced or separated. Of all the possible alternatives, mothers most often had custody, although this was the situation in only slightly over one third of the cases. In over half of the cases, only one child was being considered by the parent for abduction. Finally, with the exception of the 16–18-year-old range, the ages of the children were fairly evenly distributed across the five categories.

In regard to the in-flight parents, mothers and fathers were approximately evenly represented. As Table 5 indicates, the marital status of the in-flight parents primarily fell into one of four categories: divorced, married, separated, and never married. Custody of the child for those who were no longer married was primarily with the mother; however, fathers had custody in approximately one sixth of the cases. As with those contemplating abduction, slightly over half involved only one child and this child was most often in the 3- to 7-year-old age range. The length of the abduction ranged from one day to over four years, with three to seven months being the most frequent-occurring category.

The issue of whether there is a gender of parent by gender of child effect in child abduction was also considered. Fathers abducted boys and girls 47% and 53% of the time, respectively, and mothers abducted boys and girls 55% and 45% of the time, respectively. These findings suggest that there is little difference across fathers and mothers in terms of which sex child is abducted. In an additional three cases, a stepfather abducted a child and in all three instances the child was a girl.

Table 6 presents the most frequent reasons for being in flight (reasons cited by less than two parents are not included). Abuse or neglect of the child, followed by spouse abuse, the perception that one is a better parent, and having been denied visitation privileges were reported as the primary reasons for the abduction. Of those in flight, 27%

Table 5

Background Information (in Percent) for Parents Contemplating Abduction and in Flight

	Contemplating abduction	In flight
Parent		
Fathers	64	47
Mothers	33	44
Others	2	2
Unknown	1	7
Marital status		
Married	8	20
Married but filed for divorce	6	4
Separated	29	16
Divorced	37	38
Never married	12	15
Unknown	8	7
Custody status		
Mother sole custody	36	25
Father sole custody	12	16
Joint	7	10
Relative has custody	3	0
State has custody	5	1
Mother temporary sole custody	3	1
Father temporary sole custody	2	4
Temporary joint custody	1	2
Parents still married	13	13
Unknown	18	28
Number of children involved		
One-child families	54	54
Two-child families	21	29
Three-child families	15	5
Four-child families	3	3
Five-child families	0	1
Seven-child families	1	0
Unknown	9	8
Ages of children[a]		
Girls		
0–2 years	23	22
3–5 years	39	41
6–10 years	27	25
11–15 years	10	10
16–18 years	1	2

Table 5 (*Continued*)

	Contemplating abduction	In flight
Boys		
0–2 years	16	21
3–5 years	27	40
6–10 years	33	28
11–15 years	20	11
16–18 years	4	0
Length of abduction		
1 day or less		4
2–6 days		7
1–2 weeks		8
3–4 weeks		9
Over 1 but less than 3 months		5
Over 3 but less than 7 months		22
Over 7 but less than 12 months		6
Over 1 but less than 2 years		3
Over 2 but less than 4 years		4
Over 4 years		4
Unknown		28

[a]For 24 children it was not possible to ascertain age and/or sex. These children are not shown in the percentages reported in the table.

Table 6

Most Frequent Reasons Given for Being in Flight

Reason	Number reporting reason for being in flight
Child abuse/neglect	17
Spouse abuse	8
Better parent	8
Denied visitation with child	
Spouse on drugs	4
Lost custody	3
Other spouse threatened to take child	3
Wanted to be with child more	3
Mother is a prostitute	2

had warrants outstanding against them, 24% did not have a warrant outstanding against them, and, in 49% of the cases, the caller did not know the legal status of the abduction or did not disclose it.

Thirty-two cases were referred to one of the eight mediators working directly with Child Find of America, Inc., with one mediator handling approximately 80% of the cases. This mediator was utilized most often because he was the first mediator involved in the program, had the most expertise, and was willing and available to accept cases. In nine of the 32 cases, mediation was completed. All nine cases involved a parent in flight with one or more children. In these cases, a total of 18 children were returned to the parent from whom they were abducted. The reason mediation was not completed in the remaining 23 cases is presented in Table 7. The primary reason was that the calling parent failed to call back in order to pursue or follow through with mediation. Of the 23 cases, five were not in flight. Furthermore, in three cases the reason mediation was not completed was not viewed as being the responsibility of either parent (i.e., those in the last three categories in Table 7). Therefore, in order to form a comparison group for those for whom mediation was completed, the nine cases just delineated were eliminated, resulting in 14 cases for which mediation was not completed.

A comparison of these two group (9 and 14 cases for which mediation was and was not completed, respectively) is presented in Table 8. The most evident differences between the two groups were that, for cases in which mediation was completed, fathers were more often the in-flight parent and warrants had been issued more often. Chi-square analyses, performed on each category of data presented in Table 8, failed to reveal significant differences; however, in all cases, the computer-generated analyses cautioned that the small sample size makes the validity of the analyses questionable.

Table 7

Reason Mediation Not Completed

Reason	Number of cases
Parent calling failed to call back	10
Parent from whom child abducted unwilling to mediate	4
Mediation attempted but discontinued	2
Incorrect information given by caller	2
Mediation still in progress	2
Parent from whom child abducted could not be located	1
Mediator had parents work it out themselves	1
State had custody of child	1

TABLE 8

Characteristics (in Percent) of Families in Flight for Which Mediation Was and Was Not Completed

	Completed	Not completed
Parent		
Fathers	67	43
Mothers	22	57
Stepfather	11	0
Marital status		
Married	0	7
Separated	11	0
Divorced	89	50
Never married	0	29
Unknown	0	14
Custody status		
Mother sole custody	33	29
Father sole custody	45	29
Joint	22	14
Parents still married	0	7
Unknown	0	21
Number of children involved		
One-child families	45	64
Two-child families	33	29
Three-child families	11	7
Five-child families	11	0
Ages of children		
Girls		
0–2 years	0	0
3–5 years	33	17
6–10 years	45	17
11–15 years	22	66
16–18 years	0	0
Boys		
0–2 years	0	43
3–5 years	45	29
6–10 years	33	14
11–15 years	0	7
16–18 years	0	7
Unknown	22	0
Length of abduction		
1 day or less	0	7
2–6 days	0	0
1–2 weeks	11	0
3–4 weeks	0	7

(continued)

TABLE 8 (Continued)

	Completed	Not completed
Over 1 but less than 3 months	11	14
Over 3 but less than 7 months	22	36
Over 7 but less than 12 months	11	7
Over 1 but less than 2 years	0	7
Over 2 but less than 4 years	22	0
Over 4 years	22	14
Unknown	0	7
Warrant outstanding		
Yes	67	43
No	11	36
Uncertain	2	21

One additional set of comparisons also was made between the 9 who did complete mediation and the comparison group of 14 who did not complete mediation. The data for these comparisons were based on a set of ratings completed by the counselor accepting the phone call for Child Find. This individual completed eight 5-point Likert scale ratings on characteristics of the caller at the end of the phone conversation. The data and statistical analyses are presented in Table 9. The results indi-

TABLE 9

Means and t-Tests for Comparison of the Caller's Characteristics between Those Who Did and Did Not Complete Mediation

Characteristic[a]	Mean for completers	Mean for noncompleters	t-value
Depressed–elated	3.2	3.4	.44
Aggressive–submissive	3.5	3.2	.29
Open–reserved	3.0	2.0	2.04[b]
Relaxed–anxious	3.0	2.9	.14
Upset–calm	3.4	3.2	.39
Trusting–suspicious	2.2	2.6	.78
Cooperative–uncooperative	1.8	2.5	1.11
Optimistic–pessimistic	2.2	2.8	.11

[a]For each characteristic, 1 = very (depressed, aggressive, etc.), 2 = somewhat (depressed, aggressive, etc.), 3 = neutral, 4 = somewhat (elated, submissive, etc.), and 5 = very (elated, submissive, etc.).
[b]$p = .05$.

cate that the two groups differed on how open the caller was with the counselor.

Finally, in order to provide the reader with a better understanding of the mediation process and outcome, a brief clinical description of one case will be presented. This case involved a divorced mother who had been in flight with her three daughters (ages, 6, 5, and 3) for 6 months. (She had originally abducted her two sons also but had subsequently returned them to the father.) She had abducted the children because she was "disgusted with the court system which only gave her 2 weeks in the summer to see her children."

A total of 34 phone calls were made between the mediator and the involved parties: 16, 14, 2, 1, and 1 with the father, mother, a county investigator, the father's attorney, and a local mediator, respectively. The total phone time was 7 hours and 39 minutes with a cost of $124.22. These phone calls involved negotiation on various aspects of the children's return (e.g., when and where child would be returned). The agreement that resulted from these mediation efforts is presented in Table 10. At last contact, the family was involved in long-term mediation with a local mediator.

4. Discussion

Mediation, in cases of a parental-abducted child, can potentially provide the return of the child and assist parents in reaching an agreement on the forum they will use to resolve their differences. The results of Phase 1 of the National Project suggest that such an approach can be used successfully in returning children to the parent from whom they were abducted. These figures are encouraging and indicate that procedures other than the typically employed "search and find" strategies may assist in removing children from flight.

Of course, the success and cost effectiveness of mediation, relative to the typical procedures employed (e.g., hiring a detective, circulating a child's picture), cannot be determined from the present study. However, mediation would appear particularly attractive because it involves a cooperative resolution to a problem rather than an adversarial one. Furthermore, the data from divorce mediation research suggest that the participants are more satisfied with the process and outcome of mediation than the alternative (i.e., litigation) (Irving *et al.*, 1981; Pearson & Thoennes, 1982). Nevertheless, in regard to parental child abduction, our view at this time is that we should not be contrasting one procedure against another but rather searching for procedures like mediation to use in addition to those that have typically been utilized. In the future, it

TABLE 10
Agreement That Resulted from Mediation

The following agreement was worked out by telephone by the Child Find mediator. Both parties agreed prior to the start of the mediation that all communications between them and the mediator, other than any final agreement, would be confidential, and that he would not be called as a witness to any subsequent legal hearings in regard to this matter.

(Father) and (Mother) (Parent) agree that they are the parents of their five children: Son (1), Son (2), Daughter (1), Daughter (2), and Daughter (3). Currently, the two boys are not in contact with their mother, and the three girls are not in contact with their father; both parents want to end the current situation.

They reached the following understandings:

1. That they are both important to their children, and that their children need to know that both of their parents love them and care deeply about them; and despite any differences of opinion between the parents, neither parent will "put down" the other parent in front of the children.
2. (Mother) agrees that she will return the three girls to her mother's house in Town-name by 5 p.m. (or earlier) on DAY, DATE/MONTH, 1987, and that she will notify (Father) when she gets there. (Father) will then ask his attorney to work to insure that a felony warrant is not issued for (Mother); and he agrees that he will arrange for (Mother) to spend time with all of the children while she is in Town-name; (Mother) agrees that she will leave Town-name again by Monday night.
3. (Father) agrees that when (Mother) is visiting the children he will act as the supervisor that the current court order calls for, and not have any other member of his family present and he will work with his family, and any other individuals in the community who might be involved, to minimize any stress that (Mother) might be exposed to while she is in Town-name. (Mother) agrees to visit the children alone, and to leave promptly once the visit is over. They both agree to make these visits as pleasant as possible for the children and to not discuss any of their disagreements in front of the children.
4. (Father) agrees that he will allow (Mother) free telephone access to the children, and that if she arranges a special time with him to call, that he will have them available at that time, or to notify her if this time has to be changed. (Mother) agrees to call when she is scheduled to do so, and that if she calls them at an unscheduled time she will do so before their bedtime which is currently 8:30 p.m.
5. (Mother) agrees that under the terms of the current court order (Father) is the designated custodial parent. (Father) agrees that he will discuss with (Mother) her concerns about how the children are doing, including any serious request by one or more of the children that they be allowed to live with their mother, and that if such a move is reasonable they will attempt to work together about this change. However, they both agree that no changes can take place during this school year, or without the consent of both parents, or by an order of the court.
6. They both agree that they need to work toward an arrangement that has the children spending time during the school vacations with whichever parent that they do not live with during the school year. (Mother) recognizes that (Father) is understandably nervous about letting any of the children spend extended periods

TABLE 10 (Continued)

of time alone with her during school vacation in the near future. (Father) agrees to consider accompanying the children on a vacation this summer to where (Mother) is living and working so that they can become familiar with her home and environment; (Mother) agrees to help pay for the children's expenses. They will discuss this further once all the children are with their father, and agree how and when unsupervised visits can occur later.

7. They both agree that they need to improve their ability to cooperate with each other around their children's needs, and to develop the open and trusting relationship that is in their children's best interests. They agree that they are both equally important to the children, and that neither of them has the right to ignore the other's concerns, or to have sole say in how the children are dealt with. (Father) recognizes that in returning the three girls (Mother) is trying to be a good and responsible parent and that he will meet with a third party within six months to work out how the existing court order can be changed so that it reflects the fact that they are jointly responsible for parenting their children.

8. (Mother) agrees that she will resume the $75/month child support payments that the court has ordered as of February 1987, and that she will discuss later how, and to what extent, she can help (Father) meet the unusual expenses that he has incurred over the last six months.

9. They both agree to meet with a local mediator, in North State #2, to work out the details of a longer term and more detailed arrangement than has been possible to work out by telephone with this mediator, and that once all the children are together, and if it is possible, jurisdiction will be transferred from Named County, State #1, to Named County, State #2.

This agreement was gone over in detail by phone with both parents, and with a representative from (Father's) lawyer, Mr. _____, and they agreed to uphold the commitments that they have made. I believe it to be an accurate summary of understandings that (Mother) and (Father) reached during this mediation.

---

may be appropriate to select a "best approach." However, as the prevalence of parental abduction and the potential harm to children are so great, the resolution to the problem will likely require a multifaceted approach. Mediation would appear to have the potential to be part of such an approach.

Regardless of its effectiveness, the present results also suggest that mediation is not an easy-to-implement intervention. Success was often thwarted by one or both parents or by the complex procedure required to mediate by phone the return of an abducted child. As we noted earlier, this should not have been a surprise to us. Even when the law requires mediation as part of divorce proceedings, as occurs in California, only slightly over half of the cases are successful (McIsaac, 1982). In contrast to this type of situation, the mediation used in the present project can be far more difficult. One parent is operating outside of the law and is fearful of trusting anyone. Furthermore, typically only this parent has even considered mediation as a possible solution and, as was reflected in some of our results, the parent from whom the child was taken was not always interested. Often this parent can be hostile and resentful toward the abducting parent, potentially much more so than in mediation of child custody in divorce proceedings. Without cooperation from *both* parents, mediation cannot occur.

In addition, it is important to note that over 60% of the parents had been in flight over one month. Thus, the sample did not consist primarily of parents who were simply keeping the child for an extra day or so beyond the usual visitation privileges. Rather, the abductions constituted serious efforts to keep the child, thus potentially making mediation more difficult. Finally, mediation in divorce typically occurs face-to-face, which should facilitate the mediator's ability to establish rapport and successfully reach an agreement. In the type of mediation utilized in the present project, this was obviously not possible. All of these factors have to be viewed as potentially hindering the success of mediation for parental-abducted children.

On the other hand, phone mediation as utilized in the present project has a number of strengths that may make it the intervention of choice in some situations. It allows mediation to overcome the physical distance that may often separate parents. By at least the initial stages of negotiation being by phone, hostile physical, and possibly verbal, interchanges can be reduced. Furthermore, the two parents are more likely to have parity than in face-to-face mediation where certain aspects of one party (e.g., physical or verbal characteristics) may place him or her at an advantage. Finally, at least in the present project, the mediation was performed at no cost to the parents.

The present data also shed some light on why parents abduct a child. The results suggest that personal safety of either the child or the parent is a primary reason. This finding may well be related to the high percentage (44%) of mothers who had abducted a child and called the project. That is, although a mother may have custody of a child, she may feel compelled to flee if she feels either the child's or her safety is threatened. It is also important to note that there were a number of other reasons reported for being in flight. Although sufficient data were not available for examining the success of mediation as a function of the reason for fleeing, future research hopefully can address this issue.

We were able to make some comparisons between those who did and did not complete mediation. These comparisons tentatively suggested that in-flight fathers may be more likely to complete mediation. Furthermore, the presence of an outstanding warrant and, in phone conversations, an openness about one's situation are associated with mediation being completed. Because mothers are still the primary care-givers of children in most families, it is possible that fathers may find the daily responsibilities of childcare in an in-flight situation more stressful than mothers and, thus, wish to mediate to remove themselves from being in flight. Furthermore, a warrant outstanding against an in-flight parent may increase the motivation to reach a resolution because drop-ping the warrant could be part of the mediated agreement (but not a guarantee, as each case was treated individually). Finally, openness with the Child Find counselor probably is a reflection of one's moti-vation to terminate the in-flight situation. However, considering the small sample sizes we had for comparative purposes and the number of comparisons we made, the importance of these factors must be viewed with caution. They do, nevertheless, suggest variables to be studied in future research.

The success of the present mediation program may be evaluated in terms beyond the number of children returned. Assistance was pro-vided for an equal number of parents who were contemplating abduct-ing a child as for those who had done so. Although the effectiveness of this assistance could not be determined, it may well have prevented children from being taken in flight by a parent. If so, this is at least as important if not more so than removing a child from flight. Further-more, other parents, who were searching for an abducted child, wishing to have visitation rights enforced, and wanting information on custody, were assisted, which may well have improved the welfare of any number of children. Finally, other callers who had difficulties (e.g., drug or alcohol abuse) were provided with some assistance in terms of sug-gestions on how to find services for their needs. The fact that parents and others responded to the television, radio, and newspaper ads sug-gests that, as a source of information, the services were needed and probably beneficial.

The type of services provided to callers was varied; however, not surprising considering the legal implications of child custody, referral to the American or state Bar Association or a legal aid society for advice or assistance occurred most often. Of particular interest was the fact that many in-flight parents were not viewed as acceptable for mediation or did not want mediation. In order to be acceptable, an in-flight parent had to agree to two conditions: (1) to give the other parent's phone number so that both parties and the mediator could be involved in the mediation process, and (2) to work toward returning a child. Because of factors such as anger toward the spouse/ex-spouse, fear of prosecution, or fear of losing all contact with the child, the in-flight parent was often not willing to agree to these two conditions.

Some comparisons across this data set and the one generated by Agopian are also possible. The percentage of mothers abducting a child in our project was even higher than Agopian (1981) reported in his work (44% versus 29%). Other comparisons across these two data sets are also possible. In Agopian's study, all participants were divorced or separated, whereas in the present sample only 54% fell in these two categories. Furthermore, in Agopian's project, a higher percentage of one-child abductions (64% versus 54%) occurred and a lower percentage of children under 3 years of age (5% versus 22%) were abducted. As the method of obtaining participants (i.e., individuals who call seeking assistance versus examination of legal files) and their geographic locations, among other factors, varied substantially in two projects, differences are not surprising. Only when data are available from nationally representative samples will more definitive statements be possible about characteristics of parents who abduct a child.

It is important to emphasize that the return of an abducted child may well not be the "final answer." That is, these are children who most likely had previously been exposed to a high level of interparental and other conflict for an extended period of time with the abduction only representing the last step on the conflict continuum. Some evidence for this hypothesis is seen in the primary reasons reported for a parent going in flight, that is, parent and child abuse/neglect. Therefore, the return of a child to the home does not guarantee that such conflict between the parents, which has been shown repeatedly to be associated with disruption in the functioning of children (e.g., Emery, 1982), will dissipate. However, voluntary participation in mediation that results in the return of a child may be a first step in this direction and may lead to a better long-term outcome in terms of the level of such conflict between parents and the functioning of the child. Furthermore, the abduction *per se* has been noted in several clinical case reports to be associated with posttraumatic emotional consequences for the child (Agopian, 1984; Senior et al., 1982; Terr, 1983) and, in one experimental investigation, to be associated with an increase in short-term behavior problems (Forehand et al., 1988). Thus, additional interventions with the parents to reduce conflict with the child will often be necessary after the return.

In conclusion, the mediation program utilized in the present project appears to hold promise for the return of parental-abducted children. As has been noted, there are obvious limitations and difficulties with such an approach. Nevertheless, a complex problem like child abduction will not yield itself to simple answers. Mediation would appear to be one component of the complex solution of this issue.

ACKNOWLEDGMENTS

Appreciation is expressed to the following organizations for facilitating this research effort: William T. Grant Foundation, Rivendell Foundation, Simplicity Pattern Company, Mattel Foundation, the Spunk Fund, Inc., McCaffery and McCall, Inc. Advertising, and The Ad Council. Also, the efforts and support of Louis McCagg, Howard Davidson, John Bassett, the staff of Child Find of America, Inc., and the numerous mediators, particularly Patrick Phear, are gratefully acknowledged.

5. References

Agopian, M. W. (1980). Parental child stealing: Participants and the victimization process. *Victimology*, *5*, 263–273.

Agopian, M. W. (1981). *Parental child-stealing*. Lexington, MA: Lexington Books.

Agopian, M. W. (1984). The impact on children of abduction by parents. *Child Welfare, 63*, 511–519.

Atkeson, B. M., Forehand, R., & Rickard, K. M. (1982). The effects of divorce on children. In B. B. Lahey & A. E. Kazdin (Eds.), *Advances in clinical child psychology* (Vol. 5, pp. 255–281). New York: Plenum Press.

Bowlby, J. (1973). *Attachment and loss: Separation* (Vol. 2). New York: Basic Books.

Deutsch, M. (1973). *The resolution of conflict*. New Haven, CT: Yale University Press.

Emery, R. E. (1982). Interparental conflict and the children of discord and divorce. *Psychological Bulletin, 92*, 310–330.

Emery, R. E., & Wyer, M. M. (1987). Divorce mediation. *American Psychologist, 42*, 472–480.

Forehand, R., Long, N., Zogg, C., & Parrish, E. (1988). An examination of parent and child functioning following the return of an abducted child. Manuscript submitted for publication.

Gelles, R. J. (1984). Parent child snatching: A preliminary estimate of national incident. *Journal of Marriage and the Family, 146*, 735–739.

Irving, H., Benjamin, M., Boham, P., & MacDonald, G. (1981). *Final research report*. Toronto, Canada: Provincial Court, Family Division.

King, D. K. (1982). Custody and visitation disputes under the new mandatory mediation law. *California Law, 41*.

Levy, R. J. (1984). Comment on the Pearson-Thoennes study and on mediation. *Family Law Quarterly, 17*, 525–538.

McCoy, M. (1978). Parental kidnapping: Issues Brief No. IB77117. Washington, DC: Congressional Research Office.

McIsaac, H. (1982). Court-connected mediation. *Conciliation Courts Review, 21*, 49–56.

Pearson, J., & Thoennes, N. (1982, June). *Mediating and litigating custody disputes: A longitudinal evaluation*. Paper presented at the American Bar Association's Conference on Alternative Means of Family Dispute Resolution, Washington, DC.

Senior, N., Gladstone, T., & Nurcombe, B. (1982). Child snatching: A case report. *Journal of the American Academy of Child Psychiatry, 21*, 579–583.

Terr, L. (1983). Child snatching: A new epidemic of an ancient malady. *Journal of Pediatrics, 103*, 151–156.

6 Genetic Factors in Childhood Psychopathology

Implications for Clinical Practice

Steven G. Vandenberg and Lawson Crowe

1. Introduction

The amount of technical detail in modern genetics is so voluminous that no one is able to understand more than a fraction of it. This fraction is usually limited to a particular area, such as blood diseases ("hemaglobinopathies") or diseases of connective tissue. Yet most geneticists share a body of common understanding, which we cannot hope to condense into a few pages. All we can do is hint at it. We have chosen to spend some time on mental retardation (MR), because many believe that the area of mental illness will sometime in the future, perhaps sooner than most of us realize, begin to look like MR in its plethora of single-gene abnormalities and abnormal numbers of chromosomes as causal factors.

In addition, we believe that the growing awareness of genetic factors in mental illness needs to become an essential part of the knowledge of all clinicians in the area of child psychopathology. Awareness of the effects of genetic factors provides information about limits to treatment and, more important, leads to an informed choice of treatment.

We apologize for the lack of systematic treatment of the basic concepts of genetics. We hope that most readers will remember enough about genetics so that we will not have to take up space with basic explanations.

1.1. Advance of Genetic Knowledge

A gradual shift has occurred away from a predominantly environmentalistic view of the formation of intelligence, personality, mental

Steven G. Vandenberg and Lawson Crowe • Institute for Behavioral Genetics, University of Colorado, Boulder, Colorado 80309.

illness, alcoholism, and even criminality. First came the dramatic discovery of the nature of the genetic code by Watson and Crick. Then followed the unraveling of the cause of phenylketonuria (PKU) and its partial remediation by diet, the discovery that Down's syndrome is due to the presence of an additional chromosome 21, and the subsequent discovery of many other types of chromosomal anomalies (aneuploidies) such as Turner's syndrome (XO) and Jacobs' syndrome (XYY). Most recently, the fragile-X type of recessive sex-linked mental retardation has received considerable attention. (For details about genetic factors in these and other disorders, see Vandenberg, Singer, & Pauls, 1986.)

In a subtle way, the return of interest in cognitive processes and the turn away from the pure behavioristic to a more "mentalistic" tradition has helped to clear the way for greater acceptance of biological influences on human behavior. Watson saw his behavior-oriented approach as biologically founded, compared with the structuralist position of Wundt and Titchener. In retrospect, however, there seems to have been no inherent logic in his rejection of hereditary factors, except, perhaps, his determination to start with observable behavior only and to avoid speculative concepts. Skinner, of course, went even further in that direction. Although it has brought along the risk of drug-induced (iatrogenic) side effects such as tardive dyskinesia, a third reason for the shift from an environmentalistic to a biological perspective may be the relative success of drug therapy for some types of mental illness compared with psychotherapy of whatever orientation.

1.2. Intelligence and Genetics

At first it may appear that there is a correlation between progress in establishing genetic factors in a realm of behavior and success in measuring the behaviors in that domain. We hope to show that this is not usually the case. For example, even though there is no complete agreement on the role of genetic factors in intelligence, some consensus about its nature seems to be in sight. There is no longer any doubt that general intelligence (g) is, at the moment at least, the best and perhaps the only good predictor of various criteria for educational or vocational, though not necessarily financial, success. Nevertheless, some specific abilities may be important for predicting more specialized criteria. Unfortunately, relatively little evidence exists for this reasonable idea, mainly because the sort of data that would support such a conclusion have generally not been collected or have not been analyzed in such a way that this notion can be tested.

Progress in finding genetic factors in intelligence can be discussed in terms of normal or subnormal intelligence. The overwhelming convergence of data in support of a considerable role for genetic factors in normal intelligence need not be reviewed here (Vandenberg & Vogler, 1985). On the other hand, those genetic factors themselves are still hidden in the midst of multifactorial anonymity. As we will see, the story is different for subnormal intelligence.

Perhaps the fact that the absence of each of many genes causes mental retardation as a byproduct or as the major symptom is sufficient reason to consider all normal alleles as polygenic contributors to normal intelligence. Or are there other genetic factors in what we think of as normal individuals, so that it is not just the absence of abnormal genes that makes one intelligent? Some evidence tends to favor the latter idea. It has been shown that in PKU (Fuller & Shuman, 1974), Down's syndrome (Fraser & Sadovnick, 1976), and fragile-X mental retardation (Vandenberg & Ho, 1988), the family level of intelligence influences the ability level of the affected person. It may help to compare the situation with the one concerning physical health or longevity. Although it is true that any illness impairs health, we would not usually regard the absence of measles as a positive contribution toward health or a long life.

1.3. Mental Retardation

As mentioned before, many single-gene abnormalities that produce mental retardation are known, and some are well enough understood to be treatable or preventable. Phenylketonuria (PKU) is the best-known example of the effects of such abnormal genes. Some readers may remember seeing wall charts showing the complexities of human digestion and metabolism. Many of these pathways are vulnerable to genetic mutations of enzymes required for normal metabolic breakdown or conversion. Figure 1 shows one small section in which absence of the liver enzyme phenylalanine hydroxylase leads to accumulation of phenylpyruvic acid. This prevents the formation of myelin around neurons in the central nervous system, which, in turn, is responsible for lowered intelligence. It has been possible to develop tests for this condition in newborns who, dependent on their mothers for nutrition until birth, are not affected until they start their own digestion of phenylalanine (which is present in many foods). If placed on a diet relatively free of this substance, newborns will develop normally, though they still have the abnormality and, in the case of females, may have to return to the diet while pregnant in order not to harm the developing embryo. They also will pass on a single recessive PKU gene to their children. If these children marry a person who also carries the recessive gene, they may have affected offspring. Because it is a recessive gene, two of these abnormal genes are needed for the disorder to be expressed. PKU was

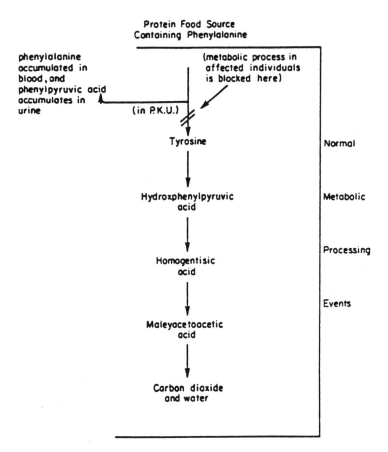

Figure 1. Metabolism of phenylalanine. From *The Heredity of Behavior Disorders in Adults and Children* (p. 32) by S. G. Vandenberg, S. M. Singer, and D. L. Pauls, 1986, New York: Plenum. Copyright 1986 by Plenum Publishing Corporation. Reprinted by permission.

one of the first single-gene abnormalities discovered because relatives who marry, such as cousins, are more likely to have inherited the same gene from a common ancestor and thereby have increased risk of having affected children. Many other errors of metabolism have been described since that time.

The cause of a second type of abnormality, formerly called "mongolism" because of the victim's distinctive facial features, was subsequently discovered. It is now called Down's syndrome after the physician who first described it, or trisomy 21, after its cause, the presence of a third chromosome 21 (or a substantial part of an extra one). (We will not discuss the rare 21-15 translocation.) Although it may be related to

Alzheimer's disease, how trisomy 21 leads to retardation is not yet fully understood. This is also not clear for other chromosomal anomalies, including fragile-X syndrome. In principle it seems that it will be only a matter of time before the details are worked out.

After the discovery of individuals with an abnormal number of chromosomes ("chromosomal aneuploidy"), there was a period of disagreement about the identity of the extra one. Methods were then developed that produce distinctive patterns of bands on each chromosome to allow definitive identification, not only of the particular chromosome but even of minor abnormalities such as deletions, inversions, and translocations (insertion of material from one chromosome into another one). (We will not discuss these minor chromosomal abnormalities because no major mental abnormalities have been attributed to these rather recent discoveries.)

Figure 2, a schematic drawing much clearer than most photographs, shows the detail that can be brought out in chromosomes by such techniques. The arrangement of chromosomes lined up in order of size is called a karyotype. What the cytogeneticist sees under the microscope is a confusing mixture of partially overlapping and unevenly bent chromosomes, some of which are "in profile" and some of which lie in a plane perpendicular to the viewer. For this reason, up to 100 cells may have to be photographed to produce a satisfactory karyotype.

One of the more controversial findings was of the XYY syndrome with an extra Y or "male" chromosome. Discovered first in inmates of maximum security prisons, it was originally hypothesized that the extra Y chromosome might cause aggressive and violent behavior as a result of the overproduction of male hormones. It has since been found that the initial studies were biased because of the unrepresentative populations studied. In other studies it has been found that this rather common abnormality does not cause abnormal aggressive behavior.

A partial list of errors of metabolism is shown in Table 1. This list is only included to give the reader some idea of the many possible causes of retardation. A full list may be constructed by consulting the latest edition of McKusick's catalog of autosomal and sex-linked genetic conditions due to single genes (McKusick, 1987). The sixth edition lists 934 "proven" dominant autosomal, 588 recessive autosomal, and 155 sex-linked conditions. This source lists 207 errors of metabolism, each due to a single mutant gene, and it also includes a map of the location of many of the genes on the 23 chromosomes. In this chapter we provide only a glimpse of the fantastic progress in human genetics that has occurred in recent years, especially after molecular techniques were introduced by which enzymes are used to cut human chromosomes at specific places. This cutting is done as a first step in the complete sequencing of the

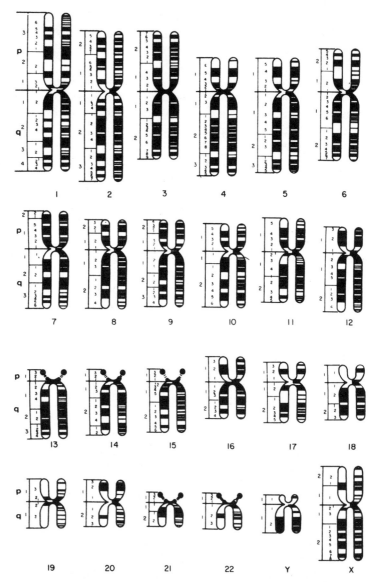

FIGURE 2. Chromosome banding patterns: (p) denotes the two upper arms of each chromosome, (q) denotes the two lower arms of each chromosome. From "High Resolution of Human Chromosomes" by J. J. Yunis, 1976, *Science, 191*, pp. 1268–1270. Copyright 1976 by the American Association for the Advancement of Science. Reprinted by permission.

TABLE 1
Errors of Metabolism

Phenylketonuria (autosomal recessive)	Pompe's disease (autosomal recessive)
Homocystinuria (autosomal recessive)	Hartnup's disease (autosomal recessive)
Tyrosinemia (autosomal recessive)	Wilson's disease (autosomal recessive)
Methylmalonic aciduria (autosomal recessive)	Tay–Sachs disease (autosomal recessive)
Maple-sugar-urine disease (autosomal recessive)	Tuberose sclerosis (autosomal dominant with variable expressivity)
Galactosemia (autosomal recessive)	Lesch–Nyan disease (X-linked recessive)
Mucolipidosis, Type I, Type II (autosomal recessive)	Menke's syndrome (X-linked recessive)
Hurler's syndrome (autosomal recessive)	Sanfilippo's syndrome (X-linked)
Hunter's syndrome (autosomal recessive)	

genetic code of the chromosome, and it led, somewhat unexpectedly, to the discovery that the lengths of resultant pieces vary for different individuals and that the cutting did not always occur at the same location. This variability, which is called restriction fragment length polymorphisms (RFLP), has been found to be Mendelian. (For a detailed treatment of the various types of enzymatic errors of metabolism, see Vogel & Motulsky, 1986.)

Many new findings of genetic disorders involve mental retardation. These findings were puzzling until it was recognized that abnormal metabolism almost always affects the most sensitive and complicated human organ—the brain. Mental retardation occurs because of a major insult to the chemistry of the developing brain. Once suitable ways have been found to identify various mental illnesses as "accurately" as intelligence tests do retardation, an equally long list of genes may be found to produce those later-occurring abnormalities of the brain. Yet it must be kept in mind that the discoveries of the various genetic causes of retardation, such as errors of metabolism or aneuploidies, did not depend on knowing the patients' IQ scores. Whether different patterns of response might have helped identify genetic factors is a moot question, because that type of information has generally been ignored or not collected.

At the same time, most researchers in this area are convinced that the role of environmental factors is larger in mental illnesses than in mental retardation. Especially convincing evidence of this is the fact that when identical twins are discordant for schizophrenia, the risk for schizophrenia in their children is the same for the healthy as for the affected twin (Fischer, 1971). Although this is generally cited as evidence for a genetic factor, it is equally potent evidence for the importance of the—admittedly unknown—environmental factors that were responsible for discordance in the identical twin parents of the children.

2. Personality and Psychopathology

2.1. Normal Personality

Before mental illnesses can be fully understood, we may need to have more agreement about normal personality, including ways to "measure" or at least characterize individual differences. It may appear that we are far from such an agreement. Nevertheless, there seems to be an emerging consensus among psychologists who have constructed personality questionnaires. Even though these researchers started from entirely different positions, they produced questionnaires that measure similar traits. For instance, Jackson started from Henry Murray's 20 needs, Cattell started with all the adjectives in the dictionary describing personality, and Eysenck related personality differences between neurotics and psychotics to ideas about conditioning and other experimental psychological findings. Three to five super factors seem to emerge from many of the tests.

One of the most promising sets of such factors is called the "robust five." The NEO Personality Inventory of Costa and McCrae (1985) is based on independent studies by Tupes and Christal (1961), Norman (1963), and Digman and Inouye (1986), all of whom used ratings by others rather than self-reports. The factors measured by the NEO are shown in Table 2. [For more details about these factors, see Digman and Inouye (1986), McCrae and Costa (1984, 1987), Noller and Law (1987), and Zuckerman, Kuhlman, and Camac (1988).] Three of the five factors are each based on six interrelated traits, as shown in Figure 3.

Evidence of genetic variance in these traits is beginning to appear, but the use of different labels by different researchers makes straightforward comparison and aggregation difficult. No really clear conceptions of pathways from genes to these behaviors have been suggested. Gray (1983) has come closest to providing a theory of a causative link between physiology and personality, whereas Eysenck (1981) has proposed ideas that are one step farther away from physiological mechanisms. More recently, Cloninger has proposed a somewhat similar three-factor model for mental abnormalities.

TABLE 2
Adjectives Describing Five Factors of Normal Personality

Factor	High scorer	Low scorer
Neuroticism	Worrying, nervous, emotional, insecure, inadequate, hypochondriacal	Calm, relaxed, unemotional, hardy, secure, self-satisfied
Extraversion	Sociable, active, talkative, socially oriented, optimistic, fun-loving, affectionate	Reserved, sober, unexuberant, task-oriented, retiring, quiet
Openness	Curious, broad interests, creative, original, imaginative, untraditional	Conventional, down-to-earth, narrow interests, unartistic, unanalytical
Agreeableness	Soft-hearted, good-natured, trusting, helpful, forgiving, gullible, straightforward	Cynical, rude, suspicious, uncooperative, vengeful, ruthless, irritable, manipulative
Conscientiousness	Organized, reliable, hard-working, self-disciplined, punctual, scrupulous, neat, ambitious, persevering	Aimless, unreliable, lazy, careless, lax, negligent, weak-willed, hedonistic

Cloninger's (1986, 1987a,b) theory is an interesting integration of biochemical, neurophysiological, and personality theories to account for individual differences in behavior, including psychopathology. He argues that most behaviors are controlled by three basic mechanisms: novelty seeking, harm avoidance, and reward dependence. Table 3 shows a schematic summary of some of his ideas. Moderation of the extreme forms of these processes might lead to the prevention of much psychopathology. It will take a good deal of theorizing and even outright speculation before we will be able to submit such ideas to testing for validity and effectiveness.

2.2. Genetic Factors in Behavioral Disorders

Recent progress in more precise diagnosis of mental illness and provision of specific checklists of criteria, rating scales, and other measuring devices is a promising sign. Yet, these improvements have not led to any clear-cut theoretical victories. In contrast, the largely empirically based use of psychotropic drugs has had considerable success. In fact, a proposal has been made to turn things upside down and base

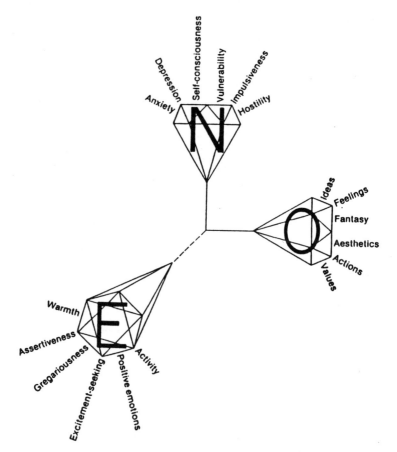

FIGURE 3. Schematic representation of the three-dimensional, eighteen-facet NEO model. From *Emerging Lives, Enduring Dispositions: Personality in Adulthood* (p. 42) by R. R. McCrae and P. T. Costa, Jr., 1984, Boston: Little, Brown & Company. Copyright 1984 by Little, Brown & Company. Reprinted by permission.

diagnostic groupings on patients' responses to drugs. Until very recently, progress in finding genetic factors in mental illness was confined to the general demonstration of the existence of genetic variance. This has been especially convincing in the case of adoption studies, most specifically for schizophrenia (Kety, Rosenthal, Wender, Schulsinger, & Jacobsen, 1975). But the precise location of the gene(s) involved remains elusive.

The search for early distinguishing signs of future mental illness, perhaps with the possibility of early intervention or even prevention, has been unrewarding. Such research is called high-risk research, not

TABLE 3

Three Major Brain Systems Influencing Stimulus–Response Characteristics

Brain system (related personality dimension)	Principal monoamine neuromodulator	Relevant stimuli	Behavioral response
Behavioral activation (novelty seeking)	Dopamine	Novelty Potential rewards or their conditioned signals Potential relief of punishment, montony, or their conditioned signals	Exploratory pursuit Appetitive approach Escape Active avoidance
Behavioral inhibition (harm avoidance)	Serotonin	Conditioned signals for punishment, novelty, or frustrative nonreward	Passive avoidance
Behavioral maintenance (reward dependence)	Norepinephrine	Conditioned signals for reward or relief of punishment	Extinction Resistance to extinction

Note. From "Neurogenetic Adaptive Mechanisms in Alcoholism" by C. R. Cloninger, 1987a, Science, 236, p. 413. Copyright 1987 by the American Association for the Advancement of Science. Reprinted by permission.

because its outcome is risky, but because the participants, or subjects, are thought to be more at risk than are randomly selected subjects. One of the best known of these research projects involves children of one or two schizophrenic parents. The estimated incidences of schizophrenia in such children are 12.8% and 46.3%, respectively (Gottesman & Shields, 1972, 1982). However, the rates observed so far in the New York High-Risk Project (Cornblatt & Erlenmeyer-Kimling, 1985; Erlenmeyer-Kimling & Cornblatt, 1987; Erlenmeyer-Kimling et al., 1987) are lower. In the case of high-risk research, one wonders whether the rather low rates of schizophrenia might be, in part, the result of the frequent minor interventions that research participation entails. Perhaps this is only true of high-risk research with children of schizophrenics, because two studies in which the risk factors were social and personal ones did not find low outcome figures (Dohrenwend et al., 1987).

The story of genetic factors in depressive disorders has several interesting aspects. For example, it has long been thought that women have a higher incidence of depression than do men. Golding (1988) has made a rather persuasive argument that the sex difference in depressive symptoms is mainly to be attributed to sex differences in social conditions that work against women, such as lower employment rates, lower wages, lower job status, and lower education. All of these factors have been shown to be related to an increase in depressive symptoms in men as well as women. Golding controlled for such social and economic conditions when she reanalyzed data from several studies of sex differences in depression and concluded that, after these corrections, there were no longer statistically significant differences in depression between the sexes. She also noted that the original differences were often due to the fact that there were more extreme outliers among women than among men. Correction for this skew also tended to cause sex differences to become nonsignificant. Feminists have been persuasive about the social determination of some of this difference. For instance, Bernard (1972) has analyzed U.S. statistics to show that being married is a good thing for men and a bad thing for women.

Ideas of sex linkage in depressive disorders have been proposed, and some support for such linkage has been found. Sex linkage, or X-linkage, is a precise term in genetics, which means that a gene (or genes) responsible for the condition is located on the X chromosome. Because women have two Xs and men have one X and one Y chromosome, a recessive condition would show up in all males who carried the abnormal gene, but women would be affected only if they had both abnormal genes, except for a complication popularized by Lyon in 1961. She argued that one of the two X chromosomes is "turned off" (inactivated) in females to compensate in part for the lesser amount of genetic material in the sex chromosomes of normal males (in whom the Y chromosome is very small). This "dosage-compensation" mechanism is evolutionarily old and is related to the fact that the location of genes on the X chromosome is more similar (constant) in mammals and some "lower" organisms than is the location of genes on the autosomes. As a consequence of the fact that the inactivation occurs early in the embryonic development and that it is a matter of chance whether the paternal or maternal X is inactivated in each of the small number of cells, a female is a mosaic for the X chromosome. This can sometimes be seen in mice, which may show patches of two coat colors. It is more difficult to demonstrate in humans, but a few women have been found who have patches of colorblind and normal retinal cells. Even though this Lyonization process may occur with respect to depression, one would still expect a lower incidence in women than in men—the opposite of the reported rates. It has been suggested that men may self-medicate depression with alcohol more often than do women, which could explain the sex differences in the two abnormalities. In the Amish, who do not exhibit alcoholism, there is no difference in depression rates between the sexes.

The gene(s) responsible for depressive disorder in the Amish was pinpointed on Chromosome 11 (Egeland et al., 1987). So far this linkage has not been found in other ethnic groups. The presence of another gene located on the X chromosome that also leads to depressive disorder remains less well established but nevertheless reasonably plausible (Baron et al., 1987). In fact, a paper by Mendlewicz and associates (1987) reports a study of 10 families in which bipolar depressive illness was closely linked to Blood Coagulation Factor IX on the long arm of the X chromosome. Because of the occurrence of father–son transmission, which tends to rule out a recessive mode of inheritance, this gene appears to be dominant. Again, it should be noted that these genetic successes were not really dependent on the refinements in diagnosis mentioned above, except that they caused a general awareness of the need for careful, detailed description and analysis of symptoms.

Next we come to neurological and psychomotor disorders, taking this grouping in a broad sense. Great progress has been made in recent years in investigating the etiology of Huntington's chorea, Alzheimer's disease, and many other conditions. In most cases, the precise diagnosis preceded the discovery of genetic factors. This may be due to the fact that neurology has always been based on careful observation of details rather than on hastily generalized axioms and ad hoc psychiatric theories.

Having thus argued that genetic discoveries have not depended on refinements in measuring relevant behaviors, it is necessary to keep in mind that the techniques and concepts had to be at least aimed in the right direction. We do not want to overemphasize the idea of a lack of correlation between precise diagnosis and genetic discoveries. The more precise the diagnosis, whether by the neurologist's hammer, by the psychometrist's ability test, or by personality questionnaire, the more likely it is that a connection with genes can be found (if there is one). On the other hand, the biological closeness of the traits to genes makes the finding of a connection more likely. The original identifications of human genes were, after all, related to blood types, which are chemical complexes related very directly to the genetic code. Subsequent discoveries of more and more minor variants, responsible for different but very similar blood-group-related illnesses and transfusion incompatibilities, have only confirmed this close relationship. Problems of measurement become more difficult in the realm of personality and mental illness because of the frequent need to rely on the patient's self-report and the possibility of lack of insight or faking by the respondent.

Considerable evidence from adoption studies indicates that genetic factors contribute significantly to alcoholism. Of course, it cannot be disputed that alcohol has to be available for the problem to arise. In that sense, an enormous environmental factor is presupposed. In respect to criminality, genetic factors have also been proposed. Eysenck (1977) has suggested predisposing personality factors that could provide a start in the search for pathways from genes to behavior. He attributes some criminality to lack of proper social conditioning, a condition he blames on individual differences in conditionability and sensitivity to pain or blame. He regards these differences as partly innate.

Christiansen (1968, 1977) has argued that early twin studies of criminality probably were flawed. He reported lower concordance rates than previous authors and, in addition, found instances where the police had arrested the wrong identical twin or assumed that one twin must have shared in the crime of the other twin. Perhaps the most convincing evidence of genetic factors in delinquency and crime comes from adoption studies in which it was found that adopted-away children of criminals had a higher rate of convictions than did controls. Most striking are the results of a Swedish study, shown in Figure 4, in which the records of adopted-away children are plotted against those of their biological fathers. The illustration also demonstrates that the more frequent the convictions of the biological fathers, the more frequent were those of the children. As discussed later, however, the idea that there may be a genetic predisposition to criminality raises ethical problems. The sample in the Swedish study was small, and many of the adopted children did not have police records. Incidentally, all such records are centralized in Sweden and are available only to approved researchers.

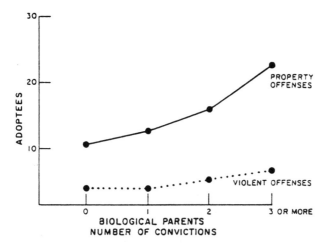

FIGURE 4. Percentage of male adoptee property offenders and violent offenders as a function of number of convictions in biological father. From "Genetic Influences in Criminal Behavior" by S. A. Mednick, W. F. Gabrielli, and B. Hutchings, in *Prospective Studies of Crime and Delinquency* (p. 66) edited by K. T. VanDusen and S. A. Mednick, 1983, Hingham, MA: Martinus Nyhoff. Copyright 1983 by Martinus Nyhoff. Reprinted by permission.

2.3. Child Psychopathology

Increasing interest in child psychopathology is illustrated by the augmented attention given to it in the third edition of the *Diagnostic and Statistical Manual* (DSM-III) and its revision (DSM-III-R) as compared to the second one. In recent years, several epidemiological surveys have helped to distinguish the truly abnormal from the merely infrequent or—from the parents' point of view—undesirable behaviors of children. Achenbach's work is perhaps the best known (Achenbach, 1986; Achenbach & Edelbrock, 1978, 1981). During the same period, research into and concern for genetic factors in psychopathology has increased considerably. Because most of this research has dealt with adult rather than with child psychopathology, we may at times have to look beyond childhood and include adult forms of abnormality, which in many cases are thought to be a continuation of childhood problems.

In discussing clinical implications of hereditary factors in child psychopathology, we should first state the obvious once again. Establishing a genetic factor for a given abnormality does not prove that each person with that genetic predisposition will express the harmful behavior. Conversely, not everyone who shows the harmful behavior does so because of the genetic factor(s) found in research studies. It is useful to distinguish between at least three levels of decreasing knowledge about genetic factors:

1a. Genetic factors are well established, and treatment by diet or other biochemical intervention is available or soon expected. For the moment this is mainly the case for a variety of metabolic abnormalities, most of which lead to mental retardation. Because the treatment is biochemical instead of psychological, we will say little about these disorders.

1b. Genetic factors are well established, but treatment by diet or medicine is not yet available. Here the clinician may be called upon to provide supportive therapy and information but can in most instances do little to slow down or stop the disorder. Examples from adult pathology are Huntington's chorea and Alzheimer's disease.

2. Genetic factors are fairly strongly suggested but are not yet pinpointed. Mood disorders provide an example. As far as clinicians are concerned, this does not differ much from category (1b) above, except that it may be desirable to keep track of advances in research that may affect the patient's future treatment.

3. Genetic factors may be suspected but are not clearly evident. This is the situation as far as most childhood abnormalities are concerned. In fact, for some types of abnormalities, the idea of genetic factors is based mainly on a presumed similarity and hypothesized continuity with an adult form of abnormality. The most extreme example of this is juvenile delinquency. Some childhood behaviors are viewed as possible precursors (and warning signals?) of adult criminality. As we have seen, there is considerable evidence of risk for criminality in children adopted away from their criminal biological fathers. Included in this class of disorders would be those, such as schizophrenia and eating disorders, with a more generally accepted genetic component.

In the case of the class of disorders for which genetic factors are known but treatment is not available (which is likely to grow in number as research proceeds to work out the details of more and more diseases), the implications for psychotherapy are limited but not nonexistent. Supportive therapy for the patient and the family can help moderate the painfulness of the problems. Groups of relatives of patients meet regularly and by sharing information and stress alleviate the pain of many of these conditions. Black and Weiss (1988) note that some of these support groups still lack genetic counseling contacts.

Although many clinicians would not have the time or inclination to provide such genetic counseling, they may need to suggest appropriate sources for such services to their clients. Clinicians may want to consider consultation in order to inform themselves of recent advances in research into the abnormality, including more precise separation of the illness from other conditions. In the case of abnormalities for which a genetic factor is certain or at least likely, the clinician should consider advising the client of the opportunity for genetic counseling. In certain types of cases, the possibility of legal action for neglecting to make such information available is increasing.

In some types of genetic disorders enough information is available in the literature to allow rather accurate prediction about the presence or absence of the abnormal gene by several prenatal diagnostic techniques, such as amniocentesis and fetoscopy. After application of such techniques, the family may face the decision whether or not to terminate the pregnancy. Most persons opting for the diagnostic process would probably also choose termination; if so, they would need supportive therapy, partly in connection with the decision whether or not to attempt to have another baby. In other cases, families may choose to accept the baby with its handicaps and wish to be kept informed of future findings concerning possible interventions and ameliorating treatments. Shaw (1977) has discussed the objectives of genetic counseling (see Table 4).

TABLE 4
Genetic Counseling Objectives

Directed at the affected individual
1. Decrease the pain and suffering of the disease
2. Advise if treatment is possible
3. Quote risk figures for offspring and other relatives
4. Reduce anxiety and guilt
5. Help patient to cope with the affliction
Directed at the parents
1. Help couples make rational decisions about their reproduction
2. Give family planning options to at-risk matings
3. Reduce anxiety and guilt in the parents
4. Educate the parents about the disease in question
5. Encourage couples to make their own decisions
6. Discourage high-risk couples from reproducing
Societal goals
1. Eliminate genetic disease
2. Prevent genetic disease
3. Reduce the incidence of genetic disease
4. Reduce the burden of genetic disease
5. Decrease the frequency of deleterious genes
6. Upgrade awareness of genetics in the public
7. Influence mate selection

Note. From "Review of Published Studies of Genetic Counseling: A Critique" by M. W. Shaw, in *Genetic Counseling* (p. 35), edited by H. A. Lubs and F. de la Cruz, 1977, New York: Raven Press. Copyright 1977 by Raven Press. Reprinted by permission.

Interest in childhood psychopathology and in genetic predisposition to childhood psychiatric problems has developed rather recently. For this reason, there is very little solid information available. As mentioned earlier, the continuity between childhood problems and adult pathology is based mainly on assumptions. Superficial resemblance of the behaviors, plus a conviction that psychopathology must have an insidious onset, form the core of these assumptions. For the somatization, obsessive-compulsive, and depression disorders, the DSM-III uses the same diagnostic criteria for children as for adults. It is interesting to note, however, that although attention deficit disorder may persist beyond childhood, it is not usually diagnosed in adults.

Earls (1987) has reviewed familial transmission of childhood psychopathology and distinguishes two types of studies: "those in which the transmission of psychiatric disorder is observed and those which explore the developmental linkages between childhood and adulthood disorders" (p. 792). He concludes that the specificity of the problems in children of parents with a given psychiatric problem seems not to be high. Could this be because, in addition to the possible "genetic loading," environmental stress is obviously produced by the parental illness? However, such an environmental factor may not always work in the same direction as the genetic factor.

In his review of developmental linkages, Earls notes that more than 50% of the children in prospective studies did not progress to become adult patients. The causes for these favorable outcomes are generally unknown. Because Earls uses the term *spontaneous recovery*, it seem unlikely that he believes the credit should go exclusively to intervention by child guidance clinics or other agencies. The fact is that we know very little about the effects of parenting behaviors. Two general factors have been found repeatedly in studies of self-reported parental behavior: affection-love-warmth versus hostility-rejection-coldness; control-discipline-supervision versus permissiveness-absence of supervision-laxness (Arrindell & van der Ende, 1984). Others have reported three or even four important dimensions of parental practices. The factor of control is frequently split into two: control versus permissiveness and consistency of control versus unpredictability or arbitrariness. A fourth factor, found in a new scale developed in Sweden, appears primarily in mothers' favoritism behavior (Perris, Jacobsson, Lindstrom, von Knorring, & Perris, 1980).

Because accurate measures of parental childrearing practices are important, we have included the Swedish questionnaire (EMBU) as an appendix to this chapter. We want to warn, however, against optimism. It is difficult to observe such behaviors and doubtful that parents can report these things objectively. It is even less likely that retrospective statements by young persons will be valid, unless verifiable by recollections of others.

While one can make some guesses about the possible effects of these parental styles, virtually nothing is known with certainty. In 1967, Vandenberg speculated about possible consequences of three dimensions of parental styles suggested by Schaefer as follows:

> Acceptance and love would lead to easy expression of emotions in children, rejection and hate to blocking of emotional expression. Encouragement of autonomy would lead to development of activity and initiative, control and intrusiveness to dependence and formation of routine habits. Firm control would favor the development of predominantly secondary function, and lax control would not—in fact it might develop opportunism and haphazard behavior. (pp. 73–78)

To our knowledge, there has been no study of parental rearing practices as predictors of children's behaviors and personalities. Ideally one would want to partial out hereditary similarity between parents and children in personality.

Secondary function is one end of a personality dimension, primary versus secondary function. The Dutch psychologist Heymans described this dimension and the other two dimensions, emotionality and activity, in papers published between 1908 and 1932. By emotionality he meant the free expression of feelings and mood rather than unemotional, cold, or overly controlled behavior. By activity he meant sustained effort and achievement rather than nervous activity such as pacing the room or inability to sit still. The primary versus secondary function refers to the length of time an experience or idea stays with a person. The person who devotes a lifetime to one idea as compared to a flighty person who jumps from one idea to another and never finishes a project represent the extremes of this dimension. The ancient Greeks made this distinction when they contrasted one person's mind as hard versus another's as soft. They used this analogy to a surface on which an inscription is made: A hard surface (such as basalt) does not take an impression easily but retains it, whereas a soft surface (such as wax) takes an impression easily but also loses it quickly. Note the similarity to Pavlov's idea of strong versus weak nervous systems.

Some very general recommendations can be made. Clinicians might well consider encouraging the child in order to build up a sense of self-worth and, to the extent possible, of competence in areas besides school achievement. Nurturing the development of artistic, athletic, and social skills, or encouraging some hobbies such as stamp collecting or taking care of an animal or simple carpentry, may be a good thing for any child, whether at risk for a serious mental illness or not. Teachers and parents may be doing this already, but the clinician's assistance could be helpful.

Perhaps the occasional co-occurrence of mental retardation and autism or of MR and psychotic behavior can provide an opening for biochemical and genetic research, which may in time branch out to illnesses in psychiatric patients of normal intelligence. Are the biological causes the same, even though they seem so different phenomenologically?

3. Prevention of Mental Illness

In fact, what we have been talking about for several pages now is prevention, a relatively recent focus in mental illness research (Rickel & Allen, 1987; Steinberg & Silverman, 1987).

One of the main problems here is that, even if we knew the best way to deal with a certain type of behavior "on the average," a particular child may respond in a paradoxical way. A shy boy, for instance, would usually benefit from group participation in an activity that he does well in, so as to increase his sense of competence, self-worth, and self-confidence. Yet some children will rebel against this and become even less confident with strangers. A very serious problem in understanding the causes of depressive conditions is the fact that there appears to be a marked increase in the incidence in recent years, particularly in young persons (Klerman, 1988). This increase is thought to be real and not due to growing awareness of the condition. Uncertainty about the future may contribute to a more frequent incidence of depressive disorders among children and adolescents. Loss of the influence of religion and of faith in political leadership may contribute even further to the stress.

In a recent book entitled *Suicide and Depression Among Adolescents and Young Adults* (Klerman, 1986), several chapter authors come close to discussing prevention by describing risk factors. No one comes out strongly assigning blame to present political and economic conditions; however, unemployment, the threat of nuclear war, and the high frequency of divorce are some of the conditions mentioned. In addition, the alarmingly high frequency of loneliness, imagined or real, is mentioned. This raises the same question again. Can one do something positive about this without evoking resistance and worsening the condition?

We are far from understanding the relationship between, for instance, social class and rates of mental illness. That a person at a low level may have to accept a job with greater physical risks to health is readily apparent, but the reality of greater psychological stress is not so obvious. In fact, many have argued that mental work, as opposed to physical labor, is more risky to one's mental health. Perhaps this is a political question, which cannot be studied objectively. Even raising such a question may be regarded as a subversive act, whether one lives in the USA or in the USSR.

The Dutch sociologist Nijhof (1979) made an ambitious attempt to develop a theory to account for the association between social class and mental illness. In their paper "The Issue of Social Class and Schizophrenia in the Netherlands," Giel, Wiersma, and deJong (1987) refer to that monograph and include a diagram in which they have translated Nijhof's terms into English. We include this diagram here, as Figure 5, to facilitate discussion.

One may summarize Nijhof's views as elaborations of four themes: Social inequality may be interpreted as due to personal defects; social problems may be attributed to personal failures; people are alone in a normless society where personal interest and power determine most actions; and in spite of reasonably comfortable situations, persons view their status relative to others as deprived. Nijhof found only partial support for his own ideas in his empirical study in Rotterdam.

Giel et al. (1987) also subjected Nijhof's ideas to an empirical test and again found only partial support for them. Rather surprisingly, depressive symptoms, unlike schizophrenia, were found to increase with higher social status, so that another process must be invoked. Perhaps there may be a mismatch between an individual's aspirations, demands on the self, and achievements. The person's social status may in that case play a complicated role, depending on whether the individual has moved up or down from the family's social position and whether he or she is in a position at, above, or below the level achieved by others with a similar education or occupation. If that were the case, one would need to know how the person sees his or her social status relative to those with whom he or she might expect to be compared.

Giel et al. (1987) also comment that personality of the individual helps to determine the person's interpretation of the situation. They cite a remark by van Praag (1984) that people who are well off are not happier than those not so well off because it is personality that counts. In their conclusion, Giel et al. favor the downward social mobility explanation over direct social causation as an explanation for the excess incidence of schizophrenia in lower social classes. The implications for intervention are less favorable, because to intervene in an individual's downward slide may be more difficult than to address general social problems that might be found to be more responsive.

The possibility that proper intervention may ameliorate and even prevent mental illness is underscored by the fact that even physical

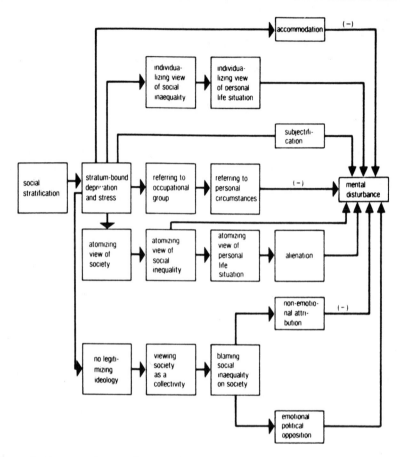

FIGURE 5. From social inequality to psychosocial complaints (free translation from Nijhof, 1979). From "The Issue of Social Class and Schizophrenia in the Netherlands" by R. Giel, D. Wiersma, and A. deJong, in *From Social Class to Social Stress: New Developments in Psychiatric Epidemiology* (p. 67) edited by M. C. Angermeyer, 1987, New York: Springer-Verlag. Copyright 1987 by Springer-Verlag. Reprinted by permission.

illnesses, such as heart conditions and multiple sclerosis, have been shown to be aggravated and in some cases perhaps even brought on by psychological factors. The same is true for typical psychosomatic conditions, such as asthma or hives. That neuroses are in large measure psychological is well known; it may surprise some to learn that movement disorders, from the Tourette syndrome to Huntington's chorea and Parkinson's disease, are also influenced by life events, as documented in chapters in the book *Interface Between Neurology and Psychiatry* (Trimble, 1985).

4. Social and Ethical Problems Raised by the New Genetic Information

What does progress in understanding the role of genetics in shaping intellectual performance contribute to our understanding of environmental influences on behavior? Can behavioral genetics help us to study how social, cultural, and other factors (such as nutrition) relate to intellectual superiority and mental retardation? Such environmental influences are likely to be the major focus of future behavioral genetic research. Clearer understanding of biological and genetic influences will permit carefully controlled study of environmental influences. Ultimately, we should be able to know precisely how particular environmental influences alter a specific genetic predisposition.

Will the finding of genetic influence on behavior result in a deterministic philosophy about life? Not necessarily. It will be a long time before we are able to understand fully the influence of our genes on specific behaviors in given situations. Even when we are able to make such accurate predictions, it is not necessarily true that we will have to resign ourselves to accepting our genetically determined "fate." The point of gaining such knowledge will be the ability to alter a genetic predisposition so that we are more able to develop as we wish. It seems reasonable that we will be able to develop environmental intervention strategies that permit us to begin with almost any combination of genetic characteristics and tailor our intervention (education) strategies so that we will help our children become as capable as possible. Increasing knowledge of the role of genetics in shaping behavior will not lead to passive acceptance of ourselves and our behaviors but will, instead, allow for educated environmental interventions.

What implications does behavioral genetic research have for the control of individuals? In a way, it is possible to use any degree of knowledge as a manipulative tool. To acquire knowledge about the genetic makeup of individuals (i.e., their various strengths and weaknesses), or even to know their IQ scores, might make it possible to take advantage of certain individuals or manipulate them so that their behavior will conform to what is desired by those in power. Such use of knowledge would be frightening. The educated professional must carefully ensure that such a development does not occur. Knowledge capable of improving the quality of life must be sought but must not be used to restrict free development. The only method we know that will ensure that such restriction does not occur is the free and rapid sharing of knowledge and the continual effort to maintain as highly educated a population as possible. In this way, knowledge will not be confined to a few who might use it dangerously but will be available to all to use it wisely.

One does not have to be deeply religious to worry about our growing ability to modify the effects of human genetic abnormalities. Are we eliminating positive side effects as well? For instance, one can think that the need for caring for the handicapped keeps us humane, as well as the possibility that fetuses aborted for some genetic defect might have grown to be unusually competent in some sphere. This might be true not only for physical defects, but occasionally also for mental abnormalities—such as a genetic condition that most of the time leads to mental retardation but occasionally may lead to the development of a special artistic or intellectual giftedness.

These worries are not without historical foundation. They are shared by behavioral geneticists, medical geneticists, genetic counselors, and their critics. Hereditarian views and emphasis on the significance of heredity for human life have often been seen as the ideological basis for a political program. Theories about the inheritance of intelligence and other "noble" traits were understood as an attempt by the aristocracy and the well-to-do to maintain the status quo and to justify the differences in wealth and privilege between themselves and the unwashed masses. The theory of hereditary superiority and inferiority expressed in concepts such as "the nobility" and "the baseborn" relieved the rich of their moral sensibilities and the necessity to consider social reforms. Social Darwinism of the late 19th century expressed these views in the guise of evolutionary theory. In our own century, the marriage of Nazi ideology and eugenics represents the most extreme abuse of hereditary theory, and, even today, genetic issues remain highly sensitive (Elias & Annas, 1987).

The society that supports genetic science hopes for benefits but fears manipulation by those who may gain the power that knowledge confers (Fletcher, 1971). As John Stuart Mill observed long ago, tyranny is limited only by lack of power. One purpose of behavioral genetic research is to expand our capacity to overcome or prevent disabilities that diminish normal development in children and consequently inhibit their growth toward self-determination (Gustaphson, 1973). Some doubt, however, that we are wise enough to conduct genetic research and apply the results without doing harm. In particular, studies of intelligence (IQ), criminality, and aggression, as well as the development of programs for genetic screening, genetic counseling (which assumes the legitimacy of abortion), and other issues related to human reproduction (prenatal diagnosis, surrogate motherhood, in vitro fertilization, etc.), have generated substantial controversy among scientists, physicians, and the general public.

For example, some critics are alarmed by the strong evidence for a genetic component in variations among members of a population in respect to intelligence, cognitive skills, memory, and so on (Kamin, 1974). They fear that the discovery or confirmation of group differences in respect to intelligence or other innate characteristics will be used to justify repressive, racist social policies, and that it will be used to encourage, as so often in the past, ethnic animosities (The *XYY* Controversy, 1980). Some critics argue that the discovery of biological determinants of behavior will produce a disregard for the value and uniqueness of the individual and will even provide justification for destroying the genetically "abnormal" (Ramsey, 1973).

Intervention in the process of reproduction has been the object of special concern, as prenatal diagnosis with its implications for abortion has improved and become more accessible (*Screening and Counseling for Genetic Conditions*, 1983). Genetic screening and genetic counseling have also raised questions about fundamental human values. Accurate, inexpensive biochemical tests have made it possible to conduct mass screening for heterozygous carriers of Tay–Sachs disease and sickle cell anemia. This has made genetic counseling possible for couples who believe that they may be "at risk" for producing offspring with these diseases. In addition, as a public health measure, heterozygous screening programs have been provided to locate carriers of recessive disorders who are themselves asymptomatic. In this way, it is hoped that some people will be able to avoid or prevent giving birth to defective children.

From the outset, the development of prenatal diagnosis made it necessary for physicians, prospective parents, and the community at large to make decisions about reproduction that were moral and nonmedical. Although most babies are born without serious difficulty either for themselves or their mothers, our society, with the enthusiastic help of the medical community, has managed to "medicalize" the reproductive process. The advance of genetic knowledge, genetic screening, and abortion technology, however, has "demedicalized" decision making about abortion and provided choices to parents in respect to the outcome of pregnancy that have hitherto been lacking.

On religious grounds, some persons and groups reject abortion for any reason. Others have feared that genetic screening programs—specifically prenatal diagnosis—will, by their availability, create social pressures to eliminate potentially diseased and handicapped children. It has been argued that social attitudes toward children that "ought not to be born" will induce guilt in the mother who bears a defective child. The willingness to abort a defective fetus has been seen as encouraging callousness toward the mentally retarded and others disabled by various genetic diseases. Some have argued that screening discriminates against the disabled and violates "fetal rights," and that it will eventually reduce our tolerance for imperfection. One ethicist has argued that a willingness to kill a defective fetus *in utero* logically entails a willingness to kill a defective child born alive (Lappe, Gustaphson, & Roblin, 1972; Raynor, 1978).

Other commentators have feared that any form of genetic screening will be coercive in its effect on parents-to-be who discover they are "at risk" for producing an affected child or who learn that the mother is carrying a fetus with some genetic disorder. They believe that such programs may also stigmatize parents who, although they understand the genetic risks, resist the implied constraints on childbearing. Such persons may be seen as "irresponsible." It is also feared that persons identified as carriers of deleterious traits or as genetically affected themselves will be stigmatized by those who do not understand the difference between being a carrier of a trait and having a disease or who do not understand the nature and causes of genetic disease (Lappe *et al.*, 1972; *Screening and Counseling for Genetic Conditions*, 1983). Some critics have worried that prenatal diagnosis and genetic screening may move from their present voluntary status to a legally mandated compulsory program and subsequently be used for eugenic purposes, specifically to "reduce the genetic load of deleterious genes" within the population (Kaback, 1982).

Most of these fears were tempered by the publication in February, 1983, of the report on "Screening and Counseling for Genetic Conditions" by the President's Commission for the Study of Ethical Problems in Medicine and Biomedical and Behavioral Research. The Report represented what now appears to be a consensus about appropriate goals for screening programs, the ethical principles on which they must be based, and the ethical guidelines for their operation. There is now general agreement that the primary goals of prenatal diagnosis are to detect genetic disease, to employ appropriate medical interventions to cure or alleviate its effects wherever possible, and to provide parents with all necessary information for making informed and responsible choices about childbearing. Secondary goals are to reduce the incidence of genetic disease, measure its frequency, and advance our knowledge about it.

The Report emphasizes the voluntary nature of screening programs. It places final moral responsibility on the parents for decisions about the appropriate course of action in the event the diagnosis reveals genetic disease. The Report emphasizes the pluralism of values in our society and argues that respect for individual self-determination requires that no one be coerced or stigmatized for following his or her own moral values. Assuming that it is medically indicated, amniocentesis should be available to those who request it, whether or not they are committed to abort a defective fetus. Respect for persons and their right to be self-determining also requires a full range of counseling prior to and after prenatal diagnosis.

No justification would found for compulsory genetic screening, with the single exception that it could be required to prevent harm to whose who were "defenseless." This is the same reasoning that justifies compulsory vaccination of school children against contagious disease. No persuasive arguments were found for any form of genetic screening as "eugenic" measures (i.e., for reducing the "genetic load" in the total population).

Although some critics of the Report have found its conclusions too cautious (Arras, 1984), it seems that earlier worries about the ethical consequences of prenatal diagnosis and other forms of genetic screening have been dealt with. Ethical standards and guidelines have been spelled out. With reasonable care there seems little likelihood that genetic screening will become mandated by law or that any of these measures can or will be used by government agencies for "eugenic" purposes. Insistence by scientists, the medical profession, the public, and the courts on ethical standards of medical practices that include the requirements of informed consent, full disclosure of diagnostic results, and confidentiality should serve to keep such programs focused on their goals of serving the health needs of parents and their offspring and advancing our knowledge of genetic disease.

5. Other Ethical Issues

Unfortunately, the search for the genetic determinants of aggression and criminality has not produced a similar ethical consensus. The notorious XYY controversy referred to above was generated by publication of prison population studies in Scotland. American investigators undertook screening programs to detect extra Y chromosomes in newborn males. It was their intention to conduct longitudinal studies of extra Y males to determine whether or not this anomaly was a correlate of violent behavior. Political pressure, personal abuse of the investigators by political activists, and methodological criticisms led to the termination of this research program.

The XYY karyotype was widely discussed as a possible genetic determinant of violence before anyone knew the incidence of the extra Y in the general population. The public, the media, lawyers, and judges— sometimes even criminals themselves (presumably for their own purposes)—were willing to believe that the presence of the extra Y chromosome was the genetic correlate of human aggressive and violent behavior ("The *XYY* Controversy," 1980). As suggested above, subsequent studies did not confirm this hypothesis.

Given our history of racial conflict and mutual distrust among races, and the fact that early studies of the anomaly were conducted in prisons and other institutions where a large part of the population was composed of African Americans and other ethnic minorities, it is not surprising that some construed interest in *XYY* research as a political program designed to confirm racist convictions. Although this particular suspicion seems to have been unfounded, other doubts about this research were raised by the fact that the early infant screening programs necessarily entailed difficult problems of combining both experimental and therapeutic considerations. The physician/investigators believed that they had to observe the development of the children and be prepared to undertake appropriate interventions as indicated. The critics claimed that this procedure amounted to a self-fulfilling prophecy or the "Pygmalion effect" between the parents, the newborn, and the researchers. Critics argued further that no experimentally satisfactory criteria were established by which the anticipated behaviors could be measured ("The *XYY* Controversy," 1980).

The belief that aggression and criminality are related to heredity has received additional support in recent years. Various studies of adopted children, their adoptive parents, and their biological parents suggest that genetic factors are among the causes of criminal behavior (Gabrielli & Mednick, 1983, 1984). There is now, in fact, a substantial body of literature supporting the theory that individual differences in the predisposition to commit crime are significantly affected by genetic factors. Despite the growing body of evidence, however, the matter is by no means settled.

Some critics of the effort to discover genetic correlates of criminal behavior reject contemporary research out of hand (Reiber, Bakan, Montagu, & Yeudall, 1980). They argue that it is impossible on the basis of present knowledge to establish a relationship between genes and anything so complex as criminal behavior, however defined. Those who support the genetic hypothesis assert that there is no "criminal gene" and speculate that a predisposition to criminal behavior will be found to be polygenic in origin. They acknowledge the substantial body of research that examines environmental variables involved in criminal behavior etiology (Gabrielli & Mednick, 1984) and generally assume that such etiology is related to gene–environment interactions (Ellis, 1982).

Gabrielli and Mednick argue that their adoption study results have implications for further research, for the attribution of responsibility for criminal acts, and for the prevention of future crimes. It is this last observation that frequently provokes strong emotional response (Reiber *et al.*, 1980). The suggestion that after accurate diagnosis some as-yet-unspecified intervention can be employed to prevent or alter undesirable behavior is often met with suspicion and hostility. Some critics allege that such views ignore the inequities and injustices responsible for many societal ills in favor of blaming the criminal poor for their misfortunes and for behavior regarded as socially deviant (Nassi & Abramovitz, 1976).

Understanding the nature of the genetic contribution to criminal behavior certainly can be expected to lead to systematic attempts (e.g., by "screening") to identify persons "at risk" for criminality, to diagnose antisocial personalities, and thus by "early detection" to prevent crime, possibly by altering the "at risk" person's environment or just possibly by altering the person. Interventions could include alteration of a neurochemical condition through the administration of drugs, a nutritional condition through dietary change (e.g., Dorfman, 1984), or even a conscious condition through psychosurgery. As discussed by Quarton (1967), he and Skinner are among those who have called for and predicted the inevitable social acceptance of these technological possibilities. Gabrielli and Mednick (1983) argue for "benign and effective intervention strategies," with the informed consent of the subject. They write, "It is clear that a better understanding of the biological processes and social-environmental influences on crime someday may permit slight restructuring of a child's development (in a positive way) so that the contingencies in favor of criminal behavior are minimized" (p. 71).

This approach raises a number of interesting ethical questions. For example, whose values will determine the "restructuring" of a child's development? At least part of the negative reaction to proposals for crime prevention through the identification and treatment of persons "at risk" for criminal behavior rises from the sorry history of past efforts to establish the heritability of criminality. Nineteenth-century theories about "moral imbeciles," persons who lacked the power to refrain from evildoing and whose moral incapacity was thought to have a physiological basis, probably did untold harm to mentally retarded persons (Scheerenberger, 1983).

In the light of history, it is doubtful that all of us will be wise enough to respect the profound variability among persons, a variability that some are inclined to regard as mere idiosyncrasy and eccentricity. We are at least as likely as our predecessors to fail to recognize the impact of our values on science and the technology that it generates. This is the basis for the claim that the use of science and technology to identify and control the behavior of persons "at risk" for criminality will be on behalf of the established power structure.

We may perhaps ask whether we should continue to accept the

recommendation that "criminal behavior" or "convictions for crimes against property" should be regarded in the same way as "polio" or "measles." Although this is by no means a new idea, is it appropriate to think that such behaviors are the same as, or at least similar to, contagious diseases, such that therapeutic interventions can be administered either voluntarily or involuntarily both for the good of the child and for the protection of society? Employing a medical model (i.e., treating crime as a "disease") suggests strong justification for preventive therapeutic interventions similar to the mandatory vaccinations of school children against contagion.

In the present state of knowledge, however, the medical model of disease can, at most, serve as a metaphor. Understanding criminality in this way tends to focus attention entirely on the criminal or potential criminal and obscures the role that social and economic status are acknowledged to play in contributing to criminal behavior. It permits those inclined to do so to deny societal responsibility for conditions also believed to be conducive to criminality, and thereby eases our conscience in respect to disparities and inequities in the social, economic, and justice systems. The "contagious disease" concept suggests the necessity for "treatment" of the criminal and only occasionally for social reform.

In this connection, we may question whether it makes moral sense to convert "criminal behavior" to behavior that is considered merely "sick." In other words, should we "medicalize" criminal acts and, thereby, relieve the criminal of moral responsibility? If the child's developmental process is restructured, and if the child commits a crime anyway, would those who did the restructuring be morally and perhaps legally accountable for "developmental malpractice"? It is possible that positive restructuring of the child's developmental process might have unanticipated effects other than "minimizing the contingencies in favor of criminal behavior." Physicians call them "side effects," but this euphemism sometimes understates their potential seriousness.

Can a person who is genetically predisposed to commit crimes be held accountable for his or her acts? In general, we do not now hold the mentally incompetent and minor children morally responsible for their actions. Should those genetically predisposed to crime be added to this group? The concept of a genetic predisposition to commit crimes, however defined, raises questions about one's moral responsibility for one's own behavior. Every person faces choices associated with society's demand for morally restrained behavior. In our society this is behavior characterized by respect for the person and property of others. For those who are genetically "predisposed" to criminality, these choices become matters of chemistry, biology, and therapy.

We suggest that being "at risk" for criminal behavior is not the same thing as being "at risk" for cancer. By virtue of their family history, persons in the latter category are well advised to undergo certain diagnostic tests from time to time. This would be merely prudent, and would bear no stigma. But what can be said of children diagnosed as being "at risk" for criminal behavior? Will they be stigmatized by preventive, therapeutic interventions? What sort of monitoring over time would restructuring of the child's development require? It seems doubtful that such persons could escape the stigma of being labeled potential social deviants. Furthermore, if we accept respect for persons as our moral duty, we may not assume that any particular person "at risk" will commit a crime. Unless it could be established with a very high degree of certainty that a particular child would commit crime (i.e., the kind of certainty associated with Trisomy 21 or PKU, where diagnosis predicts outcome with a high degree of certainty), the fact that a child's biological parents showed evidence of criminality can never serve as justification for preventive therapeutic intervention or discrimination or incarceration in the absence of an overt criminal act by the child.

Just as this society has come to reject the irrelevant criteria of race and sex as the basis for discriminating between individuals and groups, the commitment to justice and fairness prevents discrimination and disregard for personal autonomy on the basis of a person's genetic heritage. Each person must be judged on his or her own merit. It has been our ideal and persistent intuition, if not our consistent practice, to hold people capable of rational thought morally and legally accountable for their own behavior and innocent until guilt for criminal acts has been established beyond a reasonable doubt. Only if we were to change our values (i.e., designate the control of socially deviant behavior as a higher value than our respect for persons and their autonomy) and only if we were to accept finally the medical model or medical metaphor of criminality as "disease" and criminal behavior as evidence of "sickness" could we justify preventive, therapeutic interventions in the child's developmental process.

These observations should not be taken to mean that research on the genetic factors contributing to variations in behavior ought not to be done. It seems obvious that we need to know all we can about the effects of genes on behavior. On the other hand, we have adequate reasons not to be sanguine about how such knowledge may be used, and we must recognize that its use will be shaped by our values. The inherent danger of establishing, perhaps inadvertently, a "therapeutic tyranny" suggests that considerable caution should guide any prospective applications of the evidence that genetic factors contribute to certain kinds of criminal behavior in some persons.

6. Conclusions

Human genetic research, genetic counseling, and prenatal diagnosis all provide insight into human behavior. To some extent, they also provide the knowledge necessary to manipulate or redirect it. Scientists and physicians who participate in these activities, therefore, need to be ethically sensitive to the human needs of those under study. Identification of genetic anomalies and genetic disorders always raises the possibility of stigmatizing the individual—causing him or her loss of privacy, making it impossible to get a job, or even, when the identification occurs in childhood, becoming a self-fulfilling prophecy. For these reasons, personal autonomy, confidentiality, informed consent, fairness, equity, and scientific accuracy must be regarded as the highest values. These values must be taken into account in our efforts to apply what we have learned about genetic contributions to human behavior.

Appendix: The Specific Scales of the EMBU, Their Respective Items, and Coding Alternatives* for Each Item

Item No.

5	My parents refused to speak to me for a long time if I had done anything silly.	1	2	3	4
6	It happened that my parents punished me even for small offenses.	1	2	3	4
9	I think that either of my parents wished I had been different in any way.	1	2	3	4
16	I felt that my parents liked my brother(s) and/or sister(s) more than they liked me.	1	2	3	4
17	My parents treated me unjustly (badly) in comparison with how they treated my sister(s) and/or brother(s).	1	2	3	4
19	It happened that as a child I was beaten or scolded in the presence of others.	1	2	3	4
23	It happened that my parents gave me more corporal punishment than I deserved.	1	2	3	4
24	My parents would become angry if I did not help at home with what I was asked to do.	1	2	3	4

*The coding answer alternatives are: "No, never" (1); "Yes, but seldom" (2); "Yes, often" (3); and "Yes, most of the time" (4).

28	It happened that my parents narrated something I had said or done in front of others so that I felt ashamed.	1	2	3	4
33	I was treated as the "black sheep" or "scapegoat" of the family.	1	2	3	4
34	It happened that my parents wished I had been like somebody else.	1	2	3	4
37	I felt my parents thought it was my fault when they were unhappy.	1	2	3	4
44	I think my parents were mean and grudging towards me.	1	2	3	4
55	It happened that I was punished by my parents without having done anything.	1	2	3	4
57	My parents said that they did not approve of my behavior at home.	1	2	3	4
59	My parents criticized me and told me how lazy and useless I was in front of others.	1	2	3	4
61	Of my sister(s) or brother(s), I was the one whom my parents blamed if anything bad happened.	1	2	3	4
63	My parents were abrupt to me.	1	2	3	4
64	My parents would punish me hard, even for trifles.	1	2	3	4
65	It happened that my parents beat me for no reason.	1	2	3	4
68	I got beaten by my parents.	1	2	3	4
71	My parents treated me in such a way that I felt ashamed.	1	2	3	4
72	My parents let my sister(s) and/or brother(s) have things that I was not allowed to get.	1	2	3	4
76	It happened that my parents were sour or angry with me without letting me know the cause.	1	2	3	4
77	I happened that my parents let me go to bed without food.	1	2	3	4

Emotional Warmth

| 2 | My parents showed with words and gestures that they liked me. | 1 | 2 | 3 | 4 |

13	If I had done something foolish, I could then go to my parents and make everything right again by asking their forgiveness.	1	2	3	4
21	If things went badly for me, I then felt that my parents tried to comfort and encourage me.	1	2	3	4
27	I felt that it was difficult to approach my parents.	1	2	3	4
31	My parents showed that they were interested in my getting good marks.	1	2	3	4
32	If I had a difficult task in front of me, I then felt support from my parents.	1	2	3	4
39	My parents would demonstrate that they were fond of me.	1	2	3	4
41	I think that my parents respected my opinions.	1	2	3	4
43	I felt that my parents wanted to be together with me.	1	2	3	4
47	I think that my parents tried to make my adolescence stimulating, interesting, and instructive (for instance by giving me good books, arranging for me to go on camps, taking me to clubs).	1	2	3	4
48	My parents praised me.	1	2	3	4
54	I could seek comfort from my parents if I was sad.	1	2	3	4
56	My parents allowed me to do the same things as my friends did.	1	2	3	4
67	My parents engaged themselves in my interests and hobbies.	1	2	3	4
74	I felt that warmth and tenderness existed between me and my parents.	1	2	3	4
75	My parents respected the fact that I had other opinions than they had.	1	2	3	4
78	I felt that my parents were proud when I succeeded in something I had undertaken.	1	2	3	4
81	My parents bugged me.	1	2	3	4

Overprotection

| 1 | I felt that my parents interfered with everything I did. | 1 | 2 | 3 | 4 |

7	My parents tried to influence me to become something "posh."	1	2	3	4
14	My parents wanted to decide how I should be dressed or how I should look.	1	2	3	4
18	It happened that either of my parents forbade me to do things other children were allowed to do because they were afraid that something might happen to me.	1	2	3	4
20	My parents cared about what I did in the evenings.	1	2	3	4
25	My parents would look sad or in any other way show that I had behaved badly so that I got real feelings of guilt.	1	2	3	4
36	My parents criticized the friends I liked to frequent.	1	2	3	4
38	My parents tried to spur me to become the best.	1	2	3	4
45	My parents used expressions like: "If you do that you will make me sad."	1	2	3	4
46	When I came home, I then always had to account for what I had been doing to my parents.	1	2	3	4
51	It happened that I got a bad conscience towards my parents because I behaved in a way they did not desire.	1	2	3	4
52	I think that my parents put high demands on me when it came to school marks, sport performances, or similar things.	1	2	3	4
66	It happened that I wished my parents would worry less about what I was doing.	1	2	3	4
69	I was allowed to go where I liked without my parents caring too much.	1	2	3	4
70	My parents put decisive limits for what I was and was not allowed to do to which they then adhered rigorously.	1	2	3	4
73	I think that my parents' anxiety that something might happen to me was exaggerated.	1	2	3	4

Favoring Subject

3	I was spoiled by my parents in comparison to my sister(s) and/or brother(s).	1	2	3	4
10	My parents let me have things my sister(s) and/or brother(s) were not allowed to have.	1	2	3	4
29	I felt that my parents liked me more than they liked my sister(s) and/or brother(s).	1	2	3	4
79	My parents favored me in relation to my sister(s) and/or brother(s).	1	2	3	4
80	My parents took my part against my sister(s) and/or brother(s) even if I was the guilty one.	1	2	3	4

7. References

Achenbach, T. M. (1986). *Child Behavior Checklist for Ages 2–3*. Burlington: University of Vermont.

Achenbach, T. M., & Edelbrock, C. S. (1978). The classification of child psychopathology: A review and analysis of empirical efforts. *Psychological Bulletin, 85*, 1275–1301.

Achenbach, T. M., & Edelbrock, C. S. (1981). Behavioral problems and competencies reported by parents of normal and disturbed children aged four to sixteen. *Monographs of the Society for Research in Child Development, 46*(1, Serial No. 188).

Arras, J. D. (1984). Toward an ethic of ambiguity. *The Hastings Center Report, 14*, 25–33.

Arrindell, W. A., & van der Ende, J. (1984). Replicability and invariance of dimensions of parental rearing behaviour: Further Dutch experiences with the EMBU. *Personality and Individual Differences, 5*, 671–682.

Baron, M., Risch, N., Hamburger, R., Mandel, B., Kushner, S., Newman, M., Drumer, D., & Belmaker, R. H. (1987). Genetic linkage between X-chromosome markers and bipolar affective illness. *Nature, 326*, 289–292.

Bernard, J. S. (1972). *The future of marriage*. New York: World Publishers.

Black, R. B., & Weiss, J. O. (1988). A professional partnership with genetic support groups. *American Journal of Medical Genetics, 29*, 21–33.

Christiansen, K. O. (1968). Threshold of tolerance in various population groups illustrated by results from a Danish criminological twin study. In A. V. S. Reuck & R. Porter (Eds.), *The mentally abnormal offender*. Boston: Little, Brown.

Christiansen, K. O. (1977). A review of studies of criminality among twins. In S. A. Mednick & K. O. Christiansen (Eds.), *Biosocial bases of criminal behavior*. New York: Gardner.

Cloninger, C. R. (1986). A unified biosocial theory of personality and its role in the development of anxiety states. *Psychiatric Developments, 3*, 167–226.

Cloninger, C. R. (1987a). Neurogenetic adaptive mechanisms in alcoholism. *Science, 236*, 410–416.

Cloninger, C. R. (1987b). A systematic method for clinical description and classification of personality variants. *Archives of General Psychiatry, 44,* 573–588.

Cornblatt, B., & Erlenmeyer-Kimling, L. (1985). Global attention deviance as a marker of risk for schizophrenia: Specificity and predictive validity. *Journal of Abnormal Psychology, 94,* 470.

Costa, P. T., Jr., & McCrae, R. R. (1985). *The NEO Personality Inventory manual.* Odessa, FL: Psychological Assessment Resources.

Digman, J. M., & Inouye, J. (1986). Further specification of the five robust factors of personality. *Journal of Personality and Social Psychology, 50,* 116–123.

Dohrenwend, B. P., Levay, I., Shrout, P. E., Link, B. G., Skodol, A. E., & Martin, J. L. (1987). Life stress and psychopathology: Progress on research begun with Barbara Snell Dohrenwend. *American Journal of Community Psychology, 15,* 677–715.

Dorfman, A. (1984). The criminal mind: Body chemistry and nutrition may lie at the roots of crime. *Science Digest, 44,* 47, 98.

Earls, F. (1987). On the familial transmission of child psychiatric disorder. *Journal of Child Psychology and Psychiatry, 28,* 791–802.

Egeland, J. A., Gerhard, D. S., Pauls, D. L., Sussex, J. N., Kidd, K. K., Allen, C. R., Hostetter, A. M., & Housman, D. E. (1987). Bipolar affective disorders linked to DNA markers on chromosome 11. *Nature, 325,* 783–787.

Elias, S., & Annas, G. J. (1987). *Reproductive genetics and the law.* Chicago: Year Book Medical Publishers.

Ellis, L. (1982). Genetics and criminal behavior: Evidence through the end of the 1970's. *Criminology, 20,* 43–66.

Erlenmeyer-Kimling, L., & Cornblatt, B. (1987). The New York High-Risk Project: A followup report. *Schizophrenia Bulletin, 13,* 451–462.

Erlenmeyer-Kimling, L., Marcuse, Y., Cornblatt, B., Friedman, D., Rainer, J. D., & Rutschmann, J. (1987). The New York High Risk Project. In N. F. Watt, E. J. Anthony, L. C. Wynne, & J. E. Rolf (Eds.), *Children at risk for schizophrenia: A longitudinal perspective.* New York: Cambridge University Press.

Eysenck, H. J. (1977). *Crime and personality* (3rd ed.). London: Granada.

Eysenck, H. J. (1981). *A model for personality.* Berlin: Springer-Verlag.

Fischer, M. (1971). Psychoses in the offspring of schizophrenic monozygotic twins and their normal cotwins. *British Journal of Psychiatry, 118,* 43–52.

Fletcher, J. (1971). Ethical aspects of genetic controls: Designed changes in man. *New England Journal of Medicine, 285,* 776–783.

Fraser, F. C., & Sadovnick, A. D. (1976). Correlation of IQ in subjects with Down Syndrome and their parents and sibs. *Journal of Mental Deficiency Research, 20,* 179–182.

Fuller, R. N., & Shuman, J. B. (1974). Genetic divergence in relatives of PKU's: Low IQ correlation among normal siblings. *Developmental Psychobiology, 7,* 323–330.

Gabrielli, W. F., & Mednick, S. A. (1983). Genetic correlates of criminal behavior: Implications for research, attribution and prevention. *American Behavioral Scientist, 27,* 59–74.

Gabrielli, W. F., & Mednick, S. A. (1984). Urban environment, genetics and crime. *Criminology, 22,* 645–652.

Giel, R., Wiersma, D., & deJong, A. (1987). The issue of social class and schizophrenia in the Netherlands. In M. C. Angermeyer (Ed.), *From social class to social stress: New developments in psychiatric epidemiology.* New York: Springer-Verlag.

Golding, J. M. (1988). Gender differences in depression symptoms: Statistical considerations. *Psychology of Women Quarterly, 12,* 61–74.

Gottesman, I. I., & Shields, J. (1972). *Schizophrenia and genetics: A twin study vantage point.* New York: Academic Press.

Gottesman, I. I., & Shields, J. (1982). *Schizophrenia: The epigenetic puzzle.* New York: Cambridge University Press.

Gray, J. A. (1983). Anxiety, personality and the brain. In H. Gale & J. A. Edwards (Eds.), *Physiological correlates of human behavior*. New York: Academic Press.

Gustaphson, J. M. (1973). Genetic engineering and the normative view of the human. In P. N. Williams (Ed.), *Ethical issues in biology and medicine*. Cambridge, MA: Schenkman.

Heymans, G. (1908). Uber einige psychische Korrelationen. *Zeitschrift fur angewandte Psychologie, 1*, 313–381.

Heymans, G. (1932). *Inleiding tot de speciale psychologie*. Bohn: Haarlem.

Kaback, M. M. (1982). The control of genetic disease by carrier screening and antenatal diagnosis: Social, ethical, and medicolegal issues. *Birth Defects: Original Article Series, 18*, 243–254.

Kamin, L. J. (1974). *The science and politics of IQ*. Potomac, MD: Erlbaum.

Kety, S. S., Rosenthal, D., Wender, P. H., Schulsinger, F., & Jacobsen, B. (1975). Mental illness in the biological and adoptive families of adopted individuals who have become schizophrenic. In R. R. Fieve, D. Rosenthal, & H. Brill (Eds.), *Genetic research in psychiatry*. Baltimore: The Johns Hopkins University Press.

Klerman, G. L. (Ed.). (1986). *Suicide and depression among adolescents and young adults*. Washington, DC: American Psychiatric Press.

Klerman, G. L. (1988). The current age of young melancholia: Evidence for increase in depression among adolescents and young adults. *British Journal of Psychiatry, 152*, 4–14.

Lappe, M., Gustaphson, J. M., & Roblin, R. (1972). Ethical and social issues in screening for genetic disease. *New England Journal of Medicine, 286*, 1129–1132.

Lyon, M. F. (1961). Gene action in the X-chromosome of the mouse (*Mus. musculus L.*). *Nature, 190*, 372–373.

McCrae, R. R., & Costa, P. T., Jr. (1984). *Emerging lives, enduring dispositions: Personality in adulthood*. Boston: Little, Brown.

McCrae, R. R., & Costa, P. T., Jr. (1987). Validation of the five factor model of personality across instruments and observers. *Journal of Personality and Social Psychology, 52*, 81–90.

McKusick, V. A. (1987). *Mendelian inheritance in man: Catalogs of autosomal dominant, autosomal recessive, and X-linked phenotypes* (7th ed.). Baltimore: The Johns Hopkins University Press.

Mendlewicz, J., Simon, P., Sevy, S., et al. (1987). Polymorphic DNA marker on X-chromosome and manic-depression. *Lancet (1)*, 1230–1232.

Nassi, A. J., & Abramovitz, S. I. (1976). From phrenology to psychosurgery and back again: Biological studies of criminality. *American Journal of Orthopsychiatry, 46*, 591–607.

Nijhof, G. (1979). *Sociale ongelijkheid en psychiesche storingen* (Social inequality and psychic disturbances). Nijmegen: Link.

Noller, P., & Law, H. (1987). Cattell, Comrey, and Eysenck personality factors compared: More evidence for the five robust factors? *Journal of Personality and Social Psychology, 53*, 775–782.

Norman, W. T. (1963). Toward an adequate taxonomy of personality attributes: Replicated factor structure in peer nomination personality ratings. *Journal of Abnormal and Social Psychology, 66*, 574–583.

Perris, C., Jacobsson, L., Lindstrom, H., von Knorring, L., & Perris, H. (1980). Development of a new inventory for assessing memories of parental rearing behaviour. *Acta Psychiatrica Scandinavica, 61*, 265–274.

van Praag, C. (1984). Cited in: R. Veenhoven (Ed.), *Betere wereld, gelukkiger mensen* (Better world, happier people). *Swets en Zeitlinger Lisse* (pp. 70–71).

Quarton, G. C. (1967). Deliberate efforts to control human behavior and modify personality. *Daedalus, 96*, 837–853.

Ramsey, P. (1973). Screening: An ethicist's view. In B. Hilton, D. Callahan, M. Harris, P.

Condliffe, & B. Berkley (Eds.), *Ethical issues in human genetics* (pp. 147–167). New York: Plenum Press.

Raynor, C. (1978). Genetic screening. *Journal of the Royal Society of Medicine, 71,* 849–851.

Reiber, R. W., Bakan, D., Montagu, A., & Yeudall, L. I. (1980). Human nature, crime, and society: Panel discussion. *Annals of the New York Academy of Sciences, 347,* 356–364.

Rickel, A. U., & Allen, L. R. (1987). *Preventing maladjustment from infancy through adolescence.* New York: Sage.

Scheerenberger, R. C. (1983). *A history of mental retardation.* Baltimore: Brookes.

Screening and counseling for genetic conditions: A report on the ethical, social, and legal implications of genetic screening, counseling, and education programs (February, 1983). Washington, DC: President's Commission for the Study of Ethical Problems in Medicine and Biomedical and Behavioral Research.

Shaw, M. W. (1977). Review of published studies of genetic counseling: A critique. In H. A. Lubs & F. de la Cruz (Eds.), *Genetic counseling* (pp. 35–52). New York: Raven Press.

Steinberg, J. A., & Silverman, M. M. (1987). *Preventing mental disorders: A research perspective* (DHHS Publication No. ADM 87-1492). Washington, DC: U.S. Department of Health and Human Services.

Trimble, (1985). *Interface between neurology and psychiatry.* New York: Karger.

Tupes, E. C., & Christal, R. E. (1961). *Recurrent personality factors based on trait ratings* (USAF ASD Technical Report No 61-97). Lackland Air Force Base, TX: U.S. Air Force.

Vandenberg, S. G. (1967). Hereditary factors in normal personality traits (as measured by inventories). In J. Wortis (Ed.), *Recent advances in biological psychiatry* (Vol. 9, pp. 65–104). New York: Plenum Press.

Vandenberg, S. G., & Ho, H.-Z. (1988). Mental retardation due to the fragile X chromosome. Manuscript submitted for publication.

Vandenberg, S. G., Singer, S. M., & Pauls, D. L. (1986). *The heredity of behavior disorders in adults and children.* New York: Plenum Press.

Vandenberg, S. G., & Vogler, G. P. (1985). Genetic determinants of intelligence. In B. B. Wolman (Ed.), *Handbook of intelligence* (pp. 3–57). New York: Wiley.

Vogel, F., & Motulsky, A. G. (1986). *Human genetics: Problems and approaches* (2nd, completely revised ed.). New York: Springer-Verlag.

The XYY controversy: Researching violence and genetics (1980). *Hastings Center Report, 10:* Special Supplement.

Yunis, J. J. (1976). High resolution of human chromosomes. *Science, 191,* 1268–1270.

Zuckerman, M., Kuhlman, D. M., & Camac, C. (1988). What lies beyond E and N? Factor analyses of scales believed to measure basic dimensions of personality. *Journal of Personality and Social Psychology, 54,* 96–107.

7 Obesity of Infancy and Early Childhood

A Diagnostic Schema

Joseph L. Woolston and Brian Forsyth

1. Introduction

Considerable attention has been focused on the eating disorders of early childhood that result in growth failure, such as failure to thrive syndrome and rumination. In contrast, the eating disorders that result in excessive weight gain have been virtually ignored. DSM-III-R has reinforced this prejudice by refusing to classify any form of obesity as an eating disorder (American Psychiatric Association, 1987). Instead, it describes obesity as a physical disorder. As a result of this lack of interest in obesity of early childhood, there are many widely held misconceptions about its etiology, course, and even heterogeneity of subtypes. The state of clinical ignorance about the fundamentals of infantile obesity makes a scientific strategy for intervention difficult.

The first step in the elucidation of any new field of study is an operational definition that is universally accepted and phenomenologically accurate. In the study of obesity, there must be an easy, accurate, reliable method of defining the clinical condition. Because obesity implies being excessively fat, the operational definition must differentiate the condition of having excessive adipose tissue for chronological age from simply being heavy for chronological age. Triceps skinfold thickness (Garn & Clark, 1976) and an obesity index using weight gain, suprailiac skin fold, and waist circumference (Crawford, Keller, Hampton, Pacheco, & Huenemann, 1974) are two well-standardized measure-

Joseph L. Woolston • Child Study Center, Yale University School of Medicine, New Haven, Connecticut 06510. Brian Forsyth • Department of Pediatrics, Yale University School of Medicine, New Haven, Connecticut 06510.

ments that appear to satisfy the requirements for a useful, operational definition of obesity. A simpler, if slightly less valid, definition of obesity is exceeding 120% of ideal body weight for height (IBWH) for a given age and sex. IBWH is calculated by dividing actual weight by the expected weight for a given age and sex and height percentile.

2. Natural History of Infantile-Onset Obesity

2.1. Developmental Evolution

The study of the natural history of obesity in infancy and early childhood is in its beginning stages. Data about the typical course of this disorder are contradictory. The most widely held belief is that obesity of early onset is a chronic and steadily progressive disorder with very few remissions. Thirty-six percent of infants who exceeded the 90th percentile in weight were reported to be overweight as adults, as opposed to 14% of average or lightweight infants (Charney, Chamblee, McBride, Lyon, & Pratt, 1976). Eid (1970) found that infants who were gaining weight rapidly were four times more likely to be obese by age 8 than infants who were gaining weight at a normal rate. This grim prognosis has been buttressed by a network of theory and experimental data about fat-cell proliferation in early childhood and its deleterious impact on appetite and weight gain later in life.

More recent workers (Shapiro et al., 1984; Poskitt, 1980), however, have reported that obesity in infancy is a poorer predictor of obesity later in childhood than was believed previously. Poskitt (1980) showed that the relative risk of an overfat infant becoming an overfat 5-year-old was about 2.5 times that for a normal infant. Of 203 children, 40% were overweight (≥ 110% IBW) or obese (≥ 120% IBW) as infants. By age 5 years, 13.5% were overweight, and 2.5% were obese. Most overweight infants did not become overweight children, but 60% of the 27 overweight 5-year-olds also were overweight in infancy. Poskitt's findings indicate that fatness in infancy leads to an increased chance of fatness in early childhood, but this risk is less than was thought previously. Shapiro et al. (1984) studied 450 6-month-old infants whom they followed for 8½ years. They found that of the 26 children (17 boys and 9 girls) who were obese at 6 months, fewer and fewer remained obese at subsequent annual measurements, until only one remained obese at 9 years. In contrast, infants who were not obese at 6 months but who later became obese at ages 4 to 8 years were much more likely to be obese at 9 years.

This rather poor correlation between obesity in infancy and obesity in later childhood begins to call into question the notion of relentlessly progressive obesity that is triggered by fat-cell proliferation in infancy or early childhood. Rather than there being a critical phase in infancy for fat-cell proliferation, it is more likely that the degree and duration of obesity are the major determinants of total adipose cell number in humans (Kirtland & Gurr, 1979; Knittle, Timmers, Ginsberg-Fellner, Brown, & Katz, 1979). Poskitt (1980) reported that very little multiplication of adipose cells takes place in infancy. At birth, the weight of fat in the term infant is about 560 grams. By 1 year, this has increased to 2,400 grams. Over the same period, the mean weight of lipid in each adipose cell increases fom 0.12 µg to 0.50 µg. The natural increase in size of those adipose cells present at birth is sufficient to account for almost all of the increase in fat stored in the first year without any increase in cell number.

2.2. Epidemiology and Social Factors

The incidence and prevalence of obesity in early childhood is not nearly as well studied as obesity in adulthood. The few studies that have been reported indicate that the prevalence rate of obesity is 5% to 10% of preschool-aged children (Maloney & Klykylo, 1983). Occasionally, "epidemics" of infantile obesity have been reported with prevalence rates of 16.7% of infants under 12 months of age (Shukla, Forsyth, Anderson, & Marwah, 1972). These epidemics appear to be caused by culturally determined misinformation or fads about infant feeding practices (Shukla et al., 1972; Taitz, 1971). The well-publicized and best-documented epidemic occurred in England between 1960 and 1975 (Taitz, 1977). At this time, English parents were encouraged to follow the maxim that "One cannot overfeed a young baby." Parents commonly used full cream milk powder with added sucrose as baby formula. In many parts of England, mothers were encouraged to introduce solids at a very early stage. By 1973, the dangers of infantile obesity and hypertonic dehydration were well publicized. Between 1971 and 1976, the percentage of 6-week-old infants being fed unmodified milk powder went from 90 to 0, and the percentage of infants above the 50th percentile in weight went from 79 to 43 (Taitz, 1977). In a closely analogous fashion, nonorganic failure to thrive has been reported to occur as a result of parental misconceptions about diet (Woolston, 1983; Pugliese, Weyman-Daum, Moses, & Lifshitz, 1987).

Obesity appears to be related to cultural practices, since it covaries with social class. Obesity in females is nine times more common in social classes III and IV than in social classes I and II (Stunkard, d'Aquill, Fox,

& Filion, 1972). The prevalence of obesity is linked to the socioeconomic status of the parents almost as strongly as it is to the subject's own social class (Goldblatt, Moore, & Stunkard, 1965). This finding argues that socioeconomic status is linked to obesity in a casual rather than a simple associative manner.

2.3. Genetic/Familial Factors

A family-line analysis of obesity indicates that there is a strong correlation between the fatness of parents and that of their children. For example, by age 17, the children of obese parents have three times the chance of being obese as the children of lean parents. If one sibling is fat, there is a 40% chance that a second sibling will be fat (Garn & Clark, 1976). If two siblings are fat, there is an 80% chance that the third sibling will be fat. Although these data seem to support a genetic basis for obesity, one must keep other nongenetic, but family-related, factors in mind. The same study that reported the sibling data indicates that, if one spouse is fat, there is a 30% chance that the other spouse also will be fat (Garn & Clark, 1976). Obviously, this finding cannot be explained by genetic factors.

The familial factors related to infantile obesity are less clear. Poskitt (1980) reported that there was no significant difference between the number of overweight and normal-weight infants with one or both parents overweight. But by 5 years of age, 78% of the overweight and only 35% of the normal-weight children had at least one parent overweight. This was a significant difference and showed that the relative risk of a child's being overweight with at least one parent overweight was more than five times that of a child with two normal-weight parents.

2.4. Organic Factors

One of the primary foci of clinicians who are exploring the etiology of infantile obesity is the discovery of specific organic dysfunctions that produce endogenous obesity. This endogenous form of obesity is in contradistinction to exognous obesity, in which there is no physical dysfunction other than consuming an excess caloric intake. Endogenous forms are caused by discrete genetic, endocrinological or neurological syndromes, including Praeder Willi, Klinefelter's, Frohlich's, Lawrence Mood Biedl, Klein–Levin, and Mauriac syndromes. Although these organic causes of obesity frequently are searched for as an etiology for obesity in early childhood, they are quite rare. One way to distinguish between exogenous and endogenous obesity is to remember that children with endogenous obesity usually are below the 25th percentile in height and have delayed bone age, whereas children with exogenous obesity are above the 50th percentile in height and have an advanced bone age.

2.5. Psychogenic Factors

The results of studies of psychopathology in obese adults have been as contradictory as those in other areas. Although many authors have reported no objective data indicating an increased incidence of psychopathology in obese adolescents and adults (McCance, 1961; Shipman & Plesset, 1963), other authors such as Bruch (1973) and Stunkard (1975) have reported just the opposite. Silverstone (1969) attempted to reconcile these discrepant reports by differentiating between late-onset obesity secondary to a gradual accumulation of fat and early-onset obesity characterized by a sudden increase in fatness resulting from anxiety-driven overeating. Very little is known about psychopathology in infantile obesity. In one of the few reports about this problem, Kahn (1973) described a sample of 73 obese children less than 3 years old. He found that 32% of these young children showed a sudden weight gain associated with a major and traumatic separation from their primary caretakers. This report is suggestive of a discrete syndrome related to traumatic separation that results in a sudden onset of obesity. The following case example will illustrate this syndrome:

> J.L. was a 3-year, 9-month-old boy who had gained 9.1 kg in the two months before he was brought to the gastroenterology clinic. By the time he was 4 years old, he weighed 43 kg, which is the 50th percentile for a 12½-year-old-boy (Fig. 1). His history was negative for family history of obesity or pertinent illnesses. His mother reported that his weight gain began immediately upon his return from a 2-month separation from her.
>
> His medical evaluation revealed no endocrine, metabolic, neurological, or gastrointestinal disorders. His rapidly accelerating weight gain was explained fully by his enormous caloric intake. He consumed 3,700 kilocalories/day, whereas only 1,700 kilocalories were required to maintain his weight.
>
> He presented as a sad-appearing, slow-moving boy with a dejected and mistrustful mood. Despite his depressed appearance, he was able to form a therapeutic relationship rapidly. His play was characterized by a preoccupation with eating and cooking food and fixing broken things. In his play, eating was the only thing that could alleviate his anger, sadness, and anxiety. Twice-weekly psychotherapy improved his mood, and his weight stopped increasing as rapidly. However, after several months, his mother felt overwhelmed with his care. She became depressed and even more emotionally unavailable to him. Once again, his weight began to increase.
>
> As a result of these developments, his mother voluntarily placed him in a therapeutic foster home. He required several weeks to adjust to this foster home and to longing for his mother. In therapy, he then was able to describe

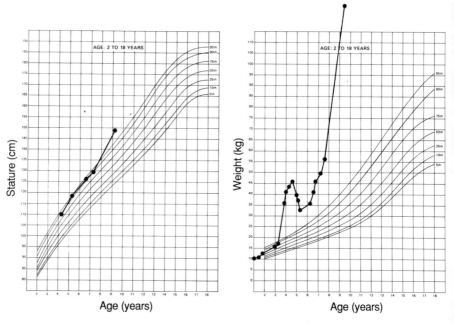

FIGURE 1. Growth curves of child with psychogenic obesity.

the trauma that had precipitated his eating disorder. Rather than abuse at his uncle's home, it was the separation from his mother that was so upsetting to him. This separation occurred at a time of immature object constancy, at a time when he was identified with his mother's depression, and at a time when their relationship was characterized by emptiness. From this point onward, J.L. continued to explore issues of his attachment, losses, feelings of emptiness, and anger. With the help of his foster mother and his therapist, he was able to lose more than 13 kg over a period of 8 months. Unfortunately he again returned to live with his mother, who was severely neglectful. In the next 3 years he gained 130 kg.

This case example highlights traumatic separation as one psychogenic cause for obesity in infancy.

A second type of psychogenic obesity occurs in the context of a disorganized family in which the child's needs are poorly perceived and even more poorly differentiated. Typically, any sign of distress in the infant or toddler is responded to by feeding and/or neglect. In this manner, it follows the pattern of a disturbance of homeostasis described by Chatoor et al. (1984). The child is taught to confuse any kind of distress as a signal to eat. The following case illustrates this second form of psychogenic obesity:

C.K. was a 2-year, 9-month-old boy reported to the state protective agency following an episode in which he was left in his home unattended.

During the period of evaluation by protective services, he was placed in a foster home for three weeks. Prior to this episode his weight had been 34 kg, and he lost 2.5 kg while in foster care (without strict dietary restrictions). He subsequently was returned to the care of his mother after arrangements were made for the family to be enrolled in a 3-month program in which psycho-therapeutic and support services were provided. At that time, he was seen by one of the authors (B.F.) for evaluation of obesity. When seen, his weight was 31.5 kg and height was greater than the 95th percentile (IBWH 165%) (Fig. 2). His blood pressure was within normal limits, and there was no evidence of organic causes of obesity. Prior growth charts demonstrated that his weight had increased to above the 95th percentile at 12 months and then had increased dramatically after 21 months.

He is the only child of a single mother who was 24 years old at the time of his birth and was receiving public assistance. She herself was obese. The pregnancy had been unplanned, and the parents had separated during the pregnancy after the mother had been abused physically by the father. Psychi-atric evaluation revealed the mother to be clinically depressed and socially isolated.

The child was reported to have frequent nightmares and, although toilet trained, was enuretic when left with others. In the pediatrician's office, he was extremely anxious, resisted examination, and was physically violent toward his mother, who was unable to set limits. Whenever upset by anxiety or angry frustration, he demanded food, to which his mother always acceded.

During the intervention period, his mother received dietary counseling in addition to psychotherapy, and his weight decreased further by 1.4 kg. His mother continued to resent the involvement of outside agencies and, although compliant with the intervention program, discontinued contact once the 3-month period ended. At follow-up in another physician's office 1 year later his weight had increased by 3.4 kg (152% IBWH).

In order to illustrate further infantile and childhood obesity of pri-mary psychogenic origin related to family disorganization, the results of

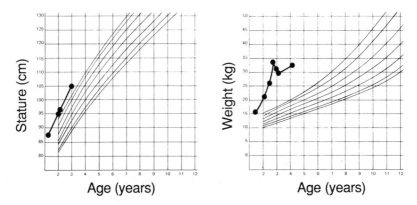

FIGURE 2. Growth curves of child with psychogenic obesity.

a clinical study of 17 patients with infantile obesity were described by Christoffel and Forsyth (1985). The majority were seen in early childhood (i.e., before 5 years of age), although some were seen in later childhood, and information about early life was obtained retrospectively. Eleven (65%) of the cases were male, six (35%) were black, six (35%) white, and four (23%) Hispanic (one was difficult to assign). Thirteen (76%) were on public assistance. The mothers were described as obese or heavy in ten cases (59%). All the children except one had a weight greater than 140% of ideal body weight for height when they were less than 4 years of age. Most of the children had become obese during infancy, although complete data were not available on all patients. One patient whose weight did not go beyond a maximum of 131% of IBWH at 2½ years of age was included because an intervention performed at that time probably prevented progression of the problem. Except for this child, all of the children later attained a weight greater than 165% IBWH. No patient had abnormal physical findings suggestive of genetic or endocrine causes of obesity. One patient had premature adrenarche, which was attributed to increased growth rate due to the obesity. All had normal thyroid function tests and all cortisol levels that were done were normal. One patient developed the Pickwickian syndrome, that is, pulmonary insufficiency due to restriction of diaphragmatic excursion and/or upper airway obstruction as a result of pharyngeal obesity.

The observed psychosocial characteristics parallel features described in failure to thrive of psychosocial origin (Barbero & Shaheen, 1967; Leonard, Rhymes, & Solnit, 1966). All of these children were from families in which there was severe disruption and disorganization. Factors that contributed to and were an expression of family dysfunction included separation of the parents, alcohol or drug abuse by the parents, and failure to maintain a stable and constant living environment. There often was denial about the severity—or even the existence—of the problem, and there often was poor medical care, failure to follow through with management plans, and, sometimes, hostility toward health professionals. The common behavioral outcome in all cases was the parent's inability to set limits, which also was evident in other parent–child interactions. Maternal depression clearly was evident in some cases.

Because these cases were seen at various ages by different clinicians, there was no uniform approach to management. One patient lost weight during hospitalization and intensive outpatient care, which involved the state child-abuse reporting agency. Other children lost weight after being placed in foster homes. In each case, this weight loss occurred without excessive restriction of caloric intake, but, along with changes in parenting and environment, the child received a more normal diet. One child lost weight during a prolonged stay in the hospital and again when, at the age of 9 years, he attended a summer weight-reduction camp but he continued to gain weight while at home in the care of his parents. The child whose maximum recorded weight was 131% of IBWH at 2 years, 5 months was placed in foster care at that age and subsequently slimmed down. Over the next 3 years of follow-up, he maintained a weight below 120% IBWH. All of the children who have remained within their families without intensive family intervention either are known to have continued to gain weight relentlessly or have been lost to follow-up. Four of the children who now are older than 11 have weights greater than 200% IBWH.

3. Proposed Classification Schema for Infantile Obesity

The current state of knowledge about obesity in infancy and early childhood is a confused and confusing picture. One of the most obvious explanations for the contradictory results of various studies is that obesity in this age group is an etiologically heterogeneous syndrome. Many authors (e.g., Maloney & Klykylo, 1983; Stunkard, 1975, 1980) have recognized multiple factors that contribute to the causation of the development of obesity, including emotional, socioeconomic, genetic, developmental, energetic, and neurological. However, virtually no attempts have been made to subdivide forms of juvenile-onset obesity into phenomenologically homogeneous groupings. Although such an attempt might be seen as oversimplified reductionism, it seems to be warranted by the clear evidence of heterogeneity in this syndrome. The first point of differentiation in this subtyping schema should be between endogenous and exogenous obesity (Figure 3). Endogenous obesity

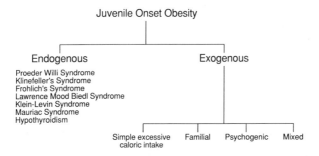

Figure 3. Diagnostic schema of obesity of infancy and early childhood.

should be classified according to specific organic etiology. Exogenous obesity should be subdivided into simple excessive caloric intake, genetic/familial, psychogenic, and mixed.

Obesity of simple excessive caloric intake results when a primary caretaker overfeeds the infant as a result of misinformation or cultural practice. There is no evidence of psychopathology in the infant or the caretaker, and there is a negative family history for obesity. This form of infantile obesity is relatively responsive to dietary intervention, assuming that the cultural attitudes that influence feeding can be modified. The age of onset can range from the neonatal period to early childhood, and the course may be rapid or gradual.

In genetic/familial obesity, there is a presumption of an underlying genetic or familial vulnerability to obesity. There is no evidence of psychopathology or nutritional misinformation, but there is a positive family history for obesity. Although both the age of onset and course are variable, most commonly the obesity is gradual and progressive, starting by the fourth or fifth year of life. Intervention has rather poor results, especially if it is introduced after the obesity has been established for several years.

In psychogenic obesity, there may be a negative family history for obesity and no evidence of nutritional misinformation, but there is strong evidence of psychopathology in the infant and/or the primary caretaker. Currently, there is evidence to describe a specific type of psychogenic obesity that is related to a traumatic separation from the primary caretaker. This form of obesity has a sudden onset (usually before age 3) and can progress rapidly. Intervention must address the psychological, as well as the nutritional, needs of the child and primary caretaker. Because the etiology is related more to psychological issues than genetics, the results of intervention will be more variable than the rather grim prognosis for familial obesity. Psychogenetic obesity also is associated with severely disorganized families in which the child's developmental needs either are ignored or misperceived.

In obesity of mixed etiology, more than one of the previously listed etiologies is found. Rather obviously, infants who are overfed, have a positive family history for obesity, and who have significant psychological disturbances will have a very resistant form of obesity. Each factor will act synergistically to maintain the obesity despite vigorous intervention. A clustering of these three etiological factors may not be uncommon.

The *raison d'être* for this diagnostic scheme is to facilitate future research and treatment. Rather clearly, children with differing types of exogenous obesity will have very different prognoses and respond to very different types of interventions. An infant or child with obesity secondary to simple excessive caloric intake may require only a simple adjustment of diet as implemented by nutritional counseling of his or her parents. Infants and children with familial obesity will require chronic supportive and dietary treatment. Engaging the parents in counseling that focuses on diet, exercise, and life-style change is crucial. This type of counseling is reported to be more successful when both the child and parents are included in groups. Children with psychogenic obesity should have the psychological issues addressed by psychotherapy for themselves and their parents.

Any research effort that fails to take various subtypes into consideration is liable to produce confusing and contradictory results. A significant finding of one subgroup might well be "washed out" by a lack of such results in another group. For example, if one examined the incidence of psychopathology in parents of obese infants and in the infants themselves, one would find rather discrepant results, depending on which subtype predominated in the sample. The same problem may be true for metabolic studies. There well may be a relatively specific metabolic profile in infants with familial obesity that is absent in other forms of obesity. Such potential heuristic value should more than outweigh the loss of complexity inherent in subcategorization of this sort.

3.1. Treatment Implications

In the past, evaluation and treatment of infantile and childhood obesity has utilized a model of linear causality. Typically, there is a search for a specific cause, especially "organic" or endogenous. This search usually is a futile one because endogenous obesity is quite rare and virtually never occurs in children over the 25th percentile in height. The focus then is turned on a very narrow nutritional approach. Although this focus is closer to the biological underpinnings of the problem, notably a positive balance between caloric intake and expenditure, it frequently ignores the powerful psychosocial influences that are permitting or encouraging the child to overeat and underexercise.

As is appropriate for any complex, multifactorial, chronic disorder, assessment and treatment must occur in the context of a multidisciplinary team approach. Ideally, this team consists of a pediatrician, developmental psychologist, child psychiatrist, social worker, nurse, and nutritionist. The team assesses the child's pediatric, developmental, psychiatric, familial, adaptive, functional, and maturational status. Because of the complexity and severity of this disorder, an inpatient evaluation may be required. Engagement of the family is the most important variable in successful treatment. A full medical assessment of the child must be performed in order to evaluate the concomitants and the sequelae of obesity, as well as the possible causes of obesity. Such disorders as slipped femoral epiphysis, diabetes mellitus, and Pickwickian syndrome may result from obesity and must be treated vigorously.

Because there appears to be a correlation between severe familial disorganization and some cases of infantile obesity, the pediatrician should evaluate the child for other problems associated with neglect, such as inadequate immunization, lead poisoning, iron deficiency, and tuberculosis. A careful developmental, cognitive, and emotional assessment needs to be done to define various psychological/developmental strengths and weaknesses. If the child is older than 30 months, the developmental psychologist should contact the appropriate educators to assess and enroll the child in an early intervention school program. The child should be evaluated for specific psychiatric disorders, such as attention deficit disorder, anxiety disorders, mood disorders, and oppositional disorder.

In addition to evaluating all aspects of family functioning, potential mental health and social resources for the family need to be assessed. The overall nutritional state of the child, the caloric intake for weight maintenance, and perhaps the nutritional status of other family members should be determined. The daily functioning of the child and family, including feeding and other mealtime behavior must be ascertained and specific behaviors that need to be eliminated or strengthened must be determined. In this manner, the team must evaluate the overall strengths and weaknesses of the child and family in order to discover the multiple factors for the child's excessive caloric intake and inadequate caloric expenditure. The various factors that contribute to the disorder then must be addressed by each member of the treatment team as is appropriate. As with other severe growth and eating disorders, removal of the child from the home sometimes is necessary. However, because the problem frequently reemerges when the child returns to the home, this most restrictive alternative should be reserved as a relatively undesirable intervention.

4. References

American Psychiatric Association (1987). *Diagnostic and statistical manual of mental disorders (DSM-III-R)*. Washington, DC: Author, 1987.

Barbero, G., & Shaheen, E. (1967). Environmental failure to thrive: A clinical interview. *Journal of Pediatrics, 73,* 690–698.

Bruch, H. (1973). *Eating disorders: Obesity, anorexia nervosa and the person within.* New York: Basic Books.

Charney, E., Chamblee, H., McBride, M., Lyon, B., & Pratt, R. (1976). The childhood antecedents of adult obesity: Do chubby infants become obese adults? *New England Journal of Medicine, 195,* 6–9.

Chatoor, I., Schaeffer, S., Dickson, L., Egan, J., Conners, C. K., & Leong, N. (1984). Pediatric assessment of non-organic failure to thrive. *Pediatric Annals, 13,* 844–850.

Christoffel, K. K., & Forsyth, B. W. C. (1985). The ineffective parent, childhood obesity syndrome. Abstract, 25th Annual Meeting of the Ambulatory Pediatric Association.

Crawford, P. B., Keller, C. A., Hampton, M. C., Pacheco, F. R., & Huenemann, R. L. (1974). An obesity index for six-month-old children. *American Journal of Clinical Nutrition, 27,* 706–711.

Eid, E. E. (1970). Follow-up study of physical growth of children who had excessive weight gain in the first six months of life. *British Medical Journal, 2,* 72–76.

Garn, S. M., & Clark, D. C. (1976). Trends in fatness and the origins of obesity. Ad Hoc Committee to Review the Ten-State Nutrition Survey. *Pediatrics, 57,* 443–456.

Goldblatt, P. B., Moore, M. E., & Stunkard, A. J. (1965). Social factors in obesity. *Journal of the American Medical Association, 192,* 1039–1044.

Kahn, E. J. (1973). Obesity in children. In N. Kiell (Ed.), *The psychology of obesity: Dynamics and treatment.* Springfield, IL: Charles C Thomas.

Kirtland, J., & Gurr, M. I. (1979). Adipose tissue hypercellularity: A review, 2. The relationship between cellulocity and obesity. *International Journal of Obesity, 3,* 15–55.

Knittle, J. C., Timmers, K., Ginsberg-Fellner, F., Brown, R. E., & Katz, D. R. (1979). The growth of adipose tissue in children and adolescents. *Journal of Clinical Investigation, 63,* 239–246.

Leonard, M., Rhymes, J., & Solnit, A. J. (1966). Failure to thrive in infants. *American Journal of Diseases of Children, 111,* 600–612.

Maloney, M. J., & Klykylo, W. M. (1983). An overview of anorexia nervosa, bulimia and obesity in children and adolescents. *Journal of the American Academy of Child Psychiatry, 22,* 99–107.

McCance, C. (1961). Psychiatric factors in obesity. Dissertation for diploma in psychological medicine. University of London.

Poskitt, E. M. E. (1980). Obese from infancy. A re-evaluation. *Topics in Paediatrics, 2,* 81–89.

Pugliese, M. T., Weyman-Daum, M., Moses, N., & Lifshitz, F. (1987). Parental health beliefs as a cause of nonorganic failure to thrive. *Pediatrics, 80,* 175–182.

Shapiro, L. R., Crawford, P. B., Clark, M. J. et al. (1984). Obesity prognosis: A longitudinal study of children from age six months to nine years. *American Journal of Public Health , 74,* 968–972.

Shipman, M. G., & Plesset, M. (1963). Anxiety and depression in obese dieters. *Archives of General Psychiatry, 8,* 530–535.

Shukla, A., Forsyth, A. A., Anderson, C. M., & Marwah, S. M. (1972). Infantile overnutrition in the first year of life: A field study in Dudley, Worcestershire. *British Medical Journal, 4,* 507–515.

Silverstone, J. T. (1969). Psychological factors in obesity. In I. M. Baird & A. N. Howard (Eds.), *Obesity: Medical and scientific aspects* (pp. 45–55). London: E & S Livingstone, Ltd.

Stunkard, A. J., (1975). Obesity. In M. F. Reiser (Ed.), *American handbook of psychiatry.* New York: Basic Books.

Stunkard, A. J. (1980). Obesity. In H. I. Kaplan, A. M. Freedman, & B. J. Sadock (Eds.), *Comprehensive textbook of psychiatry, III* (pp. 1872–1881). Baltimore, MD: Williams & Wilkins.

Stunkard, A. J., d'Aquill, E., Fox, S., & Filion, R. D. L. (1972). Influence of social class on obesity and thinness in children. *Journal of the American Medical Association, 1972, 221,* 579–584.

Taitz, L. (1971). Infantile overnutrition among artificially fed infants in the Sheffield region. *British Medical Journal, 1,* 315–316.

Taitz, L. (1977). Obesity in pediatric practice: Infantile obesity. *Pediatric Clinics of North America, 24*, 107–122.

Woolston, J. L. (1983). Eating disorders in infancy and early childhood. *Journal of the American Academy of Child Psychiatry, 22*, 114–121.

8 Developmental Differences in Depression

Alan E. Kazdin

1. Introduction

In the last decade, a great deal has been learned about childhood depression.* Specific findings from the study of depression in adults in diverse domains have served as the basis for hypotheses in evaluating depression among children. By and large, many of the findings obtained with adults have been replicated with children and adolescents. Despite many developmental continuities in the nature of depression, there remains keen interest in the evaluation and elaboration of developmental differences and points of transition from one stage to the next. From infancy through adolescence, there are, of course, remarkable and pervasive changes in biological, psychological, and social spheres. It is inevitable that the manifestations of depression will vary over the course of development.

Despite extensive discussion of the potential significance of development on the manifestations of depression (see Rutter, Izard, & Read, 1986), relatively little empirical work on the topic exists. To be sure, there are many studies of children and adolescents. Typically, studies extend theory, measures, and laboratory techniques developed in the study of depression in adults to children and adolescents. The findings permit comparison of different age groups on similar dimensions or assessment techniques. Research on childhood depression has developed relatively quickly as a result in part of the extension of theoretical and research paradigms from adults to children. There is more to the

---

*For present purposes, the term "children" will be used generically to refer to youth ages 6–18. In cases in which the distinction between children and adolescents is relevant, separate terms will be used.

ALAN E. KAZDIN • Department of Psychology, Yale University, New Haven, Connecticut 06520.

study of development than the cross-age types of comparisons. Nevertheless, such comparisons serve as a valuable point of departure for developmental research.

Many books and reviews have appeared that characterize the nature of childhood depression (e.g., Cantwell & Carlson, 1983; Kazdin, 1988; Petti, 1983; Reynolds, 1985; Trad, 1987). The purpose of the present chapter is to examine developmental differences that have been evident in research to date. The primary focus will be on differences between children and adolescents in relation to each other and to adults. The aim is not merely to enumerate differences but also to raise issues regarding the ways in which developmental differences are investigated.

Development and depression are both complex topics. The study of development encompasses the entire life span and the diverse spheres of functioning that emerge and evolve. Even the term "childhood depression" might well cover infancy through adolescence. For present purposes, the primary focus will be on children (6–11 years) and adolescents (12–18 years), which reflects the fact that the bulk of research in the field is in this age range, although infancy and toddlerhood are receiving increased attention (Trad, 1987). Similarly, the focus on depression, for present purposes, is restricted to major depressive disorder. Understanding the development of mood disorders can profit greatly from elaboration of the full range of dysfunctions in which extremes of affect play a prominent role. Yet, among mood disorders in children and adolescents, the primary research focus has been on the diagnosis, assessment, and treatment of major depressive disorder. Developmental differences in the context of major depression will serve as the central focus in this chapter. However, the broader goal is to examine the investigation of depression in the context of development. Thus, the focus on a restricted segment of development and specific type of mood disorder is designed to highlight the broader goal.

2. Historical Perspective

The idea that depression varies as a function of developmental stage is consistent with influences from several quarters including early conceptualizations of the nature of childhood depression and knowledge regarding symptoms in childhood more generally.

2.1. Psychoanalytic Theories

One of the more dramatic statements regarding developmental differences derives from early versions of psychoanalytic theory. In orthodox views, depression as a clinical disorder was not considered to be possible in children as it is in adolescents and adults (e.g., Mahler, 1961; Rie, 1966). Alternative psychoanalytic explanations of the emergence of depression have been advanced including the view that depression results from aggression directed against oneself (Rochlin, 1965), from a conflict that arouses guilt (Beres, 1966), and from low self-esteem resulting from a discrepancy between the real and ideal self (Rie, 1966). In each of these views, depression depends on a well-developed superego. Because superego development is hypothesized not to mature until adolescence, the appearance of a full clinical syndrome of depression in childhood is precluded.†

The idea that depressive disorder can appear in adulthood and adolescence but not in childhood represents a rather extreme view of developmental differences. More contemporary ego-analytic models of depression acknowledge the appearance of the disorder in childhood (Anthony, 1975; Bemporad & Wilson, 1978). Depressive states and approximations of a depressive disorder can emerge at different ages and are considered to vary as a function of psychosexual development, experience, and perceptual and cognitive skills. Thus, contemporary psychoanalytic views not only recognize depression as a clinical disorder in children but also identify possible dimensions along which developmental differences might be explored.

2.2. Masking of Symptoms in Childhood

Developmental differences were also proposed in the view that manifestations of depression in childhood may be "masked" (Cytryn & McKnew, 1972, 1974; Glaser, 1968; Malmquist, 1977; Toolan, 1962). This view began with the premise that children can experience major depression. However, the essential features, such as dysphoric mood and pervasive loss of interest, may not be present. The thought was that there is an underlying depression that is manifest in several other symptoms or forms of psychopathology. Depression was said to be "masked" or ex-

†Some forms of depression in childhood were widely acknowledged in orthodox psychoanalytic theory. For example, Spitz (1946) discussed the reactions in infancy precipitated by separation from the mother. This reaction, referred to as "anaclitic depression," may include several signs such as sadness, withdrawal, apprehension, weepiness, retarded reaction to external stimuli, slowed movement, dejection, loss of appetite and weight, and insomnia. Anaclitic depression is regarded as a result of the experience of object loss. Although many of these symptoms resemble the clinical picture of adult depression, anaclitic depression, as originally formulated, is not parallel to mood disorders in adults. Adult depression emerges in many forms only some of which might be attributed to specific environmental events.

pressed in "depressive equivalents." Children may be depressed but their mood disorder can only be inferred from the presence of other complaints evident in childhood. The symptoms that putatively mask depression included the full gamut of clinical problems evident in childhood. Temper tantrums, hyperactivity, disobedience, running away, delinquency, phobias, somatic complaints, irritability, separation anxiety, and underachievement were identified as some but not all of the depressive equivalents (see Kovacs & Beck, 1977).

The notions of masked depression and depressive equivalents have been largely rejected in part because the concepts are difficult to verify. Moreover, in recent years, diagnostic criteria developed with adults have been successfully applied in unmodified form to children (see Cantwell & Carlson, 1983). Central symptoms such as dysphoric mood and loss of interest are clearly evident upon systematic diagnostic interview. Thus, concepts such as masked depression and depressive equivalents do not seem necessary (Cytryn, McKnew, & Bunney, 1980). Nevertheless, the concepts were important historically because they underscore the possibility that depression may vary as a function of development. Also, it is often the case that children who are diagnosed as depressed meet criteria for other disorders that may be as prominent or more prominent (e.g., anxiety or conduct disorder). Thus, depression may be overshadowed or obscured by other dysfunctions. This is quite different from the original view of masked depression but points to potentially critical development issues.

2.3. Emergence of Depressive Symptoms in Childhood

Specific views of depression are not the sole or even primary basis for seeking developmental differences. The study of child development has established the dramatic changes that may take place in specific spheres of biological, psychological, and social development. For example, consideration of psychological functioning in affective, cognitive, and behavioral domains would lead to presumptive expectations of major differences in depression over the course of development (Cole & Kaslow, 1988; Dignon & Gotlib, 1985). Clinical syndromes such as depression involve large segments of functioning in these domains that would be expected to manifest themselves differently over the course of infancy, childhood, and adolescence.

The emergence of specific behaviors at different periods and their variation in frequency and intensity further underscore the likely differences in manifestations of dysfunction. Many symptoms encompassed by the syndrome of depression, as defined in current taxonomy, may be relatively common in childhood. For example, as a measure of sadness, crying has been shown to vary significantly as a function of age. At 6 years of age, approximately 18% of children have been reported to cry two to three times per week; the percentage decreases markedly by puberty to 2% (Werry & Quay, 1971). Similarly, poor appetite, another symptom of depression, is relatively common in 5-year-old girls and boys (37% and 29%, respectively) but drops sharply by age 9 (9% and 6%, respectively) (MacFarlane, Allen, & Honzik, 1954). Thus, the appearance of depression would at the very least be superimposed on youth whose normal level of affect-related characteristics vary markedly at different ages. As severity and frequency vary over the course of normal development, developmental differences in manifestations of depression would be expected as well.

2.4. Age-Specific Diagnostic Criteria

The idea of developmental differences in depression has been reflected in the delineation of diagnostic criteria unique to children. In the early 1970s, criteria for the diagnosis of depression in children were devised by Ling, Oftedal, and Weinberg (1970), and Weinberg, Rutman, Sullivan, Pencik, and Dietz (1973). The context in which these criteria were developed reflects a broader movement in the diagnosis of disorders among adults.

In the early 1970s, a group of researchers published diagnostic criteria for more general use in psychiatric research with adults (Feighner *et al.*, 1972). The criteria identified specific core symptoms and a select set of symptoms that were required from a larger list for a particular diagnosis to be present. The "Feighner criteria" were extremely influential and served as a model for subsequent development of the Research Diagnostic Criteria (RDC; Spitzer, Endicott, & Robins, 1978) as well as the criteria specified in the *Diagnostic and Statistical Manual of Mental Disorders* (DSM-III) (American Psychiatric Association [APA], 1980).

Weinberg followed the model of specifying specific symptoms to provide a standard way of diagnosing depression in children. The Weinberg criteria, as they came to be called, required the presence of dysphoric mood and self-deprecatory ideation, as well as any two of the following symptoms: aggressive behavior, sleep disturbance, change in attitude toward school, change in school performance, diminished socialization, somatic complaints, loss of usual energy, and unusual change in appetite or weight. The criteria indicate that multiple symptoms can be considered as evidence for depression as a disorder. Many of the symptoms are common with those evident in adults (e.g., dysphoric mood). However, clearly embedded in the criteria are behaviors that might be considered to mask depression (e.g., aggression). Other symptoms included dysfunction in domains obviously unique to children (e.g., school performance). The Weinberg criteria served as the basis for several investigations (Brumback, Dietz-Schmidt, & Weinberg, 1977; Brumback, Jackoway, & Weinberg, 1980; Brumback & Weinberg, 1977a,b; Weinberg et al., 1973).

Although the criteria represented an advance in operationalizing the dysfunction for children, they were somewhat broad. As a result, children who met the Weinberg criteria tended to meet the criteria for other psychiatric diagnoses as well (e.g., Carlson & Cantwell, 1980; Cytryn, McKnew, Bartko, Lamour, & Hamovitt, 1982). With the emergence of DSM-III, diagnoses became more clearly associated with more specific symptom criteria, many of which were independent of the person's age. Although children might evince unique characteristics in their manifestations of depression, the current approach is to apply the diagnosis when the core criteria have been met.

2.5. General Comments

The preceding discussion conveys some of the reasons why developmental differences in depression are expected. The orthodox psychoanalytic view of depression, the notions of masked depression and depressive equivalents, and age-specific diagnostic criteria, as noted previously, are largely of historical interest. Psychoanalytic views have been revised to recognize the existence of diagnosable depression. The notion of masked depression has been largely abandoned with repeated demonstration of the ability to diagnose depression in children and with increased recognition that the presence of other disorders (comorbidity) may complicate the diagnostic picture. The Weinberg criteria have been replaced. The notion of age-specific criteria is not necessarily abandoned. Yet, the remarkable progress evident from applying RDC and DSM-III criteria in unmodified forms to children and adolescents has attenuated the search for age-specific criteria. Application of standard diagnostic criteria to all age groups has not altered the widespread belief and the specific search for developmental differences in the disorder and its associated features.

3. Diagnostic Criteria Independent of Age

The current view that guides research is that the essential features of depression as a disorder are similar in children, adolescents, and adults. This position is evident in the *Diagnostic and Statistical Manual of Mental Disorders* (DSM-III-R) (American Psychiatric Association [APA], 1987) in which criteria for mood disorders are delineated and applied independently of age. To meet the diagnosis for major depressive disorder, an individual must show any five of the following symptoms: depressed mood, loss of interest or pleasure, significant weight loss or gain, insomnia or hypersomnia, psychomotor agitation or retardation, fatigue or loss of energy, feelings of worthlessness, diminished ability to think or concentrate, and suicidal ideation or attempt. Either depressed mood or loss of interest must be included as one of the symptoms to meet criteria for the disorder.

The statement that these symptoms can be used to diagnose depression in children, adolescents, and adults alike was made *a priori* in DSM-III (APA, 1980) and by implication raised the issue as an empirical question, namely: Can depression be diagnosed in children, adolescents, and adults using the same criteria? This question has been answered affirmatively by several investigations in which psychiatric interviews are administered to children or adolescents and their parents (e.g., Carlson & Cantwell, 1980; Chambers *et al.*, 1985; Chiles, Miller, & Cox, 1980; Kashani, Barbero, & Bolander, 1981).

The fact that depression as a clinical syndrome can be diagnosed in children, adolescents, and adults does not mean that the manifestations of the disorder are necessarily identical. DSM-III-R, representing the current criteria that are invoked for psychiatric diagnoses in the United States, recognizes that there may be different features for varying ages and developmental levels. At the outset, the criteria specify that an "irritable mood" (APA, 1987, p. 218) may be evident in children and adolescents instead of depressive affect. However, researchers generally have not reported altering the criteria in this way to diagnose major depressive disorder in children.

DSM-III-R also notes that comorbidity and concomitant behaviors may vary with age. In children, anxiety disorders and phobias are stated to be common. In adolescents, on the other hand, negativistic and antisocial behavior, use of alcohol or illicit drugs, sulkiness, uncooperativeness in relation to family activities, school difficulties, inattention to personal appearance, and sensitivity to rejection are considered to be potential concomitants. These characteristics are not to be accepted as empirically established differences in depression as a function of age. Nevertheless, they convey that invoking common essential diagnostic features does not gainsay the appearance of developmental differences.

4. Developmental Differences

Notwithstanding the application of diagnostic criteria in unmodified form to children, adolescents, and adults, there remains a keen interest in the search for developmental differences. More than interest, there are widely held views that understanding childhood depression requires a developmental perspective to consider the emergence, evolution, and organization of affective, cognitive, behavioral, and biological processes (e.g., Anthony, 1975; Cicchetti & Schneider-Rosen, 1984; Cole & Kaslow, 1988; Dignon & Gotlib, 1985; Sroufe & Rutter, 1984). There is agreement in the general case that "development" needs to be considered. The difficulty has been moving beyond this general view to the prediction of concrete ways in which differences are likely to be evident and then demonstration of these differences. This section is designed to enumerate the types of differences for which one might search and to illustrate specific findings within each type.

4.1. Prevalence

An initial type of developmental difference that may be evident is the prevalence of depression. Prevalence has been examined for depression as a symptom as well as a syndrome or disorder. As a symptom, depression refers to feelings of sadness and misery; as a syndrome or disorder, depression refers to the constellation of symptoms, as specified by the previously mentioned diagnostic criteria.

Depression as a symptom has been examined in the Isle of Wight study (Rutter, Tizard, & Whitmore, 1970). In a general population of 10–11-year-old children, 13% were found to show a depressed mood. The same children were reassessed at ages 14–15. Over 40% of the adolescents reported feelings of misery and depression. Thus, clear differences in depression as a symptom are evident in late childhood and early adolescence.

Among boys ages 14–15, the sample could be subdivided according to pubertal status (Rutter, 1986). Almost none of the prepubescent boys showed depressive feelings, whereas about one third of the postpubescent boys did so. Figure 1 conveys the sharp differences in depression (as a symptom) as a function of pubertal status. These findings are of special interest given the fact that the youth were the same sex and close in age but varied in pubertal status.

The prevalence of depression as a syndrome or disorder was also evaluated in the Isle of Wight study. Depression as a disorder was diagnosed on the basis of social impairment rather than more recently developed diagnostic criteria. At age 10, only three cases of depressive disorder were found in a sample of over 2,000 children. In contrast, at ages 14–15, there were approximately 35 cases of affective disorder.

In data obtained from the Maudsley Hospital (in England), approximately 11% of prepubertal cases showed depressive symptoms; about

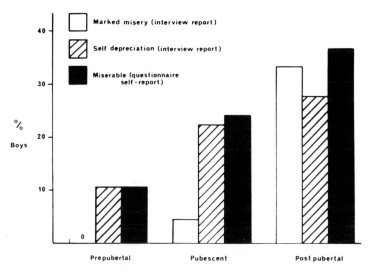

FIGURE 1. Depressive feelings as a function of stage of puberty among boys ages 14–15. (From Rutter, 1986, p. 12.)

25% of postpubertal children did so (see Rutter, 1986). The prevalence rates varied remarkably as a function of pubertal status and sex. Figure 2 shows that depressive symptoms were twice as common in boys among prepubertal children, whereas they were twice as common in girls among postpubertal children.

In the above studies, standardized diagnostic criteria (e.g., DSM, RDC) were not invoked, which make direct comparisons with current prevalence data somewhat unclear. Recent studies have utilized standardized diagnostic criteria to evaluate depression as a disorder. In the general population, approximately 2% have been identified as depressed in randomly selected child populations ages 7–12 using DSM-III criteria (Kashani et al., 1983; Kashani & Simonds, 1979). With different age groups and again using DSM-III criteria, young children (ages 1–6 years) referred for treatment may have markedly lower rates (1%) of major depression than children ages 9–12 (13%) (Kashani, Cantwell, Shekim, & Reid, 1982; Kashani, Ray, & Carlson, 1984). In clinical populations, estimates have ranged from approximately 2% to 60% (Kashani, Husain, Shekim, Hodges, Cytryn, & McKnew, 1981), although more typical estimates fall between 10% and 20% (Puig-Antich & Gittelman, 1982).

It is difficult to consider prevalence rates without acknowledging sex differences that are rather consistently found in the literature with adults. In adulthood, depression generally is more prevalent among

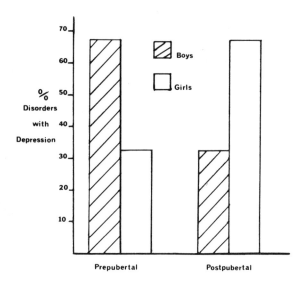

FIGURE 2. Sex ratio of disorders with depression before and after puberty. (From Rutter, 1986, p. 13.)

women than among men. To date, research has typically found no sex differences in the prevalence of depressive disorders in clinic and non-clinic samples of children (ages 6–12) (e.g., Kashani et al., 1983; Lobovits & Handal, 1985). On the other hand, research has suggested that among adolescents, the prevalence is greater in females than in males (e.g., Mezzich & Mezzich, 1979; Reynolds, 1985). Differences in severity of depression between males and females appear to begin in early adolescence and to increase over the next several years (Kandel & Davies, 1982). Differences in prevalence rates between adolescent males and females are not always found (Kaplan, Hong, & Weinhold, 1984). There remain important discrepancies in prevalence data from the currently available studies. The large discrepancies may result in part from the different measures that are used, the difficulty in administering similar measures to youth of different ages, and the different diagnostic criteria that are invoked. Consequently, further work and large-scale epidemiological studies are still needed.

4.2. Symptom Characteristics

Developmental differences may be manifest in many other ways than prevalence rates. Differences may be evident in the organization or co-occurrence of symptoms and in the presence or severity of symptoms.

4.2.1. Patterns of Symptoms

The manner in which depressive symptoms cluster or go together may vary as a function of development. Multivariate studies of children and adolescents suggest that there may well be developmental differences. For example, Achenbach and Edelbrock (1983) studied parent checklist (Child Behavior Checklist) ratings of boys and girls in different age groups (4–5, 6–11, 12–16). Because the measure is the same for each age group and both sexes, analyses of the items can address whether there are developmental differences in the patterns or constellations of symptoms.

Factor analyses were completed to identify groups of items that go together for children of different ages. A depression factor emerged in analyses of Child Behavior Checklist ratings of all groups except boys and girls ages 12–16. For boys, no depression factor emerged; for girls in this age range, the depression factor clustered with items specifically related to withdrawal, being secretive, shy, and timid, and liking to be alone. For the groups where a depression factor did emerge, the specific symptoms that clustered on this factor varied as a function of sex and age. For example, for boys ages 6–11, suicidal talk was associated with other symptoms of depression, although this was not the case at ages 4–5. For the girls ages 6–11, feeling persecuted and anxious were associated with other depressive symptoms; at ages 4–5, these symptoms were not part of the depression factor. The results suggest that depressive symptoms may be organized quite differently as a function of age and gender.

4.2.2. Severity and Relative Frequency

Severity of symptoms may also vary as a function of development. Relatively few direct comparisons have been conducted to permit evaluation of depressive symptoms among youth of different ages. In a recent exception, Ryan et al. (1987) compared children and adolescents who met RDC for major depressive disorder based on a standardized diagnostic interview. Comparisons revealed that prepubertal children showed somewhat greater depressive appearance, somatic complaints, psychosomatic agitation, and hallucinations than did adolescents. In contrast, adolescents showed greater anhedonia, hopelessness, hypersomnia, weight change, and lethality of suicide attempt. These findings are especially interesting given the fact that all youth met diagnostic criteria for depression. Thus, invoking standard diagnostic criteria readily permits variation in the expression of symptoms over the course of development. It is important to note as well that for most of the symptoms of depression, frequency and severity were no different between children and adolescents.

In a recent study, Mitchell, McCauley, Burke, and Moss (1988) also compared depressive symptoms in children (7–12 years old) and adolescents (13–17 years old). Evaluation of symptoms, based on diagnostic interviews, compared youth of different ages (e.g., 7–8, 9–10) in an effort to identify variations in symptom presentation. Data were collapsed to form the child and adolescent groups after identifying no discernible differences with the subgroups. The results indicated no clear differences in symptom distribution with the exception of hypersomnia. This latter symptom, although more frequent in adolescents, reflects a single difference that might be expected by "chance," given the number of comparisons.

At this point, further research is needed to clarify the developmental differences in symptom presentation. The findings of Ryan *et al.* (1987) and Mitchell *et al.* (1988) would appear to reflect major discrepancies. However, each study reported that children and adolescents were similar on most symptoms. The developmental differences that were found in the former but not in the latter study are of special interest, given some similarities in the studies such as the use of the same diagnostic interview to assess symptoms of depression. Yet there are several methodological differences as well, including the basis for classifying youth (pubertal stage versus age) and variation in the distribution of inpatient and outpatient cases. The differences between the two studies warrant further investigation. In each study, it is clear that diagnostic criteria developed with adults can be applied to children and adolescents and also permit the evaluation of potential differences in symptoms of depression and associated features.

Direct comparisons of symptoms as a function of age or developmental status are infrequent. Nevertheless, clear differences can be found in the patterns for select symptoms. For example, suicide is often associated with psychopathology and, among alternative diagnoses, primarily depression. In the general population, suicide before the age of 12 or 14 years is quite rare (Hawton, 1986). The rate rises sharply during adolescence, continues throughout adulthood, and reaches a peak in old age. Attempted suicide (parasuicide) is also rare before puberty and shows a marked rise during adolescence. Given the different base rates over the course of development, suicidal attempt is less likely to be included in the syndrome in childhood than in adolescence and adulthood.

There are no doubt other symptoms where severity of dysfunction varies over the course of development. The pattern may vary with individual symptoms but a general expectation might be increased severity and intensity from childhood to adolescence. For example, loss of interest or pleasure (anhedonia) is a central symptom for the diagnosis of depression. Preliminary evidence suggests that anhedonia varies as a function of age, with older children (10–13) showing greater anhedonia (reduced pleasure) across a large number of potentially rewarding events than children (6–9) (Kazdin, 1989).

4.3. Additional Characteristics of Dysfunction

4.3.1. Associated Features

Several characteristics of depression have been studied as correlates of the syndrome, although they are not part of the diagnostic criteria. Many features studied include a variety of cognitive processes, biological markers, and patterns of interpersonal behavior, to mention a few. Within each of these areas of research, multiple constructs and measures have been examined. For example, diverse cognitive processes have been studied in adults including helplessness, hopelessness, negative self-statements, and locus of control. Many biological markers have been examined including urinary metabolites of monoamines, measures of blood and plasma, cell membrane characteristics, neuroendocrine function, and sleep characteristics. Studies of social behavior have evaluated nonverbal behavior, solitary activity, and degree and type of social interaction with others.

The multiple characteristics sampled here have been evaluated in several studies with adults. In a relatively short period of time, tests have evaluated the extent to which these characteristics are evident in children and adolescents. In general, research has shown marked similarities among children, adolescents, and adults in cognitive, biological, and interpersonal spheres. These continuities have been reviewed elsewhere (e.g., Kazdin, 1988; Puig-Antich, 1986; Trad, 1987) and hence are not reiterated here.

Differences occasionally have been evident. For example, studies of adults with major depressive disorder show several sleep characteristics including decreased latency to initial rapid eye movement (REM) periods, decreased slow-wave sleep time, increased REM density, and decreased sleep efficiency. These characteristics do not appear to be evident in depressed children and adolescents (e.g., Goetz et al., 1983; Young, Knowles, MacLean, Boag, & McConville, 1982). However, there remain some ambiguities. Sleep characteristics in depressed children and adolescents have been similar to those in depressed adults, with inconsistencies in whether age, pubertal status, and method of assessing sleep characteristics affect the relations (Emslie, Roffward, Rush,

Weinberg, & Parkin-Feigenbaum, 1987; Lahmeyer, Poznanski, & Bellur, 1983). In general, the weight of current evidence suggests that sleep characteristics associated with depression vary as a function of age. However, the issue remains under investigation, given the different points of evaluation in relation to a depressive episode (before, during, after) and the range of sleep characteristics that can be evaluated.

Other differences in associated characteristics have been suggested. Among adults, the efficacy of imipramine (IMI) has been well established (Mindham, 1982). Moreover, treatment response has been related to plasma concentrations of medication. Similar findings have been obtained for children (6–12) diagnosed with major depressive disorder (e.g., Preskorn, Weller, & Weller, 1982; Puig-Antich et al., 1987). The findings for adolescents appear to differ.

Ryan et al. (1986) evaluated IMI among adolescents (mean age = 14.25, range = 10–17 years) who met RDC for major depression. Only 44% improved significantly in response to treatment. Moreover, no clear relation was evident between plasma concentrations and therapeutic response. The results could not be explained by the subtypes of depression evident in the sample. Endogenous depressives, for whom IMI is considered to be especially effective, generally did not respond to treatment (33% improved significantly). The authors raise the possibility that the high level of sex hormones during adolescence and young adulthood may interfere with the antidepressive effects of IMI. Clearly, further tests of the responsiveness of adolescents to medication and the specific hypotheses regarding interactions with level of sex hormones warrant additional study.

4.3.2. Comorbidity

Among the associated features, there may be developmental differences in the presence of other (nondepressive) symptoms and disorders that co-occur with major depression. The presence of more than one disorder, or comorbidity, is an area where interesting continuities and developmental differences have been found. In both children and adults, there is a consistent co-occurrence of major depressive and anxiety disorders. Thus, individuals with a diagnosis of one of these types of disorders is likely to meet criteria for the other as well (Bernstein & Garfinkel, 1986; Norvel, Brophy, & Finch, 1985; Strauss, Last, Hersen, & Kazdin, 1988; Wolfe et al., 1987). The specific anxiety disorders appear to vary. Among adults, agoraphobia, panic, and generalized anxiety disorders are often associated with depression. Among children, school phobia and separation anxiety have been found. Some developmental differences have been reported in relation to children and adolescents. For example, anxiety disorders and conduct disorders appear to be more likely in children than in adolescents (Ryan *et al.*, 1987). In addition, antisocial behavior and conduct disorder may be more likely to co-occur with depression in boys than in girls (McGee & Williams, 1988; Mitchell *et al.*, 1988).

Comorbidity involving multiple mood disorders has also been evident in childhood and adult depression. Thus, children often meet diagnostic criteria for both major depression and dysthymic disorder (Kovacs, Feinberg, Crouse-Novak, Paulauskas, & Finkelstein, 1984a; Kovacs *et al.*, 1984b). Among adults, those with a diagnosis of major depression often meet criteria for depressive personality (Weissman *et al.*, 1986). Further work is needed to examine developmental differences in comorbidity of mood disorders.

4.3.3. *Prognosis*

Few studies have evaluated the course or prognosis of children and adolescents with major depressive disorder over time. In a longitudinal prospective study, Kovacs *et al.* (1984a) found that the mean duration of major depressive disorder was 32 weeks among youth ages 8–13. Approximately 1.5 years later, 92% had recovered. This rate appears somewhat higher than the rate for adults, which is approximately 50% over a period of one year (Keller, Shapiro, Lavori, & Wolfe, 1982). Within childhood, the rate of recovery appears to be associated with age. Children who were older at first onset of major depressive disorder recovered more rapidly than children with an earlier onset (see Kovacs *et al.*, 1984a,b). Sex differences have also been reported with greater persistence of depressive symptoms among boys than girls (McGee & Williams, 1988).

4.4. *General Comments*

The preceding discussion does not exhaust the range of developmental differences that have been sought or found. One area of potential interest is in alternative subtypes of depression. The classification of subtypes is by no means resolved in the literature on adult depression (Carlson & Garber, 1986). Nevertheless, applying diagnostic criteria in unmodified form has revealed many of the subtypes (e.g., endogeneous, psychotic depression) evident in children as they have been in adults. Developmental differences in the prevalence of subtypes and whether subtype characteristics vary across developmental periods have not been thoroughly studied. Some evidence suggests that psychotic depression may be more frequent before than after puberty (Ryan *et al.*, 1987). Clearly, further work is needed.

Several other specific developmental differences might be noted in relation to depression and its correlates. For example, Blumberg and Izard (1985) found that depressed children (ages 10–11) were similar on measures of emotional experience to the profiles obtained with depressed adults. Thus, sadness, self-directed hostility, shame, anger, and other emotions significantly correlated with depression. Yet the pattern for girls was more similar than for boys to the profiles of depressed adults. The findings are of interest because they raise significant questions about differences between boys and girls of the same age and because they follow in a program of research where parallel data have been obtained for adults. However, the results also point to more general issues in relation to identifying developmental differences. The initial task in evaluating depression is to describe differences over the course of development and to track changes across periods. However, demonstration of differences is only an initial step. Further work is needed to explain the basis (i.e., mechanisms) for such differences as well as their theoretical and clinical significance.

5. Issues and Obstacles

Developmental differences remain a topic of great interest and in need of major research efforts. Several issues and obstacles inherent in the subject matter make the task of revealing the process of development difficult. Although the study of child psychopathology in general raises special issues, the focus on differences and similarities across childhood, adolescence, and adulthood raises additional obstacles.

5.1. Assessment Issues

Assessment raises manifold obstacles because of the manner of obtaining information about dysfunction at different points in development and the impact of other influences on the information that is derived. First, youth of different ages may vary greatly in their capacity to report on their emotions, cognitions, and behaviors. From the standpoint of assessment, this means that a given measure may not be available for use for the full age range of interest (e.g., 4–18 years). To evaluate similar characteristics across a given age span may require the development of different measures or variations of the same measures. Alteration of assessment procedures to assess a given characteristic at different points in development may influence the results and conclusions. Even administration of the same measure at different ages may introduce indeterminacies in the informational yield. The same items may be interpreted in systematically different ways as a function of developmental stage. For example, young children (5 years of age and younger) are likely to deny the presence of any sadness (Glasberg & Aboud, 1981, 1982). Items designed to assess sadness might yield different responses among children of different ages.

The assessment problems of different measures across the age span are by no means insurmountable. If the measures yield similar findings across different developmental periods, interpretive problems are minimal. For example, measures of cognitive style and anhedonia yield similar findings in children and adults (e.g., Kazdin, 1989; Seligman & Peterson, 1986). The use of different measures is not problematic in this context. However, discrepancies in findings between children and adults would raise questions about the possibility of true developmental differences or whether assessment procedures are difficult to equate across the ages.

Second, and related to the first point, information from others (e.g., parents, teachers) is relied upon differentially across childhood and adolescence. With children in particular, assessment often relies heavily on parental report. Use of parents as a source of information is often a procedural substitute for information that might not be as readily obtained from the child. However, from a methodological standpoint, self-report and parent-report measures may yield quite different information. To begin with, evidence suggests that children report fewer symptoms and lower estimates of symptom severity than do their parents (Kazdin, French, Unis, & Esveldt-Dawson, 1983; Orvaschel, Puig-Antich, Chambers, Tabrizi, & Johnson, 1982; Tisher & Lang, 1983). In addition, measures completed by the parent often are influenced by a variety of factors that have little to do with the child's functioning. Several studies have shown that maternal perceptions of child adjustment and functioning are related to maternal psychopathology (especially anxiety and depression), marital discord, stressors, and social support outside the home (e.g., Forehand, Lautenschlager, Faust, & Graziano, 1986; Mash & Johnston, 1983; Moretti, Fine, Haley, & Marriage, 1985). Thus, the information obtained may be influenced by a number of factors other than child dysfunction. In general, conclusions about differences in development may vary as a function of the reliance upon different sources of input in characterizing child behavior.

5.2. Age versus Developmental Status or Stage

The search for developmental differences usually consists of identifying children of different ages and making comparisons on a set of measures in various contexts (e.g., clinic, home, school). However, using age as a measure of development may obscure important differences. Evidence reviewed previously suggests that depression as a symptom and syndrome may vary markedly as a function of pubertal status. The failure of most research to delineate pubertal status when this could vary within the ages studied has important consequences. Thus, the presence or absence of developmental continuities may be obscured by equating children according to age or grade level, if their pubertal status differs.

The use of age as a sole or primary basis to study developmental differences raises another issue. Age is conceptually neutral in the sense that it is not encumbered by a specific conceptual view or approach. This means that age is likely to be employed widely to delineate youth among researchers of diverse theoretical persuasions. Yet, the advantage of widespread use bears a heuristic cost. Age as a way of delineating groups does not point directly to mechanisms that might account for any developmental differences. Other methods of staging are likely to be conceptually richer.

For example, already mentioned was pubertal status as a way of delineating developmental status. A myriad of changes take place with puberty. Consequently, differences in depression and related symptoms as a function of pubertal status do not direct attention to a narrow band of mechanisms that might account for such differences. On the other hand, within a particular approach (e.g., neuroendocrine), one can point to possible mechanisms as likely leads. For example, when Ryan *et al.* (1986) found that adolescents did not respond to IMI when given in doses within the therapeutic range, it was reasonable to suggest that sex hormone differences may influence the efficacy of medication in ways not evident in children or adults. Research can directly test this hypothesis by correlating sex-hormone level and therapeutic response or specific biochemical processes through which IMI is moderated.

Age and pubertal status are only two among an indefinite number of ways of delineating stages for studying development. Alternative areas of research and conceptual views pose stages that correlate but cannot be equated with age. For example, stages of psychosexual development, moral reasoning, and Piagetian cognitive development, among others raise important prospects for studying developmental differences. Perhaps more broadly, developmental processes (e.g., holism, differentiation) can be used as a basis for delineating developmental periods (e.g., Cicchetti & Schneider-Rosen, 1984; Sroufe & Rutter, 1984). To the extent that stages can be reliably measured, they warrant evaluation in relation to developmental differences. The reason is not only to go beyond the simplistic search that age differences may foster, but also to identify the possible reasons or critical mechanisms that can account for such differences. Exploring the mechanisms will greatly enhance knowledge of developmental differences and continuities and the progressions of symptoms from one stage to the next.

6. Strategies for Evaluating the Interface of Development and Depression

Understanding the impact of development and depression can be accomplished in different ways. At least two separate strategies can be identified. These are referred to here as the investigation of cross-age commonalities and age-specific characteristics.

6.1. Cross-Age Commonalities

In the first strategy, a particular construct or domain of functioning of interest is identified. The construct is then evaluated among persons varying in age or developmental stage. For example, one might evaluate sleep characteristics, learned helplessness, or performance of positively reinforcing activities in children, adolescents, and adults. In such research, the construct of interest is extended across developmental periods. The specific measures to assess the domain of interest are similar or occasionally even identical across the developmental spectrum.

The key feature of this approach is the search for developmental continuities. The implied assumption of the approach is that the methodology, technique, or construct is meaningfully applied or appropriate across age groups. Clearly, the bulk of research on childhood depression reflects the cross-age commonalities approach. Such large bodies of research of this ilk would include work on biological markers, cognitive processes, and social interaction. In each area, theories of depression, measures, and laboratory techniques developed from research with adults have been extended to children. It is not surprising that to date the research suggests that there are remarkable continuities in depression and its associated features across the developmental spectrum. The usual conclusion from this research is that depression and its features in children, adolescents, and adults are more similar than different.

6.2. Age-Specific Characteristics

In the second research approach, age- or stage-specific characteristics are investigated. Characteristics of the individual or the specific situations or settings in which they are placed that are unique to the period of interest are examined. Here continuities using the same or similar measures are not sought because the search focuses on unique features peculiar to each stage. The focus is on elaborating age- or stage-specific manifestations.

Research of this approach begins by identifying characteristics or situations that may be unique and in which novel manifestations of depression and related characteristics might be evident. For example, infancy is associated with special interactions with the mother (e.g., as in breast feeding), exploration of the environment, the emergence of language, and so on. Are there special characteristics here that relate to or reflect current depressive affect or that predict subsequent major depressive disorder? Answers to the question can be pursued empirically by developing special methods to evaluate those characteristics.

The age-specific approach emphasizes the differences, not necessarily discontinuities, of developmental periods by focusing on unique characteristics of a given age or stage. At each stage of development, including infancy, toddlerhood, childhood, adolescence, and adulthood unique intrapersonal and interpersonal characteristics may emerge. A specific theoretical framework for classifying development may be used to delineate the stages for such an evaluation. Yet, in any case, the goal is to elaborate stage-unique characteristics. There is relatively little of this type of work one can identify in the context of depression. As a consequence, it is no surprise that the widely held notion that depression varies as a function of development has relatively little data in its support.

Developmental research requires elaborating the unique characteristics within a given age period. This approach is obviously difficult because it requires knowledge of the specific developmental periods as well as psychopathology and perhaps the ability to develop new measures to assess unique characteristics or circumstances. The approach bears a potentially great yield because this type of work can elaborate the progressions of a particular dysfunction over the course of development. Thus, one can identify that in infancy, depression (or pre-depressive signs) may include certain attachment, feeding, or verbal or nonverbal patterns. In toddlerhood and childhood, unique parent–child interactions, peer-group contacts, and types of solitary activity may be relevant. Continuation of this line of work elaborates different manifestations. The differences across periods provide a more in-depth understanding of development and psychopathology.

6.3. General Comments

The cross-age and age-specific approaches toward developmental research are dichotomized artificially for purposes of presentation. The former approach emphasizes continuities in the sense of beginning research with a selected construct, measure, or laboratory technique from research on one developmental period (e.g., adulthood) and applying this elsewhere in development (e.g., childhood). The latter approach emphasizes developmentally unique characteristics and evaluates the different processes and situations and their interface over the course of development.

The approaches are not entirely distinct. For example, one might extend a particular construct across developmental periods. The application suggests that the cross-age strategy is adopted. However, extensions to another age or stage of development may require major alterations in the specific ways in which the construct is operationalized and assessed. As an illustration, nonverbal behavior (e.g., eye contact, gestures) has been frequently studied in depressed adults. Extension of this research to children might utilize similar constructs and measures. However, extension to infants is likely to be very different because the usual context for assessing nonverbal behavior (e.g., interviews) would be inapplicable. Direct comparisons across infancy and adulthood might be difficult for a given set of nonverbal behaviors because the measures are so different. In short, a common focus (nonverbal behavior) may lead to age-specific evaluation depending on the developmental stage.

The broader issue is to search for the full gamut of characteristics that might be associated with a particular dysfunction such as depression. Perhaps the initial stage of research is identification of commonalities across the developmental spectrum. The commonalities are not only important to chart but also reflect the most obvious step. Evaluation of stage-specific and unique characteristics requires the clear integration of knowledge of development into the study of dysfunction. Both approaches are obviously necessary. In the case of depression, the paucity of research on age-specific characteristics is important to note. Research of this strategy is more likely to elaborate developmental differences.

7. Conclusions

The present chapter has considered several issues related to the search for developmental differences in depression. The focus was limited in a number of ways that may have critical implications for the overall objectives. To begin with, only a limited segment of development, specifically childhood and adolescence, was examined. With a restricted focus, it is easy to lose sight of the broader issue. Developmental psychopathology entails the full course of development. Omitted from the chapter was any discussion of infancy and the elderly. Understanding depression from a developmental perspective obviously will require consideration of the entire life course.

Second, the chapter was limited in the focus to major depressive disorder. There are, of course, a range of mood disorders as well as reactions (e.g., adjustment disorder, bereavement) with similar clinical presentations. Understanding depression will require an examination of the full range of related conditions. Indeed, from a developmental perspective, it may be especially important to focus on the full range of mood disorders in an attempt to understand any single disorder more fully. It is likely that progressions from one developmental stage to another will entail greater specificity in the clinical picture. Thus, early in life, signs of dysfunction may be more diffuse and not meet criteria for specific disorders. Over time, the symptom picture may crystallize. To focus on a narrowly, albeit carefully, defined syndrome and to search for this particular syndrome at different stages may well miss antecedent conditions from which the syndrome emerges. Related, developmental progressions may well involve the movement from one form of mood disorder to another. Thus, assessment of such progressions may require considering the full range of mood disorders beyond the limited focus of the present chapter.

Given the limitations, perhaps little can be said about developmental differences in relation to major depression. However, the present chapter was not designed to catalogue such differences. There are critical issues related to the search for differences and the manner in which this search is proceeding. A great deal has been learned about depression and other mood disorders in years of research with adults. Multiple theoretical models, assessment devices, laboratory techniques, and treatments have been evaluated. The large and continually expanding body of knowledge serves as a strong basis for extending research across the full range of development. Current research on mood disorders spans the full developmental spectrum from infants to the elderly. The knowledge gained may not only be of obvious interest in understanding depression but also serve as a broader paradigm for developmental psychopathology more generally.

In searching for developmental differences, it is critical not to lose perspective on the larger goal. The purpose is not to generate isolated findings that youth of different ages or youth in relation to adults differ on a particular construct or measure. To be sure, the initial stage of understanding development is descriptive. Consequently, isolated findings of differences are not to be demeaned. Yet even in the initial descriptive stage, a purely phenomenological focus is not the only or perhaps even the more advantageous approach. Theory-based research helps to focus on the domains of potential significance and with implications that will further develop theory and experimentation. A predicted developmental difference as, for example, based on a particular cognitive or biological theory, may greatly enhance our understanding of the dysfunction, its changing course, and key transition points.

This chapter highlighted some of the differences in depression over the course of childhood and adolescence. The differences to date are largely analogous to still photographs drawn from the moving picture that development represents. Longitudinal studies that evaluate alternative stages, transitions, and symptom progressions are required to chart the course of depression.

Acknowledgments

Completion of this research was supported by a Research Scientist Development Award (MHOO353) and by a grant (MH35408) from the National Institute of Mental Health.

8. References

Achenbach, T. M., & Edelbrock, C. S. (1983). *Manual for the Child Behavior Checklist and Revised Child Behavior Profile*. Burlington, VT: University Associates in Psychiatry.

American Psychiatric Association. (1980). *Diagnostic and statistical manual of mental disorders* (3rd ed.). Washington, DC: Author.

American Psychiatric Association. (1987). *Diagnostic and statistical manual of mental disorders-Revised*. Washington, DC: Author.

Anthony, E. J. (1975). Childhood depression. In E. J. Anthony & T. Benedek (Eds.), *Depression and human existence* (pp. 231–277). Boston: Little, Brown.

Bemporad, J. R., & Wilson, A. (1978). A developmental approach to depression in childhood and adolescence. *Journal of the American Academy of Psychoanalysis, 6*, 325–352.

Beres, D. (1966). Superego and depression. In R. M. Lowenstein, L. M. Newman, M. Scherr, & A. J. Solnit (Eds.), *Psychoanalysis—A general psychology* (pp. 479–498). New York: International Universities Press.

Bernstein, G., & Garfinkel, B. (1986). School phobia: The overlap of affective and anxiety disorders. *Journal of the American Academy of Child Psychiatry, 25*, 235–241.

Blumberg, S. H., & Izard, C. E. (1985). Affective and cognitive characteristics of depression in 10- and 11-year-old children. *Journal of Personality and Social Psychology, 49*, 194–404.

Brumback, R. A., Dietz-Schmidt, S. R., & Weinberg, W. A. (1977). Depression in children referred to an educational diagnostic center: Diagnosis and treatment and analysis of criteria and literature review. *Diseases of the Nervous System, 38*, 529–535.

Brumback, R. A., Jackoway, M. K., & Weinberg, W. A. (1980). Relation of intelligence to childhood depression in children referred to an educational diagnostic center. *Perceptual and Motor Skills, 50*, 11–17.

Brumback, R. A., & Weinberg, W. A. (1977a). Childhood depression: An explanation of a behavior disorder of children. *Perceptual and Motor Skills, 44*, 911–916.

Brumback, R. A., & Weinberg, W. A. (1977b). Relationship of hyperactivity and depression in children. *Perceptual and Motor Skills, 45,* 247–251.

Cantwell, D. P., & Carlson, G. A. (Eds.). (1983). *Affective disorders in childhood and adolescence: An update.* New York: Spectrum.

Carlson, G. A., & Cantwell, D. P. (1980). Unmasking masked depression in children and adolescents. *American Journal of Psychiatry, 137,* 445–449.

Carlson, G. A., & Garber, J. (1986). Developmental issues in the classification of depression in children. In M. R. Rutter, C. E. Izard, & P. B. Read (Eds.), *Depression in young people: Developmental and clinical perspectives* (pp. 399–434). New York: Guilford Press.

Chambers, W. J., Puig-Antich, J., Hirsch, M., Paez, P., Ambrosini, P. J., Tabrizi, M. A., & Davies, M. (1985). The assessment of affective disorders in children and adolescents by semistructured interview: Test-retest reliability. *Archives of General Psychiatry, 42,* 696–702.

Chiles, J. A., Miller, M. L., & Cox, G. B. (1980). Depression in an adolescent delinquent population. *Archives of General Psychiatry, 37,* 1179–1184.

Cicchetti, D., & Schneider-Rosen, K. (1984). Toward a transactional model of childhood depression. In D. Cicchetti & K. Schneider-Rosen (Eds.), *Childhood depression: New directions for child development* (pp. 5–27). San Francisco: Jossey-Bass.

Cole, P. M., & Kaslow, N. J. (1988). Interactional and cognitive strategies for affect regulation: Developmental perspective on childhood depression. In L. B. Alloy (Ed.), *Cognitive processes in depression* (pp. 310–343). New York: Guilford Press.

Cytryn, L., & McKnew, D. H. (1972). Proposed classification of childhood depression. *American Journal of Psychiatry, 129,* 149–155.

Cytryn, L., & McKnew, D. H. (1974). Factors influencing the changing clinical expression of the depressive process in children. *American Journal of Psychiatry, 131,* 879–881.

Cytryn, L., McKnew, D. H., Bartko, J. J., Lamour, M., & Hamovitt, J. (1982). Offspring of patients with affective disorders: II. *Journal of the American Academy of Child Psychiatry, 21,* 389–391.

Cytryn, L., McKnew, D. H., & Bunney, W. E. (1980). Diagnosis of depression in children: A reassessment. *American Journal of Psychiatry, 137,* 22–25.

Dignon, N., & Gotlib, I. H. (1985). Developmental considerations in the study of childhood depression. *Developmental Review, 5,* 162–199.

Emslie, G. J., Roffward, H. P., Rush, A. J., Weinberg, W. A., & Parkin-Feigenbaum, L. (1987). Sleep EEG findings in depressed children and adolescents. *American Journal of Psychiatry, 144,* 668–670.

Feighner, J. P., Robins, E., Guze, S. B., Woodruff, R. A., Winokur, G., & Munoz, R. (1972). Diagnostic criteria for use in psychiatric research. *Archives of General Psychiatry, 26,* 57–63.

Forehand, R., Lautenschlager, G. J., Faust, J., & Graziano, W. G. (1986). Parent perceptions and parent-child interactions in clinic-referred children: A preliminary investigation of the effects of maternal depressive moods. *Behaviour Research and Therapy, 24,* 73–75.

Glasberg, R., & Aboud, F. (1981). A developmental perspective on the study of depression: Children's evaluative reactions to sadness. *Developmental Psychology, 17,* 195–202.

Glasberg, R., & Aboud, F. (1982). Keeping one's distance from sadness: Children's self-reports of emotional experience. *Developmental Psychology, 18,* 287–293.

Glaser, K. (1968). Masked depression in children and adolescents. In S. Chess & A. Thomas (Eds.), *Annual progress in child psychiatry and child development* (Vol. 1, pp. 345–355). New York: Brunner/Mazel.

Goetz, R. R., Goetz, D. M., Hanlon, C., Davies, M., Weitzman, E. D., & Puig-Antich, J.

(1983). Spindle characteristics in prepubertal major depressives during an episode and after sustained recovery: A controlled study. *Sleep, 6*, 369–375.

Hawton, K. (1986). *Suicide and attempted suicide among children and adolescents.* Beverly Hills, CA: Sage.

Kandel, D. B., & Davies, M. (1982). Epidemiology of depressive mood in adolescents: An empirical study. *Archives of General Psychiatry, 39*, 1205–1212.

Kaplan, S. L., Hong, G. K., & Weinhold, C. (1984). Epidemiology of depressive symptomatology in adolescents. *Journal of the American Academy of Child Psychiatry, 23*, 91–98.

Kashani, J. H., Barbero, G. J., & Bolander, F. D. (1981). Depression in hospitalized pediatric patients. *Journal of the American Academy of Child Psychiatry, 20*, 123–134.

Kashani, J. H., Cantwell, D. P., Shekim, W. O., & Reid, J. C. (1982). Major depressive disorder in children admitted to an inpatient community mental health center. *American Journal of Psychiatry, 139*, 671–672.

Kashani, J. H., Husain, A., Shekim, W. O., Hodges, K. K., Cytryn, L., & McKnew, D. H. (1981). Current perspectives on childhood depression: An overview. *American Journal of Psychiatry, 138*, 143–153.

Kashani, J. H., McGee, R. O., Clarkson, S. E., Anderson, J. C., Walton, L. A., Williams, S., Silva, P. A., Robins, A. J., Cytryn, L., & McKnew, D. H. (1983). Depression in a sample of 9-year old children. *Archives of General Psychiatry, 40*, 1217–1223.

Kashani, J. H., Ray, J. S., & Carlson, G. A. (1984). Depression and depression-like states in preschool-age children in a child development unit. *American Journal of Psychiatry, 141*, 1397–1402.

Kashani, J., & Simonds, J. F. (1979). The incidence of depression in children. *American Journal of Psychiatry, 136*, 1203–1205.

Kazdin, A. E. (1988). Childhood depression. In E. J. Mash & L. G. Terdal (Eds.), *Behavioral assessment of childhood disorders* (2nd ed., pp. 157–195). New York: Guilford.

Kazdin, A. E. (1989). Evaluation of the Pleasure Scale in the assessment of anhedonia in children. *Journal of the American Academy of Child and Adolescent Psychiatry, 28*, 364–372.

Kazdin, A. E., French, N. H., Unis, A. S., & Esveldt-Dawson, K. (1983). Assessment of childhood depression: Correspondence of child and parent ratings. *Journal of the American Academy of Child Psychiatry, 22*, 157–164.

Keller, M. B., Shapiro, R. W., Lavori, P. W., & Wolfe, N. (1982). Relapse in major depressive disorder: Analysis with the life table. *Archives of General Psychiatry, 39*, 911–915.

Kovacs, M., & Beck, A. T. (1977). An empirical clinical approach towards a definition of childhood depression. In J. G. Schulterbrandt & A. Raskin (Eds.), *Depression in children: Diagnosis, treatment, and conceptual models* (pp. 1–25). New York: Raven Press.

Kovacs, M., Feinberg, T. L., Crouse-Novak, M., Paulauskas, S. L., & Finkelstein, R. (1984a). Depressive disorders in childhood I. A longitudinal prospective study of characteristics and recovery. *Archives of General Psychiatry, 41*, 229–237.

Kovacs, M., Feinberg, T. L., Crouse-Novak, M., Paulauskas, S. L., Pollock, M., & Finkelstein, R. (1984b). Depressive disorders in childhood II. A longitudinal study of the risk for a subsequent major depression. *Archives of General Psychiatry, 41*, 643–649.

Lahmeyer, H. W., Poznanski, E. O., & Bellur, S. N. (1983). Sleep in depressed adolescents: Comparison with age-matched controls. *American Journal of Psychiatry, 140*, 1150–1153.

Ling, W., Oftedol, G., & Weinberg, W. (1970). Depressive illness in childhood presenting as a severe headache. *American Journal of Diseases of Children, 120*, 122–124.

Lobovits, D. A., & Handal, P. J. (1985). Childhood depression: Prevalence using DSM-III criteria and validity of parent and child depression scales. *Journal of Pediatric Psychology, 10,* 45–54.

MacFarlane, J. W., Allen, L., & Honzik, M. P. (1954). *A developmental study of the behavior problems of normal children between 21 months and 14 years.* Berkeley: University of California Press.

Mahler, M. (1961). On sadness and grief in infancy and childhood. *Psychoanalytic Study of the Child, 16,* 332.

Malmquist, C. P. (1977). Childhood depression: A clinical and behavioral perspective. In J. G. Schulterbrandt & A. Raskin (Eds.), *Depression in children: Diagnosis, treatment and conceptual models* (pp. 35–59). New York: Raven Press.

Mash, E. J., & Johnston, C. (1983). Parental perception of child behavior problems, parenting self-esteem, and mothers' reported stress in younger and older hyperactive and normal children. *Journal of Consulting and Clinical Psychology, 51,* 86–89.

McGee, R., & Williams, S. (1988). A longitudinal study of depression in nine-year-old children. *Journal of the American Academy of Child and Adolescent Psychiatry, 27,* 342–348.

Mezzich, A. C., & Mezzich, J. E. (1979). Symptomatology of depression in adolescence. *Journal of Personality Assessment, 43,* 267–275,

Mindham, R. H. S. (1982). Tricyclic antidepressants and amine precursors. In E. S. Paykel (Ed.), *Handbook of affective disorders* (pp. 231–245). New York: Guilford Press.

Mitchell, J., McCauley, E., Burke, P. M., & Moss, S. J. (1988). Phenomenology of depression in children and adolescents. *Journal of the American Academy of Child and Adolescent Psychiatry, 27,* 12–20.

Moretti, M. M., Fine, S., Haley, G., & Marriage, K. (1985). Child and adolescent depression: Child-report versus parent-report information. *Journal of the American Academy of Child Psychiatry, 24,* 298–302.

Norvel, N., Brophy, C., & Finch, A. J. (1985). The relationship of anxiety to childhood depression. *Journal of Personality Assessment, 49,* 151–153.

Orvaschel, H., Puig-Antich, J., Chambers, W., Tabrizi, M. A., & Johnson, R. (1982). Retrospective assessment of prepubertal major depression with Kiddie-SADS-E. *Journal of the American Academy of Child Psychiatry, 21,* 392–397.

Petti, T. A. (Ed.). (1983). *Childhood depression.* New York: Haworth Press.

Preskorn, S. H., Weller, E. B., & Weller, R. A. (1982). Depression in children: Relationship between plasma imipramine levels and response. *Journal of Clinical Psychiatry, 43,* 450–453.

Puig-Antich, J. (1986). Psychobiological markers: Effects of age and puberty. In M. Rutter, C. E. Izard, & P. B. Read (Eds.), *Depression in young people: Developmental and clinical perspectives* (pp. 341–381). New York: Guilford Press.

Puig-Antich, J., & Gittelman, R. (1982). Depression in childhood and adolescence. In E. S. Paykel (Ed.), *Handbook of affective disorders* (pp. 379–392). New York: Guilford Press.

Puig-Antich, J., Perel, J., Lupatkin, W., Chambers, W. J., Tabrizi, M. A., King, J., Davies, M., Johnson, R., & Stiller, R. (1987). Imipramine in prepubertal major depressive disorders. *Archives of General Psychiatry, 44,* 81–89.

Reynolds, W. M. (1985). Depression in childhood and adolescence: Diagnosis, assessment, intervention strategies, and research. In T. R. Kratochwill (Ed.), *Advances in school psychology* (Vol. 4, pp. 133–189). Hillsdale, NJ: Erlbaum.

Rie, H. E. (1966). Depression in childhood: A survey of some pertinent contributions. *Journal of the American Academy of Child Psychiatry, 5,* 653–685.

Rochlin, G. (1965). *Griefs and discontents.* Boston: Little, Brown.

Rutter, M. R. (1986). The developmental psychopathology of depression: Issues and perspectives. In M. Rutter, C. E. Izard, & P. B. Read (Eds.), *Depression in young people: Developmental and clinical perspectives* (pp. 3–30). New York: Guilford Press.

Rutter, M. R., Izard, C. E., & Read, P. G. (Eds.) (1986). *Depression in young people: Developmental and clinical perspectives.* New York: Guilford.

Rutter, M. R., Tizard, J., & Whitmore, K. (1970). *Education, health, and behavior.* London: Longmans.

Ryan, N. D., Puig-Antich, J., Ambrosini, P., Rabinovich, H., Robinson, D., Nelson, B., Iyengar, S., & Twomey, J. (1987). The clinical picture of major depression in children and adolescents. *Archives of General Psychiatry, 44,* 854–861.

Ryan, N. D., Puig-Antich, J., Cooper, T., Rabinovich, H., Ambrosini, P., Davies, M., King, J., Torres, D., & Fried, J. (1986). Imipramine in adolescent major depression: Plasma level and clinical response. *Acta Psychiatrica Scandinavica, 73,* 275–288.

Seligman, M. E. P., & Peterson, C. (1986). A learned helplessness perspective on childhood depression: Theory and research. In M. Rutter, C. E. Izard, & P. B. Read (Eds.), *Depression in young people: Developmental and clinical perspectives* (pp. 223–249). New York: Guilford Press.

Spitz, R. (1946). Anaclitic depression. *Psychoanalytic Study of the Child, 2,* 113–117.

Spitzer, R. L., Endicott, J., & Robins, E. (1978). Research Diagnostic Criteria: Rationale and reliability. *Archives of General Psychiatry, 35,* 773–782.

Sroufe, L. A., & Rutter, M. (1984). The domain of developmental psychopathology. *Child Development, 55,* 17–29.

Strauss, C. C., Last, C. G., Hersen, M., & Kazdin, A. E. (1988). Association between anxiety and depression in children and adolescents with anxiety disorders. *Journal of Abnormal Child Psychology, 16,* 57–68.

Tisher, M., & Lang, M. (1983). The Children's Depression Scale: Review and further developments. In D. P. Cantwell & G. A. Carlson (Eds.), *Childhood depression* (pp. 181–203). New York: Spectrum.

Toolan, J. M. (1962). Depression in children and adolescents. *American Journal of Orthopsychiatry, 32,* 404–414.

Trad, P. V. (1987). *Infant and childhood depression: Developmental factors.* New York: Wiley.

Weinberg, W. A., Rutman, J., Sullivan, L., Pencik, E. C., & Dietz, S. G. (1973). Depression in children referred to an education diagnostic center. *Journal of Pediatrics, 83,* 1065–1072.

Weissman, M. M., Merikangas, K. R., Wickramaratne, P., Kidd, K. K., Prusoff, B. A., Leckman, J. F., & Pauls, D. L. (1986). Understanding the clinical heterogeneity of major depression using family data. *Archives of General Psychiatry, 43,* 430–434.

Werry, J. S., & Quay, H. C. (1971). The prevalence of behavior symptoms in younger elementary school children. *American Journal of Orthopsychiatry, 41,* 136–143.

Wolfe, V. V., Finch, A. J., Saylor, C. F., Blount, R. L., Pallmeyer, R. P., & Carek, D. J. (1987). Negative affectivity in children: A multitrait-multimethod investigation. *Journal of Consulting and Clinical Psychology, 55,* 245–250.

Young, W., Knowles, J. B., MacLean, A. W., Boag, L., & McConville, B. J. (1982). The sleep of childhood depressives. *Biological Psychiatry, 17,* 1163–1168.

9 Recommendations for Research on Disruptive Behavior Disorders of Childhood and Adolescence

ROLF LOEBER AND BENJAMIN B. LAHEY

1. Introduction

Researchers in the area of Disruptive Behavior Disorders of childhood and adolescence face a frustrating paradox. Until we know how many distinct disorders or dimensions constitute the domain of Disruptive Behavior Disorders and until we have reached a consensus on classificatory criteria and measurement strategies, it is extremely difficult to conduct meaningful research on these disorders. On the other hand, until meaningful research has been conducted, we will not have the empirical basis from which to construct classificatory criteria and to evaluate the relative merits of different measurement strategies.

As a result, after 25 years of intensive research efforts, consensus among researchers can be reached on only the most general issues concerning the Disruptive Behavior Disorders. The recent publication of the revised, third edition of the *Diagnostic and Statistical Manual of the Mental Disorders* (DSM-III-R) (American Psychiatric Association [APA], 1987) provides an important case in point. Although revisions of the diagnostic categories comprised by the domain called the Disruptive Behavior Disorders of childhood and adolescence were based on the recommendations of many of the most respected scholars in the field, the new categories and criteria are at least as controversial as the original catego-

ROLF LOEBER • Department of Psychiatry, Western Psychiatric Institute and Clinic, School of Medicine, University of Pittsburgh, Pittsburgh, Pennsylvania 15213.   BENJAMIN B. LAHEY • Department of Psychology, University of Georgia, Athens, Georgia 30602.

ries provided in the DSM-III (American Psychiatric Association [APA], 1980). A close inspection of the database available to these scholars makes quite clear the reasons why no other outcome could be expected. One cannot develop a set of unambiguous and widely endorsed diagnostic criteria using an empirical base that is disparate, fragmented, not comparable across studies, and mixed liberally with clinical impressions.

As understandable and inevitable as the difficulties in developing criteria for DSM-III-R were, the disappointment felt by researchers and clinicians at its publication is equally understandable. For all of its faults in the area of the Disruptive Behavior Disorders, DSM-III provided researchers with a standard set of categories against which their subjects could be defined. It was hoped by many that DSM-III-R would provide even more successful definitional anchor points. In retrospect, those hopes were unrealistic. The difficulties and ambiguities in DSM-III have been compounded by the new criteria of DSM-III-R, which are not only substantially different for all the Disruptive Behavior Disorders, but in some instances appear to be inadequate and empirically unfounded.

It was in this atmosphere that a number of researchers met to discuss improved strategies for research on disruptive disorders. A first seminal meeting was chaired by Jan Loney and J. Gerald Young at the 1986 meeting of the American Academy of Child and Adolescent Psychiatry. Out of this meeting, an interdisciplinary group of concerned researchers was formed that held a subsequent meeting in Athens, Georgia, in February 1987. The conference was attended by Howard Abikoff, Susan B. Campbell, Caryn L. Carlson, E. Jane Costello, Mina K. Dulcan, Rex Forehand, Steven P. Hinshaw, David J. Kolko, Marcus Kruesi, Benjamin B. Lahey, Rolf Loeber, Richard Milich, William E. Pelham, Robert L. Sprague, and James M. Swanson. Several other meetings subsequently took place over the following year and were attended by Howard Abikoff, Benjamin B. Lahey, Rolf Loeber, Jan Loney, and William E. Pelham.

It quickly became obvious, given the current state of available research, that this group would encounter difficulties in reaching consensus similar to that experienced by the DSM-III-R committee in its attempts to agree on the specific diagnostic criteria for Disruptive Behavior Disorders (such as criteria and cutting scores). Thus, no attempt was made to create an "alternative DSM-III-R" for researchers. However, cogent and illuminating discussions illustrated the issues and research strategies that divided the group. Understandably, these discussions often led to unresolvable points of disagreement because of the absence of critical empirical evidence. This chapter presents the recommendations of two participants at those meetings for research strategies in studies of Disruptive Behavior Disorders to collect the kinds of data that will allow future resolution of current differences in opinion.

1.1. Current Diagnostic Terminology in the Domain of Conduct Problems

Since the formulation of Conduct Disorder as a separate disorder in the first edition of the DSM (American Psychiatric Association [APA], 1952), clinicians and researchers have questioned whether or not it is appropriate to conceptualize conduct problems as a single dimension or whether more than one dimension can be distinguished (Achenbach & Edelbrock, 1978; Dreger, 1982; Garber, 1984; Yule, 1981). The second edition of DSM referred to distinctions among three types of Conduct Disorder: unsocialized–aggressive reaction, group–delinquent reaction, and runaway reaction (American Psychiatric Association [APA], 1968). This was later changed in DSM-III to four types: undersocialized aggressive, socialized aggressive, undersocialized nonaggressive, and socialized nonaggressive (APA, 1980). The publication of DSM-III also introduced a new category of conduct problems, termed Oppositional Disorder.

The latest version of the DSM (DSM-III-R) renamed Oppositional Disorder as Oppositional Defiant Disorder and replaced the four subtypes of Conduct Disorder with a classification that recalled two of the three types from DSM-II: group type, solitary aggressive type, and undifferentiated type, which is a remainder category (APA, 1987). Whereas DSM-III allowed the concurrent diagnoses of Oppositional Disorder and Conduct Disorder, DSM-III-R states that the diagnosis of Conduct Disorder hierarchically precludes the diagnosis of Oppositional Defiant Disorder.

DSM-III-R's distinction between Oppositional Defiant Disorder and Conduct Disorder is based largely on the seriousness of the acts involved. Oppositional Defiant Disorder refers to "a pattern of negativistic, hostile, and defiant behavior without the more serious violations of the basic rights of others that are seen in Conduct Disorder" (APA, 1987, p. 53). The diagnosis is developmentally defined in the loose sense that it applies only to those children whose oppositional behavior is more pronounced than in other children of the same age. Behaviors characteristic of Oppositional Defiant Disorder include temper tantrums, chronic disobedience, irritability, and provocative behavior patterns that are more extreme than is typical for youngsters of a given age.

Conduct Disorder refers to the presence of a "persistent pattern of conduct in which the basic rights of others and major societal norms or

rules are violated" (APA, 1987, p. 56). These behaviors include the inflic-
tion of physical or mental harm, such as physical cruelty and physical
assault, as well as property loss, such as theft or forgery. Although
many of these behaviors are considered delinquent acts because they
violate criminal laws, not all symptoms of Conduct Disorder are suffi-
ciently serious to fall into this category. Further, there are a number of
symptoms of Conduct Disorder that do not lead to direct victimization of
others; examples of these are truancy, substance abuse, and running
away from home.

1.2. Current Diagnostic Terminology in the Domain of Attention Deficits/Hyperactivity

The patterns of behavior in the attention deficit/hyperactivity domain have been referred to formerly as Minimal Brain Damage and
Minimal Brain Dysfunction. These highly inferential terms were replaced in the second version of the DSM by Hyperkinetic Reaction of
Childhood (APA, 1968). With the publication of DSM-III, the term Attention Deficit Disorder (ADD) was introduced, which made a distinction among three putative dimensions of maladaptive behavior: inattention, impulsivity, and hyperactivity. Based on these three dimensions,
two diagnostic categories were distinguished in DSM-III. Children with
difficulties in all three dimensions were given the label of Attention
Deficit Disorder with Hyperactivity (ADD/H), whereas children with
deficits in attention and impulsivity only were said to exhibit Attention
Deficit Disorder without Hyperactivity (ADD/WO).

In DSM-III-R, the distinction among the three dimensions was
dropped in favor of a single, unidimensional list of symptoms, with
children receiving a diagnosis of Attention Deficit–Hyperactivity Disorder (AD-HD) when they scored over criterion on the symptom list. An
additional diagnostic category of Undifferentiated Attention Deficit Disorder (UADD) was created, which partially approximates the former
ADD/WO diagnosis. Because the new diagnostic categories of AD-HD
and UADD are based on logically contradictory assumptions and are not
defined in mutually exclusive terms, they will likely create confusion for
researchers. This issue, and proposed solutions, will be discussed
below.

1.3. Definitions of Other Terms Used

Although we primarily will use in this chapter diagnostic terms
from DSM-III and DSM-III-R, we also will need to use other terms
whose precise meanings vary considerably in the literature. Therefore,

to minimize confusion it may be helpful to define those other terms as they are used herein. Diagnostic categories will continue to be capitalized; uncapitalized terms will refer to more general and more continuous patterns of deviant behavior as may emerge from factor analyses of parent or teacher ratings. Thus, the term *conduct problems* refers to the broad domain of disruptive, noncompliant, disturbing, and antisocial behaviors, whereas the term *attention deficit/hyperactivity* refers to the broad domain of behavioral and cognitive difficulties associated with deficits in attention, impulsivity, and overactivity.

1.4. Criteria for Distinctions between Disorders and Subtypes

There are several forms of evidence to substantiate distinctions between disorders and distinctions between subtypes within a disorder. First, different forms of psychopathology, obviously, should have distinct characteristics. Second, different forms of psychopathology should be associated with different correlates of patient behavior (such as handicaps other than the psychopathology) and different background factors (such as familial psychopathology). These correlates and background factors may or may not reflect etiological differences unique to one disorder but not to another. Third, distinctions between disorders can be strengthened when each disorder is associated with or predictive of discrete outcomes over time. Fourth, distinctions between disorders may be based on patients' selective response to one but not to other forms of treatment. Because of space limitations, this chapter concentrates on the first three categories of evidence.

2. Recommendations for the Study of the Disruptive Disorders

Six general types of recommendations are proposed concerning (1) dimensions of behavior that should be included in studies of the Disruptive Behavior Disorders and distinctions that should be made among those dimensions, (2) the frequent and highly important overlap among dimensions/disorders, (3) optimal measurement strategies, (4) exclusionary criteria in selecting subject samples, (5) optimal reporting standards, and (6) needed research on the developmental nature of the Disruptive Behavior Disorders.

2.1. Recommendations Concerning Dimensions of the Disruptive Behavior Disorders

Confusion exists concerning the number of dimensions that should be distinguished in both the conduct problem domain and the attention deficit/hyperactivity domain. The general nature of this confusion will be described separately for each domain, and preliminary evidence will be presented suggesting that a number of distinctions can be made within each domain. Some of these distinctions may greatly improve our ability to predict the developmental course of Disruptive Behavior Disorders and may make more fruitful studies of etiology and treatment possible. Therefore, it is suggested that the distinctions best supported by current evidence be made in future studies. The empirical basis for most of the distinctions that will be recommended is modest at best, but it is precisely for this reason that it is suggested that they be made. It is only by providing more evidence that researchers will be able to make rational decisions in the future on, for example, the possible existence of distinct subtypes of conduct disorder. This will make it possible to increase the comparability among studies, while not impeding the development of alternative, empirically based distinctions.

2.1.1. Dimensions of the Conduct Problems Domain

A review of the current evidence suggests that several rather than one dimension will eventually be distinguished. Indeed, the current evidence from factor analytic and other studies lends some tentative support to some of the distinctions made in DSM-III-R. Factor analytic studies of elementary-school-aged children often reveal at least two factors in the conduct problem domain: a oppositional/defiant factor and one (or more) conduct disorder factors (Dreger, 1981). On the other hand, some factor analytic studies of children in this age range occasionally have failed to distinguish between the two dimensions and showed one combined oppositional defiant and conduct disorder factor (Quay, 1979). This probably indicates that youngsters who show conduct disorder also tend to show many of the oppositional behaviors that are characteristic of younger children. However, there is a clear need for additional research to test the hypothesis that Conduct Disorder and Oppositional–Defiant Disorder are distinct entities, even though they overlap in some children.

In contrast to studies of elementary-school-age children, factor analytic studies of preschool children have more consistently yielded a single "externalizing" factor composed only of oppositional defiant behaviors (Fowler & Park, 1979; Kohn, 1977; McDermott, 1983; O'Donnell & Van Tuinan, 1979). However, these studies do not provide strong evidence against the distinction of separate conduct behavior and oppositional defiant behavior. Frequently, the more serious antisocial behaviors, which are considered to be symptomatic of Conduct Disorder, do not emerge until later in childhood or even adolescence (Loeber, 1988; Robins, 1985). As a result, most factor analytic studies on the behavior of preschoolers do not include many items referring to Conduct Disorder in the item pools, and those that do find that the items are endorsed by raters so infrequently that they do not load strongly on any factor. Thus, it may well be that there is a single oppositional defiant dimension of conduct problems during the preschool years but that at least one other dimension of more serious antisocial behaviors (Conduct Disorder) emerges during the elementary school years.

Other multivariate studies have looked for possible subclassifications within the conduct disorder dimension. Studies have documented separate aggressive and nonaggressive conduct disorder factors or clusters (Aman, Werry, Fitzpatrick, Lowe, & Waters, 1983; Burdsal, Force, & Campbell, 1984; Glow, Glow, & Rump, 1982; McGee et al., 1985; Pelham, Atkins, Murphy, & White, 1981; Quay, 1979; Werry, Sprague, & Cohen, 1975). The emergence of these distinct factors may reflect the gradually increasing prevalence and stability of nonaggressive conduct problems during late childhood and adolescence (Gersten, Langner, Eisenberg, Simcha-Fagan, & McCarthy, 1976; Glow et al., 1982; Lindholm & Touliatos, 1981; Loeber, 1982).

Loeber and Schmaling examined the large number of factor analytic studies based on ratings of child psychopathology (ranging from preschooler to adolescents), covering either male or male/female samples (Loeber & Schmaling, 1985a). They noticed that in many instances conduct problems fell out in two factors. By using multidimensional scaling they found that conduct problems could be represented by one scale with two distinct poles. One pole consisted of overt conduct problems, such as argues, teases, attacks people, irritable, and the like. The other pole consisted of nonaggressive, more concealed conduct problems such as alcohol and/or drug use, truancy, theft, or fire setting. Behaviors at the respective poles were labeled *overt* and *covert* conduct problems; more restricted labels, however, would be *aggressive* and *nonaggressive* conduct problems. It should be noted that disobedience appeared as a feature of both poles as it was situated in the middle of the problem scale.

Factor analyses on teacher ratings, however, usually show one conduct disorder factor instead of two. Systematic comparisons by Lachar, Gdwoski, and Snyder between teacher and parent ratings on the same children showed two conduct disorder factors derived from the parent ratings and one factor derived from the teacher ratings (Lachar, Gdowski, & Snyder, 1984). This may suggest that the common finding of only one factor in teacher ratings is a methodological artifact, perhaps reflecting either teachers' limited ability to observe low-rate, concealed behaviors or the setting-specificity of problem behavior in some children.

Several reservations should be expressed about the findings of factor analytic studies. First, it remains to be seen whether the antisocial dimension is identical when exclusively female samples are considered. Second, it must be emphasized that factor analytic studies shed light on the clustering of *behaviors* only and not directly on the clustering or classification of *subjects*. Third, factor analytic studies do not directly reveal the presence of subjects who score high on more than one factor and whose generalized behavior problems may have a particularly poor prognosis (see below). Fourth, many of the studies deleted low-frequency conduct disorder items from inclusion in the factor analyses because of infrequent endorsement. Fifth, results from factor analyses can vary greatly with the nature and sex of subject samples (e.g., clinic versus community samples). Finally, the data used by researchers often violate the underlying assumptions of factor analyses because of categorical behavior categories, severely restricted ranges of such categories, highly skewed distributions, and non-normality.

Factor analytic studies are not the only source of empirical evidence concerning the validity of distinctions among putative dimensions of the conduct problems domain, however. Comparisons between categorically defined Conduct Disorder and Oppositional Defiant Disorder are few in number, but some relevant information is available. Several studies have shown that some children who do not meet the diagnostic criteria for Conduct Disorder do receive DSM-III diagnoses of Oppositional Disorder, suggesting a degree of independence of these two dimensions/disorders (Anderson, Williams, McGee, & Silva, 1987; Reeves, Werry, Elkind, & Zametkin, 1987; Rey *et al.*, 1988; Werry, Methven, Fitzpatrick, & Dixon, 1983). However, the interdiagnostician agreement for the diagnosis of Oppositional disorder was low and disagreements tended to occur primarily with the diagnosis of Conduct Disorder.

Although the more distinct DSM-III-R criteria for these two disorders may result in improved reliability of differential diagnosis, these studies raise concern about the validity of the distinction. Furthermore, the only study that has directly compared children with sole DSM-III diagnoses of Conduct Disorder and Oppositional Disorder found that they differed only in the magnitude of social impairment and the severity of antisocial behavior (Rey *et al.*, 1988). If confirmed by future studies, such findings suggest that the oppositional defiant and conduct disorder dimensions may not be qualitatively distinct, although important quantitative distinctions may be present. If so, the systematic scaling of the severity of children's behavior problems that has been in existence since the 1920s may be useful in making significant quantitative distinctions (Vidoni, Fleming, & Mintz, 1983; Wickman, 1928). However, it must be emphasized strongly that our knowledge of the status of Oppositional Defiant Disorder as an independent dimension of conduct problems is too sketchy at the present time to make anything more than preliminary guesses as to its nature.

Other studies have compared children who exhibit both aggressive and nonaggressive aspects of conduct disorder. Robins and Loeber and Schmaling hypothesized that the risk for psychopathology would be substantially higher when individuals' repertoires consisted of both aggressive and nonaggressive conduct problems as compared with youngsters whose problem behavior was confined to only aggressive or nonaggressive acts (Loeber & Schmaling, 1985b; Robins, 1966). Loeber and Schmaling (1985b) distinguished among those boys who fought and stole (called versatiles), those who stole only, those who fought only, and a remainder group. They found that the risk of delinquency, particularly repeated offending, was highest among the versatiles, followed by the exclusive stealers, the exclusive fighters coming next, and the remainder coming last. These results held at a follow-up five years later (Stouthamer-Loeber, Loeber, & Green, 1988). The extremely deviant behavior of the versatiles (involving numerous conduct problems in addition to fighting and stealing) and arrest for delinquent acts have been confirmed in a number of studies (Junger-Tas & Junger, 1984; Lewis, 1954; Roff, 1986). It is possible, however, that these findings mean only that children whose Conduct Disorder is more severe (i.e., exhibit more symptoms of any type) have a poorer prognosis.

In DSM-III, the social aspects of Conduct Disorder were captured by the distinction between Socialized and Undersocialized Conduct Disorder, based on children's attachment to others. Research evidence for this distinction has not been strong (but see Jenkins, 1966). The distinction was not pursued further in DSM-III-R; instead, a solitary aggressive type was distinguished from a group type, depending on whether or not youngsters engage in antisocial behavior by themselves or in the company of peers. As far as we know, however, reliable procedures for classifying youngsters on this basis are not yet available. The review of juvenile co-offending by Reiss (1986) illustrates the many difficulties in establishing whether antisocial acts are habitually committed in groups or not and whether youngsters can be classified on that basis. Some research findings indicate that solitary offenders tend to be more at risk for delinquent careers than those who commit crime in the company of others (Chaiken & Chaiken, 1982; Osborn & West, 1980); whether this also applies to conduct problems in younger children is far from clear, however.

Another way of approaching the justification for distinct disorders or subclassification in diagnostic categories is to examine the convergent and divergent validity of behavioral items selected as criteria for a diagnosis or for the summary score for a dimension. We were not able to find many studies on the divergent and convergent validity of the summary scores used in DSM-III diagnoses (but see Loney, 1984, 1985, 1987; Stewart & deBlois, 1984).

So far, the validity of potential subclassifications has been examined in terms of risk for delinquency, but a number of other relevant outcomes, such as schizophrenia, drug abuse, and alcohol abuse, are all associated with early conduct problems (Robins, 1966; Rutter & Giller, 1983). It remains to be seen, however, which subclassifications would contribute further to specify the risk for these outcomes as well.

2.1.2. Summary

There is a scarcity of studies on Oppositional Defiant Disorder, and its divergent validity from Conduct Disorder is unclear. Factor analytic and group comparison studies have lent some tentative support to the distinction between aggressive and nonaggressive conduct problems; but at this time, research is lacking to distinguish between solitary and group type in Conduct Disorder. Much work still needs to be done to determine the convergent and divergent validity of the defining criteria for these disorders.

It is recommended that studies of the conduct problems domain include measures of the differences between, and the degree of overlap among, the three putative dimensions of oppositional–defiant behavior, aggressive conduct problems, nonaggressive conduct problems, and solitary versus group-committed conduct problems. Particular attention should be paid to those individuals who exhibit both aggressive and nonaggressive conduct disorder. These youngster are apparently more prevalent in clinical populations, whereas exclusively aggressive and exclusively nonaggressive conduct problem children are more common in community samples. Future studies would do well to examine more closely the changing relationships among the dimensions of disruptive behavior over the course of childhood and adolescence.

2.2. Recommendations Concerning Dimensions of the Attention Deficits/Hyperactivity Domain

2.2.1. Inattention as Distinct from Hyperactivity

It is probable that the maladaptive behaviors that constitute the attention deficits/hyperactivity domain are also multidimensional in nature. Existing research suggests that, when sufficient numbers of items descriptive of both dimensions are included in the item pools and when subject samples are employed in which there is sufficient variance on those items, two dimensions of ADD generally are extracted in factor analytic studies (see reviews by Carlson & Lahey, 1983; Hinshaw, 1987; Quay, 1986). One dimension primarily describes inattention and disorganization and the other contains items that refer mostly to motor hyperactivity and impulsivity. Only rarely is a separate impulsivity factor reported (Lambert & Hartsough, 1987).

Current research, however, is less clear about the placement of specific items on these two factors, largely for two reasons. There is considerably more variation across studies in the inclusion of specific items in the item pool than in the general nature of the factors extracted. Thus, although it is possible to portray these two dimensions in general terms, there is only partial agreement about their descriptors. However, representative item lists for the two factors can be found in several studies (Conners, 1969, 1973; Lahey et al., in press; Neeper & Lahey, 1986; Quay & Peterson, 1983; Ullman, Sleator, & Sprague, 1984). Some studies failed to extract separate factors, especially when a relatively small number of descriptors of inattention and motor hyperactivity were included in the measurement instrument (Furlong & Fortman, 1984; Loney, Langhorne, & Paternite, 1978). Other cases of inconsistent findings are less explicable, however. For example, factor analyses of the Conners Teacher Rating Scale have sometimes yielded separate inattention and motor hyperactivity factors (Conners, 1969; Goyette, Conners, & Ulrich, 1978; O'Leary, Vivian, & Nisi, 1985; Werry & Hawthorne, 1976) and sometimes have not (Trites, Blouin, & LaPrade, 1982; Werry et al., 1975).

Similarly, factor analysis of teacher-completed Child Behavior Checklists yielded separate factors (Edelbrock & Achenbach, 1984), but factor analysis of parent-completed scales did not, in spite of only minor differences in the item pools for the parent and teacher versions (Achenbach, 1978). On the other hand, factor analysis of the Revised Behavior Problem Checklist (Quay & Peterson, 1983) yielded separate factors when completed by parents but not when completed by teachers (Hinshaw, Morrison, Carte, & Cornsweet, 1987). However, the weight of evidence supports the distinction between inattention and motor hyperactivity factors (Carlson & Lahey, 1983; Quay, 1986).

It is important to note that this two-dimensional description of the attention deficit/hyperactivity domain based on factor analytic evidence is not consistent with the definition of the attention deficit disorders used in DSM-III, which distinguished three dimensions (inattention, impulsivity, and motor hyperactivity) (Campbell & Werry, 1986). The distinction between the inattention and motor activity dimensions is both warranted and important, but insufficient evidence exists to determine whether a third dimension of impulsivity should be distinguished. At this time, it appears that descriptors of what was termed impulsivity in DSM-III are actually components of both the inattention and motor hyperactivity dimensions. Those DSM-III items from the impulsivity factor descriptive of disorganization and need for supervision load rather consistently with the inattention items (Lahey, Schaughency, Hynd, Carlson, & Nieves, 1987; Neeper & Lahey, 1986). On the other hand, the descriptors of what appears to lie more directly at the core of Kagan's (1966) concept of impulsive tempo ("acting before thinking") tend to load on the motor hyperactivity items. (Lahey, Stempniak, Robinson, & Tyroler, 1978; Lahey, Schaughency, Hynd, Carlson, & Nieves, 1987; Neeper & Lahey, 1986).

Caution should be exercised, however, in accepting any conclusion regarding the items grouped under the impulsivity dimension in DSM-III. This caution is warranted for at least three reasons. First, the factor loadings of some of these items varied somewhat among the different factor analyses (Healy et al., 1987; Lahey et al., in press). Second, when descriptors of conduct disorder are also included in the factor analysis, some of these so-called impulsivity items sometimes factor with conduct disorder rather than motor hyperactivity (Pelham et al., 1981). Third, our ability to define and measure impulsivity is fraught with difficulties (Milich & Kramer, 1984). Thus, it appears that ADD is best characterized by two dimensions, inattention–disorganization and motor hyperactivity–impulsivity, but the role of impulsivity in these factors is still unclear.

This two-factor conceptualization of ADD is similarly inconsistent with the DSM-III-R criteria for Attention Deficit–Hyperactivity Disorder (AD-HD). On the one hand, as the text description in DSM-III-R of AD-HD clearly states, AD-HD is conceptualized as a disorder involving *both* inattention and hyperactivity/impulsivity (APA, 1987, p. 50). On the other hand, however, to qualify for this diagnosis, the child must manifest *any* 8 of the list of 14 symptoms of inattention, motor hyperactivity, and impulsivity. Such a unidimensional definition would be an appropriate psychometric strategy if all the symptoms of AD-HD could be said to be interchangeable manifest markers of the *same* latent trait. However, the large body of empirical evidence that suggests that the attention deficit/hyperactivity domain is not unidimensional implies that the DSM-III-R criteria for AD-HD may well not accomplish its stated aim.

Comparing DSM-III and DSM-III-R, the former had a much more explicit multidimensional definition of ADD and therefore constituted stricter criteria for diagnosis than are currently held by DSM-III-R. This implies that some children, who according to DSM-III criteria did not previously qualify for the multidimensional diagnosis of ADD/H, may under DSM-III-R qualify for a diagnosis of AD-HD. For example, one study of a school-based population has shown that 37.5% of children who meet DSM-III-R criteria for AD-HD do *not* meet DSM-III criteria for ADD/H (Newcorn *et al.*, 1987). In contrast, only 9.1% of the children diagnosed as ADD/H failed to qualify for a DSM-III-R diagnosis of AD-HD. Although replications of this finding with clinic–referred samples are clearly needed, these findings certainly strengthen the concern that the DSM-III-R category of AD-HD will be considerably more heterogeneous than the DSM-III category of ADD/H.

2.2.2. Inattention without Hyperactivity

Both DSM-III and DSM-III-R allow for some children to be diagnosed as ADD without hyperactivity. Clearly, children are referred to clinics who have problems in attention and disorganization, but not in motor hyperactivity and impulsive behavior (Carlson, Lahey, Frame, Walker, & Hind, 1987; Lahey *et al.*, in press; Lahey *et al.*, 1987). The framers of DSM-III posited that there may be meaningful differences between those children labeled ADD/H who are deviant on all three dimensions of ADD (inattention, impulsivity, and motor hyperactivity) and those who are deviant on only the inattention and the impulsivity dimensions (APA, 1980). A number of studies employing both epidemiological (King & Young, 1982; Lahey, Schaughency, Strauss, & Frame, 1984) and clinic-referred samples (Edelbrock, Costello, & Kessler, 1984; Lahey *et al.*, 1987) have documented consistent differences between the DSM-III subtypes of ADD/H and ADD/WO. Children who exhibit ADD/H have been found to exhibit more conduct problems, particularly aggression, and to be more rejected by peers, whereas children with ADD/WO are more shy, anxious and depressed, sluggish, drowsy, and less successful academically (Carlson, 1986).

In the transition from DSM-III to DSM-III-R, the ADD/WO diagnosis was replaced by that of Undifferentiated Attention Deficit Disorder (UADD) for children with difficulties only in attention. Unfortunately, DSM-III-R provides no criteria for UADD. Therefore, we need either to develop *ad hoc* diagnostic criteria for UADD or to use the DSM-III definition of ADD/WO.

If clinical diagnostic classifications are to be employed, the factor analyses of DSM-III and DSM-III-R symptom lists provided by Healy *et al.* (1987) and Lahey *et al.* (in press) yielded very similar separate inattention–disorganization and motor hyperactivity–impulsivity factors in each case. These lists could be used as guidelines for selecting an *ad hoc* list of defining characteristics for UADD. However, no information is available upon which to base decisions concerning cutting scores for number of symptoms.

If teacher and parent rating scales are used to define experimental groups, rating scales should be employed that have separate inattention and motor hyperactivity factors, such as the Revised Behavior Problem Checklist (Quay & Peterson, 1983) or the Comprehensive Behavior Scale for Children (Neeper & Lahey, 1988). Using this approach, children who show elevated scores on both factors could be experimentally defined as exhibiting ADD/H or AD-HD, whereas children with elevated scores on only the inattention factor could be experimentally classified as exhibiting ADD/WO or UADD.

2.2.3. Summary

For studies of the domain of attention deficit/hyperactivity, it is recommended that the inattention–disorganization dimension and the motor hyperactivity–impulsivity dimension be distinguished and measured separately. In particular, children showing deviance on both dimensions (ADD/H or AD-HD) should be distinguished from children showing deviance on only the inattention–disorganization dimensions (ADD/WO or UADD). It is probable that these two disorders differ so substantially that UADD should not be considered a Disruptive Behavior Disorder, but the possibly distinct, long-term, sequelae of AD-HD and UADD remain to be investigated.

3. Justifying Distinctions between and within Disruptive Behavior Disorders: Different Correlates and Background Factors

As mentioned above, justification for distinctions between and within Disruptive Behavior Disorders can be strengthened when different disorders are associated with distinct correlates of child behavior (such as handicaps other than psychopathology) and different background factors (such as familial psychopathology). Most work in this area concerns the distinction between conduct problems and attention deficit/hyperactivity. Because these two entities are correlated, it is important to gauge which correlates or background factors are uniquely associated with one and not with the other. This requires the use of research methods that experimentally or statistically control the association between the dependent variable (e.g., parental substance abuse) and one disorder while assessing the degree of association with the other disorder. One example is the use of partial correlations where the relationship between a background factor and conduct problems is examined, while statistically controlling for attention deficit/hyperactivity, and vice versa. Only a few studies have attempted this (Farrington, Loeber, & van Kammen, in press; Loeber, Brinthaupt, & Green, in press). Using this and other methods, parents' child-rearing and socialization practices with their children appear uniquely associated with conduct problems and *not* with attention deficit/hyperactivity (Loney *et al.*, 1978; Taylor, Schachar, Thorley, & Wieselberg, 1986).

Likewise, parental problems in coping, alcoholism, and substance use were more related to children's conduct problems rather than attention deficits/hyperactivity (Lahey *et al.*, 1988; Loeber *et al.*, in press; Stewart, deBlois, & Cummings, 1980; Taylor *et al.*, 1986). On the other hand, studies that examined parental psychopathology in children identified as hyperactive (but that did not distinguish those children who also exhibited Conduct Disorder for the purpose of statistical analyses) found a high frequency of paternal antisocial personality and substance use (Cantwell, 1972; Morrison & Stewart, 1971). Within the domain of conduct problems, there are indications that aggressive and nonaggressive conduct problems are associated with distinct socialization processes within families (Loeber & Stouthamer-Loeber, 1986). But also in this instance, more systematic research is needed to confirm existing findings and explore other potential etiological variables, which distinguish between different disorders and their subtypes.

4. Recommendations Concerning the Overlap among the Different Forms of Disruptive Behavior Disorders

There is reason to believe that overlap among the various forms of the Disruptive Behavior Disorders is of considerable significance. Loney and Milich (1982), in a sample of elementary-school-age children, showed the importance of the overlap between "aggression" (actually oppositional behaviors) and hyperactivity. The oppositional–hyperactive children were more deviant in several dimensions than those children who were oppositional only or those who were hyperactive only.

Turning to conduct disorder, a number of studies have demonstrated that children with conduct disorder who also exhibit features of ADD/H display far more serious and persistent antisocial behaviors than children with any other codiagnosis or with only conduct problems (August & Stewart, 1982; Offord, Sullivan, Allen, & Abrams, 1979; Schachar, Rutter, & Smith, 1981; Walker, Lahey, Hynd, & Frame, in press). Two analyses have been conducted to ensure that this exacerbation of conduct disorder is associated specifically with ADD/H rather than with attention deficits only. First, the pattern of conduct disorder is more severe in children with conduct disorder and coexisting ADD/H than in children with conduct disorder and coexisting ADD/WO (Lahey *et al.*, 1987). Second, when ratings of inattention, impulsivity, and motor hyperactivity are correlated with the number of conduct disorder symptoms, significant correlations are found for motor hyperactivity and impulsivity, but not for inattention (Sandberg, Rutter, & Taylor, 1978; Walker *et al.*, in press).

Longitudinal studies have shown that the presence of ADD/H, or its experimentally defined research equivalent, occurring in conjunction with aggression or Conduct Disorder, increases the probability of later delinquency (Loeber *et al.*, in press; Loeber, 1987; Loney, Kramer, & Milich, 1982; Magnusson, 1988) and probably the risk for antisocial personality in adulthood.

A problem in past research is that the findings did not establish whether AD-DH contributed to later maladjustment *independent* of Conduct Disorder and vice versa. For that reason, Farrington *et al.* (in press) examined the course of these syndromes in the Cambridge Study in Delinquent Development, which followed up London boys from age 8 to age 25. Briefly, the results show that an index of hyperactivity/impulsivity/attention deficits (HIA) at ages 8–10 significantly predicted later chronic offending (more than six convictions) independently of conduct problems at that age. HIA best predicted early offending and rarely applied to males who started their delinquent career in adulthood. Separate analyses showed that almost all of the results held when background variables were controlled. The association between early onset of delinquency and the presence of HIA has been confirmed by Loeber *et al.* (in press). Although neither study refers to psychiatric diagnoses, they provide strong support for research criteria that distinguish between Conduct Disorder and AD-HD in terms of different outcomes over time.

Scholarly reports vary enormously in their reporting of other common codiagnoses, such as Major Depressive Disorder, Substance Abuse Disorder, and Learning Disability. Each of these three disorders, by itself, suggests risk of later deviant outcomes, but when they occur in conjunction with Conduct Disorder, the comorbity may alter the risk of persistence of the Conduct Disorder. The sequential nature of codiagnoses and their co-occurrences often is expressed through common behavior patterns in children that easily can lead to confusion in diagnoses. Therefore, it is deemed essential to determine whether or not such codiagnoses apply.

4.1. Summary

It is recommended that studies of *either* the conduct problems domain or the attention deficit/hyperactivity domain include measures of the relevant dimensions in *both* domains. At a minimum, for example, it is essential that, in a study using subjects given the diagnosis of AD-HD compared with nonreferred controls, the number of those clinic-referred subjects who would also qualify for a diagnosis of Conduct Disorder be reported. Similarly, a study that experimentally classified a group of subjects as AD-HD on the basis of teacher ratings should also report the mean ratings on the conduct disorder factor of the teacher rating scale.

The developmental outcomes of individuals who exhibit either Conduct Disorder or AD-HD alone apparently differ dramatically from those children who are deviant in both domains. In particular, the combination of Aggressive Conduct Disorder and AD-HD appears to be both very common and virulent. The importance of the overlap with UADD and other disorders such as depression and anxiety is less well understood, but of enough potential importance to warrant the measurement of these dimensions in studies of Conduct Disorder as well. Studies examining the domains of conduct problems or attention/deficits alone (i.e., without consideration of both dimensions) in the past have led to serious confusion and should be avoided in the future. There is a need for research to determine objective criteria to assess which disorder is primary and which disorder is secondary.

5. Recommendations Concerning Measurement Strategies

Many of the following recommendations are unique to Disruptive Behavior Disorders, although some apply to other disorders as well (Kupfer & Rush, 1983).

5.1. Multiple Measurement Strategies

There are many approaches to the measurement of conduct problems and attention deficits/hyperactivity, including structured interviews, teacher, peer, and parent rating scales, and direct observation in classroom and analog classroom or playroom situations with and without structured tasks. No one strategy is favored by even a simple majority of researchers, however. For this reason, *more than one assessment strategy should be used in each study.* For example, researchers who use structured interviews to obtain symptom-by-symptom information to make clinical diagnoses or who use direct observations should also report teacher and parent rating scales to document the degree of deviance of the groups using these continuous metrics. The opposite is true for researchers who use rating scales to define groups. In this way, the results of each new study can be combined with those in other studies, which used either measurement strategy.

It is not yet clear which conduct problems require independent observations to arrive at sound research diagnoses. Many aggressive conduct problems lend themselves to direct observation (Patterson, 1982), which has the added advantage of avoiding biases in caretaker's ratings (see below). Many nonaggressive conduct problems, however, occur at a low base rate and are actively concealed by youngsters; therefore, the observation of these acts is either impractical or very expensive. In this realm, there is certainly a place for the use of court records of delinquent acts and for school records of suspensions or explusions. Some studies, especially large-scale epidemiological studies, do not have the opportunity or funds to accomplish observations or to contact several informants; methodological research is needed to establish which types of measurement are most valid for epidemiological surveys.

Obtaining and reporting multiple criteria for the determination of discrete Disruptive Behavior Disorders is of paramount importance in allowing researchers using diverse methods of assessment to compare experimental findings. In addition, the reporting of multiple criteria eventually will lead to data that will allow an empirical determination of the optimal methods of classification. That is to say, some methods of assessment ultimately will be demonstrated to be more reliable and valid than others. Studies that are conducted using a single assessment strategy run the risk that the method that was employed will be deemed unacceptable by future studies, whereas studies using multiple methods are far more likely to make an enduring contribution.

5.2. Multiple Informant Strategies

The identification of abnormal patterns of behavior can be likened to a signal-detection problem, whereby the use of multiple informants increases the chances that relevant behavioral characteristics will be identified. Moreover, because children do not act the same in different settings, it is critical to obtain information from informants in different settings.

It should be recognized, however, that not all informants appear equally suitable to report on every aspect of Disruptive Behavior Disorder. For example, many caretakers are unaware of children's concealing, nonaggressive conduct problems, such as theft and truancy (Janes,

Hesselbrock, Myers, & Penniman, 1987; Kashani, Orvaschel, Burk, & Reid, 1985; Loeber & Schmaling, 1985b), making children themselves better informants. Studies on adolescents' self-reported delinquency appear to have reasonable validity when compared with official arrest records (Hindelang, Hirschi, & Weis, 1981). Some nonaggressive conduct problems such as lying and fire setting, however, often are inadequately reported by children compared with information provided by parents (Edelbrock, Costello, Dulcan, Conover, & Kala, 1986; Kolko & Kazdin, in press). In those cases, adults' reports probably are more valid.

Research reports suggest that not all children are able to accurately assess the degree or frequency of their own aggressive or violent behavior and that some tend to underreport these behaviors; the degree of underreporting appears directly related to the severity of the child's aggression (Cairns & Cairns, 1984; Eron, Walder, & Lefkowitz, 1971; Kazdin, Esveldt-Dawson, Uris, & Rancurello, 1983; Ledingham, Younger, Schwartzman, & Bergeron, 1982; Verhulst, Althaus, & Berden, 1987). For that reason, it is more sensible to rely on adults' assessment in this realm or to make use of peer ratings (Pelham & Bender, 1982).

Children's ability to report on their own problem behavior and emotions apparently improves with increasing age. Edelbrock and associates, for example, have shown that the low short-term test–retest reliabilities for children between ages 6 and 9 reporting on aggressive conduct problems improved with age (Edelbrock, Costello, Dulcan, Kalas, & Conover, 1985).

It should be noted that under certain conditions, caretakers may overreport the child's conduct problems, for example, when the caretaker is depressed or experiences marital disruptions (Forehand, Brody, & Smith, 1986; Griest, Wells, & Forehand, 1979; Schaughency & Lahey, 1985). In these instances, additional information may be sought from a nondepressed caretaker or teacher. Thus, although it makes sense to collect information from multiple informants, careful consideration should be given to the question of which informants can provide the best estimates of each particular problem behavior.

There are other important reasons why the collection of information from more than one adult in multiple settings is highly desirable. First, Disruptive Behavior Disorders appear to be genuinely situation specific. That is to say, children usually are described as being deviant in some rather than all socially important situations. This can be the result of informants (principally parents and teachers) failing to detect deviant behavior. However, because of differing situational demands on behavior, ADD behaviors and disruptive behaviors in general are believed to differ genuinely from situation to situation. For some research purposes, for example, children need not exhibit AD-HD behavior in all relevant situations to be classified as AD-HD, but it is not clear in how may situations the child must be deviant. Barkley's (Barkley, 1982) comments on the measurement of situation specificity and the Werry-Weiss-Peters scale (Werry, 1968) are useful in dealing with this issue. Second, even within a particular setting, children's disruptive behavior may vary considerably over time depending on the tasks they perform.

Third, different informants are more likely to observe the child in different situations, and in the case of parents and teachers, may have different abilities to compare the child's behavior with that of other children. Several studies have found that teachers were better informants than parents on AD-HD (Loeber et al., in press; Loney, 1982; Sandberg, Wieselberg, & Shaffer, 1980). This may reflect the greater opportunity teachers have compared with parents to compare the behavior of children. Clinician ratings may be desirable, but the behavior of children with these disorders in clinic settings is notoriously atypical, unless structured tasks are undertaken that somehow tap the problem behaviors. For this reason, in most cases, clinic ratings should be given less weight than parent and teacher ratings.

5.3. Summary

It is strongly recommended that studies of the conduct problem and attention deficit/hyperactivity domains not be conducted using a single measurement mode. Because so little agreement exists at present as to the best measurement mode, the use of *multiple* measurement strategies appears to be the most reasonable compromise. It is recommended further that multiple informants from multiple situations be employed to obtain these measures in order to improve their reliability and validity. However, it should be noted that not all informants may provide the most optimal or reliable information on all dimensions of disruptive disorders. In fact, there is considerable opportunity in the realm of Disruptive Behavior Disorders to undertake research to compare the yields of different data-gathering techniques. Different informants are usually also necessary to gauge the setting-specificity of the child's problem behavior.

6. Recommendations Concerning Exclusionary Criteria

Children should be excluded from studies of the disruptive disorders when they exhibit other disorders that may create the impression of

AD-HD or Conduct Disorder. These would include all psychotic disorders, pervasive developmental disorders, severe neurological disorders, and mental retardation. For example, although it certainly appears that children with low normal intelligence can exhibit AD-HD, because of the possibility that adult informants will confuse low intelligence with attention deficits, children with intelligence quotients less than 70 should either be excluded or care should be taken to independently verify the existence of ADD behaviors that are not attributed to low intelligence. In some cases, even higher cut offs for intelligence scores would be appropriate.

Age cut offs and age of onset (or age of recognition) criteria cannot currently be justified on the basis of existing information. The criteria provided by DSM-III and DSM-III-R provide useful guidelines in this respect, except that the onset (or at least the discovery) of many cases of what has been termed ADD/WO is clearly later than that of ADD/H (Lahey et al., 1987). However, care should be taken to report age of onset and to distinguish between early-onset Conduct Disorder and AD-HD and later-onset disorders as they may constitute entirely different entities. Studies should not be limited to only one gender, but when possible, analyses should be conducted separately for boys and girls.

6.1. Summary

It is recommended that subjects not be selected for studies of either conduct problems or attention deficits/hyperactivity if they exhibit pervasive developmental disorders, psychotic disorders, severe neurological disorders, or mental retardation. Studies of children specifically selected because they exhibit both conduct problems (and/or attention deficit/hyperactivity) and any of these excluded disorders might well be of interest, of course, but the inclusion of a few subjects in larger samples with these excluded disorders would be potentially confusing. Care should be taken to report age of onset and to conduct analyses separately for boys and girls.

7. Other Recommendations Concerning Information to Be Reported in Assessment

It is highly desirable that future reports of research on the Disruptive Behavior Disorders include the following information:

1. The measurement and reporting, to the degree possible, of *impairments in functioning* (such as general intelligence, social status, em-

ployability, and educational achievements) that often co-occur with Disruptive Behavior Disorders. It appears to be most important to assess and report general intelligence to rule out the possibility of confusing low intelligence with AD-HD in subject selection and to assess the role of intelligence in the prognosis of all of the Disruptive Behavior Disorders.

2. Mention of the *referral source* and other inclusion criteria for youngsters with Disruptive Behavior Disorders. The nature of this source—school counselor, probation officer, pediatrician, parents—reflects both the concerns of adult caretakers and the particular constellation of problem behaviors presented by youngsters.

3. Because many children receive *medications* that can influence their behavior and the accuracy of diagnosis, it is deemed essential that research reports include information on both current and past medications. Particularly relevant is the type of medication, the absolute and mg/kg dosage, frequency and duration of administration, and whether or not assessments were done while the medication was active.

4. Other formal treatments need to be documented as well, such as cognitive or social skills training programs for the child and parent training.

5. As in all psychological research with children and their families, the socioeconomic status of the family should be indexed.

7.1. Summary

It is recommended that all studies of the conduct problems and attention deficits/hyperactivity domain report general measures of adaptive functioning (particularly intelligence), socioeconomic status, educational attainment, referral source, medication, and other treatments. Improved research methods and more systematic data collection and reporting of the characteristics of the subjects will further our understanding of Disruptive Behavior Disorders and will improve diagnostic practices for both research and clinical purposes.

8. Recommendations Concerning Developmental Issues in Assessment

Current diagnostic criteria for the Disruptive Behavior Disorders pay little more than lip service to their developmental nature. The clearest difficulty is in the absence of age-appropriate definitions of symptoms and disorders. For example, DSM-III-R states as of one the criteria "has used a weapon in more than one fight" (APA, 1987, p. 55). Does this imply that a 6-year-old who has used a large stick in a fight should be included in the same way as a 12-year-old who used such weapons as a knife, brass knuckles, or weapons more commonly used by adults? At present, little information is available to answer such questions, but a study could be designed to determine whether using objects as weapons that were not designed to be weapons is more predictive of antisocial outcome at earlier than later ages. Examples of other questions that remain to be answered are the extent to which Oppositional Defiant Disorder predicts Conduct Disorder (or for one of its subclassifications but not another) and how aggressive and nonaggressive Conduct Disorders develop over time and combine in some youngsters. The developmental sequences among Attention Deficit Hyperactivity Disorder, Oppositional Defiant Disorder, and Conduct Disorder remain to be elucidated (Loeber, 1988).

It also remains to be seen whether, as activity level decreases with age (Abikoff, Gittleman-Klein, & Klein, 1977; Richman, Stevenson, & Graham, 1982), ADD/H evolves into ADD/WO or into ADD-residual. Little is known about transitions among other common codiagnoses, such as Depressive Disorder, and various forms of Disruptive Behavior Disorders. Knowledge of these transitions should make it possible to better document and distinguish between normal and deviant development (Garber, 1984). Also, it remains to be seen whether shifts in diagnosis over time are sufficient to document developmental progressions or whether more detailed measurements can serve a better purpose.

8.1. Summary

The pressing need for additional research on developmental changes in the nature of the various Disruptive Behavior Disorders and developmental changes in the relations among these disorders was recognized. It was recommended that research on developmental considerations be considered a priority.

9. General Conclusions

Researchers in the area of the Disruptive Behavior Disorders of Childhood sometimes seem to be on a frustrating fishing expedition; we are not quite sure which bait and tackle to use because we know very little about the fish we hope to catch. In the coming years, we need to learn much more about the dimensions that constitute the domain of

Disruptive Behavior Disorders, but until we achieve greater consensus on classificatory criteria and measurement strategies, it will be understandably difficult to conduct meaningful research. Conversely, however, we will not be able to evaluate effectively the relative merits of proposed classificatory criteria and different measurement strategies until meaningful research has been conducted on these disorders.

Because of the dilemmas posed by this all-too-familiar "bootstrap" irony, strategies for future research were recommended that may facilitate systematic increases in knowledge. In one sense, it is premature to attempt to define categories and subcategories using specific diagnostic criteria as in DSM-III-R. However, if a number of the directions for future research recommended above are taken, the empirical basis for such classificatory decisions may be available in the near future. Proposals were made concerning putative dimensions of the Disruptive Behavior Disorders that are most promising for study, the need to study the importance of overlap among the Disruptive Behavior Disorders, the need to use multiple strategies of measurement that obtain information from multiple sources, necessary exclusionary criteria, optimal standards for reporting information in published papers, and the need for further study of the developmental nature of these disorders.

We strongly recommend that these objectives be incorporated in a major epidemiological study on Disruptive Behavior Disorders in childhood and adolescence. Such a study would have to have multiple, overlapping cohorts with the youngest of preschool age, so that nonclinical precursors to the disorders can be traced, in addition to etiological factors specific to each subclassification within the Disruptive Behavior Disorders domain. The study's samples preferably should be selected from geographic communities with varying risk for the disorders and include youngsters of both sexes with early risk factors, some of whom may already have been referred to either psychiatric or pediatric clinical services. In order to replicate findings, such a major epidemiological study would need to be undertaken in different sites, taking, possibly, as a model the Epidemiological Catchment Area Project (Weissman, Myers, & Ross, 1986).

One of the major advantages of such a concerted effort is the opportunity to determine developmentally appropriate and inappropriate behaviors at different ages. Although, an initial study could examine present behavior patterns and past development, another goal is to use such a study as the beginning of a longitudinal study in which the development of disruptive behaviors can be traced over time. Such a study, especially if it is a collaborative effort among scholars from different disciplines, can contribute immensely to improved measurement and analysis strategies and make it possible to build empirical foundations for diagnostic distinctions within the Disruptive Behavior Disorders domain. The study would also elucidate potential etiological factors that are unique to AD-HD or Conduct Disorder, or unique to subtypes within each, and inform more precisely on prognostic features for different disorders or subtypes.

A concerted multisite investigation is all the more necessary because the Disruptive Behavior Disorders, compared with many other disorders in childhood and adolescence, are of a chronic nature, often persisting into adulthood, and are largely insensitive to most long-range therapeutic interventions (Kazdin, 1987), creating multiple impairments and frustrations for the children themselves, their victims, and the adults who try to raise them.

ACKNOWLEDGMENTS

This chapter evolved from a paper prepared under Grant No. 86-JN-CX-0009 from the Office of Juvenile Justice and Delinquency Prevention, Office of Justice Programs, U.S. Department of Justice, and Grant No. MH42529 of the National Institute of Mental Health. Points of views or opinions in this document are those of the authors and do not necessarily represent the official position or policies of the U.S. Department of Justice or the National Institute of Mental Health. The conference that preceded the paper was supported by the University of Georgia at Athens. A second meeting of the authors of this manuscript was graciously supported in part by the Department of Child Psychiatry of the Schneider Children's Hospital of Long Island-Jewish Medical Center. The contributions of members of the Study Group, both at the original meeting in Athens and subsequent meetings, are an integral part of this manuscript and are, of course, gratefully acknowledged. The authors also are most appreciative of the helpful comments of Howard Abikoff, James Breiling, Susan B. Campbell, Dennis Cantwell, David P. Farrington, Rachel Klein, David Kolko, Jan Loney, Richard S. Milich, William P. Pelham, Magda Stouthamer-Loeber, and Christopher Thomas on an earlier draft of this manuscript. The authors also are particularly grateful to Celia Nourse-Eatman for her assistance in perfecting the manuscript. Any fault for erroneous recommendation in this manuscript, however, rests with the authors and not with the individual members of the Study Group.

10. References

Abikoff, H., Gittelman-Klein, R., & Klein, D. F. (1977). Validation of a classroom observation code for hyperactive children. *Journal of Consulting and Clinical Psychology, 45*, 772–783.

Achenbach, T. M. (1978). The Child Behavior Profile: I. Boys aged 6–11. *Journal of Consulting and Clinical Psychology, 46,* 478–488.

Achenbach, T. M., & Edelbrock, C. S. (1978). The classification of child psychopathology: A review and analysis of empirical efforts. *Psychological Bulletin, 85,* 1275–1301.

Aman, M. G., Werry, J. S., Fitzpatrick, J., Lowe, M., & Waters, J. (1983). Factor structure and norms for the revised Behavior Problem Checklist in New Zealand children. *Australian and New Zealand Journal of Psychiatry, 17,* 354–360.

American Psychiatric Association. (1952). *Diagnostic and statistical manual of mental disorders* (1st ed.). Washington, DC: Author.

American Psychiatric Association. (1968). *Diagnostic and statistical manual of mental disorders* (2nd ed.). Washington, DC: Author.

American Psychiatric Association. (1980). *Diagnostic and statistical manual of mental disorders* (3rd ed.). Washington, DC: Author.

American Psychiatric Association. (1987). *Diagnostic and statistical manual of mental disorders* (3rd ed. rev.). Washington, DC: Author.

Anderson, J. C., Williams, S., McGee, R., & Silva, P. A. (1987). DSM-III disorders in preadolescent children: Prevalence in a large sample from the general population. *Archives of General Psychiatry, 44,* 69–76.

August, G. J., & Stewart, M. A. (1982). Is there a syndrome of pure hyperactivity? *British Journal of Psychiatry, 140,* 305–311.

Barkley, R. A. (1982). Guidelines for defining hyperactivity in children: Attention Deficit Disorder with Hyperactivity. In B. B. Lahey & A. E. Kazdin, (Eds.), *Advances in clinical child psychology: Vol. 5.* (pp. 137–180). New York: Plenum Press.

Burdsal, C., Force, R. D., & Campbell, J. (1984). Behavioral dimensions in fourth-, fifth-, and sixth-grade students as rated by teachers. *Journal of Clinical Psychology, 40,* 172–184.

Cairns, R. B., & Cairns, B. D. (1984). Predicting aggressive patterns in girls and boys: A developmental study. *Aggressive Behavior, 10,* 227–242.

Campbell, S. B., & Werry, J. S. (1986). Attention deficit disorder (hyperactivity). In H. C. Quay & J. S. Werry (Eds.), *Psychopathological disorders of childhood* (3rd ed., pp. 111–155). New York: Wiley.

Cantwell, D. P. (1972). Psychiatric illness in the families of hyperactive children. *Archives of General Psychiatry, 27,* 414–417.

Carlson, C. L. (1986). Attention deficit disorder without hyperactivity: A review of preliminary experimental evidence. In B. B. Lahey & A. E. Kazdin (Eds.), *Advances in Clinical Child Psychology* (pp. 153–175). New York: Plenum Press.

Carlson, C. L., & Lahey, B. B. (1983). Factor structure of teacher rating scales for children. *School Psychological Review, 12,* 285–291.

Carlson, D. L., Lahey, B. B., Frame, C. L., Walker, J., & Hind, G. W. (1987). Sociometric status of clinic-referred children with attention deficit disorders with and without hyperactivity. *Journal of Abnormal Child Psychology, 15,* 537–547.

Chaiken, J. M., & Chaiken, M. R. (1982). *Varieties of criminal behavior,* Santa Monica, CA: Rand.

Conners, C. K. (1969). A teacher rating scale for use in drug studies with children. *American Journal of Psychiatry, 126,* 152–156.

Conners, C. K. (1973). Rating scales for use in drug studies for children. *Psychopharmacology Bulletin,* Special Issue: Pharmacotherapy with Children, *24,* 24–29.

Dreger, R. M. (1981). First-, second-, and third-order factors from the children's Behavioral Classification project instrument and an attempt at rapprochement. *Journal of Abnormal Psychology, 90,* 242–260.

Dreger, R. M. (1982). The classification of children and their emotional problems: An overview—II. *Clinical Psychology Review, 2,* 349–386.

Edelbrock, C., & Achenbach, T. M. (1984). The teacher version of the Child Behavior Profile: I. Boys aged 6–11. *Journal of Consulting and Clinical Psychology, 52,* 207–217.

Edelbrock, C., Costello, A. J., Dulcan, M. K., Conover, N. C., & Kala, R. (1986). Parent–child agreement on child psychiatric symptoms assessed via structured interview. *Journal of Child Psychology and Psychiatry, 27,* 181–190.

Edelbrock, C., Costello, A. J., Dulcan, M. K., Kalas, R., & Conover, N. C. (1985). Age differences in the reliability of the psychiatric interview of the child. *Child Development, 56,* 265–275.

Edelbrock, C. S., Costello, A. J., & Kessler, M. D. (1984). Empirical corroboration of the attention deficit disorder. *Journal of American Academy of Child Psychiatry, 23,* 285–291.

Eron, L. D., Walder, L., & Lefkowitz, M. M. (1971). *Learning of aggression in children.* Boston: Little, Brown.

Farrington, D. P., Loeber, R., & van Kammen, W. B. (in press). *Long-term criminal outcomes of hyperactivity-impulsivity-attention deficit and conduct problems in childhood.* In L. N. Robins & M. R. Rutter (Eds.), *Straight and devious pathways to adulthood.* New York: Cambridge University Press.

Forehand, R., Brody, G., & Smith, K. (1986). Contributions of child behavior and marital dissatisfaction to maternal perceptions of child maladjustment. *Behaviour Research & Therapy, 24,* 43–48.

Fowler, P. O., & Park, R. M. (1979). Factor structures of the preschool behavior questionnaire in a normal population. *Psychological Reports, 45,* 599–606.

Furlong, M. J., & Fortman, J. B. (1984). Factor analyses of the abbreviated Conners Teacher Rating Scale: Implications for the assessment of hyperactivity. *Psychology in the Schools, 21,* 289–293.

Garber, J. (1984). Classification of childhood psychopathology: A developmental perspective. *Child Development, 55,* 30–48.

Gersten, J. C., Langner, T. S., Eisenberg, J. G., Simcha-Fagan, D., & McCarthy, E. D. (1976). Stability and change in types of behavioral disturbances of children and adolescents. *Journal of Abnormal Child Psychology, 4,* 111–127.

Glow, R. A., Glow, P. H., & Rump, E. E. (1982). The stability of child behavior disorders: One year test-retest study of Adelaide versions of the Conners Teacher and Parent Rating Scales. *Journal of Abnormal Child Psychology, 10,* 33–60.

Goyette, C. H., Conners, C. K., & Ulrich, R. F. (1978). Normative data on revised Conners Parent and Teacher Rating Scales. *Journal of Abnormal Child Psychology, 6,* 221–136.

Griest, D., Wells, K. G., & Forehand, R. (1979). An examination of predictors of maternal perceptions of maladjustment in clinic-referred children. *Journal of Abnormal Psychology, 88,* 277–287.

Healy, J. M., Halperin, J. M., Newcorn, J., Wolf, L. E., Pascualvaca, M. A., O'Brien, J., Morganstein, A., & Young, J. G. (1987). *The factor structure of ADD items in DSM-III-R.* Read at the Annual Meeting of the American Academy of Child and Adolescent Psychiatry, Washington, DC.

Hindelang, M. J., Hirschi, T., & Weis, J. (1981). *The measurement of delinquency by the self report method.* Beverly Hills: Sage.

Hinshaw, S. P. (1987). On the distinction between attentional deficits/hyperactivity and conduct problems/aggression in child psychopathology. *Psychology Bulletin, 101,* 443–463.

Hinshaw, S. P., Morrison, D. C., Carte, E. T., & Cornsweet, C. (1987). Factorial dimensions of the Revised Behavior Problem Checklist: Replication and validation within a kindergarten sample. *Journal of Abnormal Child Psychology, 15,* 309–327.

Janes, C. L., Hesselbrock, V. M., Myers, D. G., & Penniman, J. H. (1987). Problem boys in young adulthood—Teacher ratings and 12-year follow-up. *Journal of Youth & Adolescents, 8,* 453–472.

Jenkins, R. L. (1966). Psychiatric syndromes in children and their relationship to family background. *American Journal of Orthopsychiatry, 36,* 450–457.

Junger-Tas, J., & Junger, M. (1984). *Juvenile delinquency.* Ministry of Justice: The Hague, The Netherlands.

Kagan, J. (1966). Reflection-impulsivity: The generality and dynamics of conceptual tempo. *Journal of Abnormal Psychology, 71,* 17–24.

Kashani, J. H., Orvaschel, H., Burk, J. P., & Reid, J. C. (1985). Informant variance: The issue of parent–child disagreement. *Journal of American Academy of Child Psychiatry, 24,* 437–441.

Kazdin, A. E. (1987). *Conduct disorder in childhood and adolescence.* New York: Sage.

Kazdin, A. E., Esveldt-Dawson, K., Uris, A. S., & Rancurello, M. D. (1983). Child and parent evaluations of depression and aggression in psychiatric inpatient children. *Journal of Abnormal Child Psychology, 11,* 401–414.

King, C., & Young, R. D. (1982). Attentional deficits with and without hyperactivity: Teacher and peer perceptions. *Journal of Abnormal Child Psychology, 10,* 483–495.

Kohn, M. (1977). *Social competence, symptoms and underachievement in children: A longitudinal perspective.* Washington, DC: Winston.

Kolko, D. J., & Kazdin, A. E. (in press). Parent–child correspondence in identification of fire-setting among child psychiatric patients. *Journal of Child Psychology and Psychiatry.*

Kupfer, D. J., & Rush, A. J. (1983). Recommendations for scientific reports on depression. *American Journal of Psychiatry, 140,* 1327–1328.

Lachar, D., Gdowski, C. L., & Snyder, D. K. (1984). External validation of the Personality Inventory for Children (PIC) profile and factor scales: Parent, teacher, and clinician ratings. *Journal of Consulting and Clinical Psychology, 2,* 155–164.

Lahey, B. B., Pelham, W. E., Schaughency, E. A., Atkins, M. S., Murphy, H. A., Hynd, G. W., Russo, M., Hartdagen, S., & Lorys-Vernon, A. (in press). Dimensions and types of attention deficit disorder. *Journal of American Academy of Child Adolescent Psychiatry.*

Lahey, B. B., Piacentini, J. C., McBurnett, K., Stone, P., Hartdagen, S., & Hynd, G. (1988). Psychopathology in the parents of children with conduct disorder and hyperactivity. *Journal of American Academy of Child Adolescent Psychiatry, 27,* 163–170.

Lahey, B. B., Schaughency, E. A., Hynd, G., Carlson, C. L., & Nieves, N. (1987). Attention deficit disorder with and without hyperactivity: Comparison of behavioral characteristics of clinic-referred children. *Journal of American Academy of Child Adolescent Psychiatry, 26,* 718–723.

Lahey, B. B., Schaughency, E. A., Strauss, C. C., & Frame, C. L. (1984). Are attention deficit disorders with and without hyperactivity similar or dissimilar disorders? *Journal of American Academy of Child Adolescent Psychiatry, 23,* 302–310.

Lahey, B. B., Stempniak, M., Robinson, E. J., & Tyroler, M. J. (1978). Hyperactivity and learning disabilities as independent dimensions of child behavior problems. *Journal of Abnormal Psychology, 87,* 333–340.

Lambert, N. M., & Hartsough, C. S. (1987). The measurement of attention deficit disorder with behavior ratings of parents. *American Journal of Orthopsychiatry, 57,* 362–370.

Ledingham, J. E., Younger, A., Schwartzman, A., & Bergeron, G. (1982). Agreement among teacher, peer, and self-ratings of children's aggression, withdrawal, and likability. *Journal of Abnormal Child Psychology, 10,* 363–372.

Lewis, H. S. (1954). *Deprived children.* London: Oxford University Press.

Lindholm, B. W., & Touliatos, J. (1981). Development of children's behavior problems. *Journal of Genetic Psychology, 139,* 47–53.

Loeber, R. (1982). The stability of antisocial and delinquent child behavior: A review. *Child Development, 53,* 1431–1446.

Loeber, R. (1987). Behavioral precursors and accelerators of delinquency. In W. Buikhuisen & S. A. Mednick (Eds.), *Explaining crime.* Leyden: Brill.

Loeber, R. (1988). National histories of juvenile conduct problems, delinquency, and associated substance use: Evidence for developmental progressions. In B. B. Lahey & A. E. Kazdin (Eds.), *Advances in clinical child psychology.* New York: Plenum Press.

Loeber, R., Brinthaupt, V. P., & Green, S. M. (in press). Attention deficits, impulsivity, and hyperactivity with or without conduct problems: Relationships to delinquency and unique contextual factors. In R. J. MacMahon & R. DeV. Peters (Eds.), *Behavioral disorders of adolescence: Research, intervention, and policy in clinical and school settings.* New York: Plenum Press.

Loeber, R., & Schmaling, K. B. (1985a). Empirical evidence for overt and covert patterns of antisocial conduct problems: A metaanalysis. *Journal of Abnormal Child Psychology, 13,* 337–352.

Loeber, R., & Schmaling, K. B. (1985b). The utility of differentiating between mixed and pure forms of antisocial child behavior. *Journal of Abnormal Child Psychology, 13,* 315–336.

Loeber, R., & Stouthamer-Loeber, M. (1986). Family factors as correlates and predictors of juvenile conduct problems and delinquency. In N. Morris & M. Tonry (Eds.), *Crime and justice* (Vol. 7, pp. 29–149). Chicago: University of Chicago Press.

Loney, J. (1982). *Research diagnostic criteria for childhood hyperactivity.* Paper presented at the meeting of the American Psychopathological Association, New York.

Loney, J. (1984). *A short parent scale for subgrouping childhood hyperactivity and aggression.* Paper presented at the meeting of the American Psychological Association, Toronto, Canada.

Loney, J. (1985). *Oppositional disorder: yes or no?* Paper presented at the meeting of the American Academy of Child Psychiatry, San Antonio, Texas.

Loney, J. (1987). Hyperactivity and aggression in the diagnosis of attention deficit disorder. In B. B. Lahey & A. E. Kazdin, (Eds.), *Advances in clinical child psychology.* New York: Plenum Press.

Loney, J., Kramer, J., & Milich, R. S. (1982). The hyperactive child grows up: Predictors of symptoms, delinquency, and achievement at follow-up. In K. D. Gadow & J. Loney (Eds.), *Psychosocial aspects of drug treatment for hyperactivity* (pp. 381–415). Boulder, CO: Westview.

Loney, J., Langhorne, J. E., & Paternite, C. E. (1978). An empirical basis for subgrouping the hyperkinetic/minimal brain dysfunction syndrome. *Journal of Abnormal Psychology, 87,* 431–441.

Loney, J., & Milich, R. (1982). Hyperactivity, inattention, and aggression in clinical practice. In M. Wolraich & D. K. Routh (Eds.), *Advances in behavioral pediatrics* (Vol. 3, pp. 113–147). Greenwich, CT: JAI Press.

Magnusson, D. (1988). *Individual development from an interactional perspective: A longitudinal study.* Hillsdale, NY: Erlbaum.

McDermott, P. A. (1983). A syndrome topology for analyzing school children's disturbed social behavior. *School Psychological Review, 12,* 250–259.

McGee, R., Williams, S., Bradshaw, J., Chapel, J., Robins, A., & Silva, P. A. (1985). The Rutter scale for completion by teachers: Factor structure and relationships with cognitive abilities and family adversity for a sample of New Zealand children. *Journal of Childhood Psychology and Psychiatry, 26,* 727–739.

Milich, R., & Kramer, J. (1984). Reflections on impulsivity: An empirical investigation of impulsivity as a construct. *Advances in Learning and Behavioral Disabilities, 3,* 57–94.

Morrison, J. R., & Stewart, M. A. (1971). A family study of the hyperactive child syndrome. *Biological Psychiatry, 3,* 189–195.

Neeper, R., & Lahey, B. B. (1986). The Children's Behavior Rating Scale: A factor analytic developmental study. *School Psychology Review, 15,* 277–288.

Neeper, R., & Lahey, B. B. (1988). *The Comprehensive Behavior Rating Scale for Children.* San Antonio, TX: Psychological Corporation.

Newcorn, J., Halperin, J. M., Healy, J., O'Brien, J., Morganstein, A., Sharma, V., & Young, J. G. (1987). *Are ADDH and ADHD children the same or different?* Paper presented to the annual meeting of the American Academy of Child and Adolescent Psychiatry, Washington, DC.

O'Donnell, J. P., & Van Tuinan, M. (1979). Behavior problems of preschool children: Dimensions and congenital correlates. *Journal of Abnormal Child Psychology, 7,* 61–75.

Offord, D. R., Sullivan, K., Allen, N., & Abrams, N. (1979). Delinquency and hyperactivity. *Journal of Nervous and Mental Diseases, 167,* 734–741.

O'Leary, K. D., Vivian, D., & Nisi, A. (1985). Hyperactivity in Italy. *Journal of Abnormal Child Psychology, 13,* 485–500.

Osborn, S. S., & West, D. J. (1980). Do young delinquents really reform? *Journal of Adolescence, 3,* 99–114.

Patterson, G. R. (1982). *A social learning approach, Vol. 3: Coercive family process.* Eugene, OR: Castalia.

Pelham, W. E., Atkins, M. S., Murphy, H. A., & White, K. S. (1981). *Operationalization and validation of attention deficit disorders.* Read at the Annual Meeting of the Association for the Advancement of Behavior Therapy, Toronto, Canada.

Pelham, W. E., & Bender, M. E. (1982). Peer relationships in hyperactive children: Description and treatment. *Advances in learning and behavioral disabilities, 1,* 356–436.

Quay, H. C. (1979). Classification patterns of aggression, withdrawal and immaturity. In H. C. Quay & J. S. Werry (Eds.), *Psychopathological disorders of childhood* (3rd ed.). New York: Wiley.

Quay, H. C. (1986). Classification. In H. C. Quay & J. S. Werry (Eds.), *Psychopathological disorders of childhood* (3rd ed.). (pp. 1–34). New York: Wiley.

Quay, H. C., & Paterson, D. R. (1983). *Interim manual for the Revised Behavior Problem Checklist.* Coral Gables, FL: University of Miami.

Reeves, J. C., Werry, J. S., Elkind, G. S., & Zametkin, A. (1987). Attention deficit, conduct, oppositional, and anxiety disorders in children: II. Clinical characteristics. *Journal of American Academy of Child Adolescent Psychiatry, 26,* 144–155.

Reiss, A. J. (1986). Group influences on criminal career parameters. In A. Blumstein, J. Cohen, J. A. Roth & C. A. Visher (Eds.), *Criminal careers and career criminals.* Washington, DC: National Academy of Sciences.

Rey, J. M., Bashir, M. R., Schwarz, M., Richards, I. N., Plapp, J. M., & Stewart, G. W. (1988). Oppositional disorder: Fact or fiction? *Journal of American Academy of Child Adolescent Psychiatry, 27,* 157–162.

Richman, N., Stevenson, J., & Graham, P. J. (1982). *Pre-school to school: A behavioural study.* London: Academic Press.

Robins, L. N. (1985). The epidemiology of antisocial personality. In J. O. Cavenar (Ed.), *Psychiatry.* Philadelphia: Lippincott.

Robins, L. N. (1966). *Deviant children grow up: A sociological and psychiatric study of sociopathic personality.* Baltimore: Williams & Wilkins.

Roff, J. D. (1986). Identification of boys at high risk for delinquency. *Psychological Reports, 58,* 615–618.

Rutter, M., & Giller, H. (1983). *Juvenile delinquency: Trends and perspectives.* Middlesex, England: Penguin.

Sandberg, S. T., Rutter, M., & Taylor, E. (1978). Hyperkinetic disorder in psychiatric clinic attenders. *Developmental Medicine and Child Neurology, 20,* 279–299.

Sandberg, S. T., Wieselberg, M., & Shaffer, D. (1980). Hyperkinetic and conduct problem children in a primary school population: Some epidemiological considerations. *Journal of Child Psychology & Psychiatry, 21,* 293–311.

Schachar, R., Rutter, M., & Smith, A. (1981). The characteristics of situationally and pervasively hyperactive children: Implications for syndrome definition. *Journal of Child Psychology & Psychiatry, 22*, 375–392.

Schaughency, E. A., & Lahey, B. B. (1985). Mothers' and fathers' perceptions of child deviance: Roles of child behavior, parental depression, and marital satisfaction. *Journal of Consulting and Clinical Psychology, 53*, 718–723.

Stewart, M. A., & deBlois, C. S. (1984). *Diagnostic criteria for aggressive conduct disorder*, Unpublished manuscript, Department of Psychiatry, University of Iowa College of Medicine, Iowa City.

Stewart, M. A., deBlois, C. S., & Cummings, C. (1980). Psychiatric disorder in the parents of hyperactive boys and those with conduct disorder. *Journal of Child Psychology and Psychiatry, 21*, 283–292.

Stouthamer-Loeber, M., Loeber, R., & Green, S. (1988). *The utility of different classifications of problem behavior in predicting male delinquency.* Manuscript in preparation.

Taylor, E., Schachar, R., Thorley, G., & Wieselberg, M. (1986). Conduct disorder and hyperactivity: I. Separation of hyperactivity and antisocial conduct in British child psychiatric patients. *British Journal of Psychiatry, 149*, 760–767.

Trites, R. L., Blouin, A. G. A., & LaPrade, K. (1982). Factor analysis of the Conners Teacher Rating Scale based on a large normative sample. *Journal of Consulting and Clinical Psychology, 50*, 615–623.

Ullmann, R. K., Sleator, E. K., & Sprague, R. L. (1984). A new rating scale for the diagnosis and monitoring of ADD children. *Psychopharmacology Bulletin, 20*, 160–164.

Verhulst, F. C., Althaus, M., & Berden, F. M. G. (1987). The Child Assessment Schedule: Parent-child agreement and validity measures. *Journal of Child Psychology and Psychiatry, 28*, 455–466.

Vidoni, D. O., Fleming, N. J., & Mintz, S. (1983). Behavior problems of children as perceived by teachers, mental health professionals, and children. *Psychology in the Schools, 20*, 93–98.

Walker, J. L., Lahey, B. B., Hynd, G. W., & Frame, C. L. (in press). Comparison of specific patterns of antisocial behavior in children with conduct disorder with or without coexisting hyperactivity. *Journal of Consulting and Clinical Psychology.*

Weissman, M. M., Myers, J. K., & Ross, C. E. (Eds.). (1986). *Community surveys of psychiatric disorders.* New Brunswick, NJ: Rutgers University Press.

Werry, J. S. (1968). Developmental hyperactivity. *Pediatric Clinics of North America, 15*, 581–599.

Werry, J. S., & Hawthorne, D. (1976). Conners Teacher Questionnaire: Norms and validity. *Australian and New Zealand Journal of Psychiatry, 10*, 257–262.

Werry, J. S., Methven, R. J., Fitzpatrick, J., & Dixon, H. (1983). The interrater reliability of DSM-III in children. *Journal of Abnormal Child Psychology, 11*, 341–354.

Werry, J. S., Sprague, R. L., & Cohen, M. N. (1975). Conners' Teacher Rating Scale for use in drug studies—An empirical study. *Journal of Abnormal Child Psychology, 3*, 217–229.

Wickman, E. K. (1928). *Children's behavior and teacher's attitudes.* New York: Commonwealth Fund.

Yule, W. (1981). The epidemiology of child psychopathology. In B. B. Lahey & A. E. Kazdin (Eds.), *Advances in clinical child psychology* (Vol. 4). New York: Plenum Press.

Index